Reinventing Education

The need for change in the education system is obvious and overwhelming. But each stakeholder group has its own ideas about why the system is broken and how to fix it. Competing priorities, political inertia and diminishing budgets maintain the dysfunctional status quo. This essential text examines the underlying causes behind the key challenges facing schools and argues that we need to move from knowledge transfer systems to a deliberately developmental approach that transforms capabilities including emotional regulation, systems thinking, critical analysis, creativity and collaborative capability.

The chapters provide a framework for designing, constructing and implementing school systems that can transform the outcome in a classroom, school or trust. Topics covered include:

- Why education is a 'wicked' problem
- Why development must be central and sit alongside knowledge transfer (as AI takes over 'expertise')
- How motivation and value systems evolve and are key to change
- How to drive behaviour change to transform outcomes
- What human-centred means now in a reinvented system

Offering much-needed insights, guidance and solutions for teachers, school leaders and policy-makers, this book will be valuable reading for all those interested in school improvement and education policy.

Alan Watkins is the CEO and Founder of Complete, a consultancy that specialises in developing exceptional leadership, globally, through individual and team development.

Matt Silver is the CEO and Founder of The Glass House Leadership Lab, an educational coaching and co-consultancy group that believes the catalyst to system transformation is the personal development of leaders, teachers and learners.

Reinventing Education

Beyond the Knowledge Economy

Alan Watkins and Matt Silver

Routledge
Taylor & Francis Group
LONDON AND NEW YORK

Designed cover image: Lucy Turner

First published 2025
by Routledge

4 Park Square, Milton Park, Abingdon, Oxon OX14 4RN
and by Routledge

605 Third Avenue, New York, NY 10158

Routledge is an imprint of the Taylor & Francis Group, an informa business

© 2025 Alan Watkins and Matt Silver

The right of Alan Watkins and Matt Silver to be identified as authors of this work has been asserted in accordance with sections 77 and 78 of the Copyright, Designs and Patents Act 1988.

All rights reserved. No part of this book may be reprinted or reproduced or utilised in any form or by any electronic, mechanical, or other means, now known or hereafter invented, including photocopying and recording, or in any information storage or retrieval system, without permission in writing from the publishers.

Trademark notice: Product or corporate names may be trademarks or registered trademarks, and are used only for identification and explanation without intent to infringe.

British Library Cataloguing-in-Publication Data
A catalogue record for this book is available from the British Library

Library of Congress Cataloging-in-Publication Data
Names: Watkins, Alan, 1961– author. | Silver, Matt, author.
Title: Reinventing education : beyond the knowledge economy / Alan Watkins and Matt Silver.
Description: Abingdon, Oxon ; New York, NY : Routledge, 2025. | Includes bibliographical references.
Identifiers: LCCN 2024030214 (print) | LCCN 2024030215 (ebook) | ISBN 9781032870816 (hardback) | ISBN 9781032870809 (paperback) | ISBN 9781003530831 (ebook)
Subjects: LCSH: Educational change—Great Britain. | Education—Aims and objectives—Great Britain.
Classification: LCC LB2806 .W2945 2025 (print) | LCC LB2806 (ebook) | DDC 371.2/070941—dc23/eng/20241015
LC record available at https://lccn.loc.gov/2024030214
LC ebook record available at https://lccn.loc.gov/2024030215

ISBN: 978-1-032-87081-6 (hbk)
ISBN: 978-1-032-87080-9 (pbk)
ISBN: 978-1-003-53083-1 (ebk)

DOI: 10.4324/9781003530831

Typeset in Melior
by Apex CoVantage, LLC

Contents

About the Authors   viii
Acknowledgements   x

Introduction   1
Let's Start at the Very Beginning   6
The First Great Leap Forward   8
The Emergence of the Principle Wave   10
The Root of the Performance Wave (Leading Edge)   12
The Emergence of the Progressive Wave   14
Glimmers of the Polarities Wave   16
No Longer Fit for Purpose   17

Part One: The State of the Education System

1   Current Reality in Education   23
    How Does the Current Reality Impact Young People?   26
    How Does the Current Reality Impact Educators?   30
    How Does the Current Reality Impact Parents?   32
    How Does the Current Reality Impact Society and the Economy?   33
    Education as a Wicked Problem for the 21st Century   34
       Multi-Dimensional   35
       Multiple Stakeholders   37
       Multiple Causes   37
       Multiple Symptoms   38
       Multiple Solutions   39
       Constantly Evolving   40

2   Glimmers of Change   43
    John Dewey   45
    Jean Piaget   46
    Howard Gardner   47
    Montessori, Steiner and International Baccalaureate (IB)   49
    Finland's Education System   53

Part Two: Diagnosis and Treatment

3 Awareness Before Change 59
   A Word on Change 62

4 Individual Development in Theory 67
   The Disconnect Between Learning and Development 75
   Understanding the Mental Health Crisis 82

5 Individual Development in Practice 85
   Developing Greater Physical and Emotional Intelligence 87
      Level 1 of ESQ – Energy Awareness 88
      Level 2 of ESQ – Energy Management 90
      Level 3 of ESQ – Emotional Awareness 91
      Level 4 of ESQ – Emotional Intelligence 92
      Level 5 of ESQ – Emotional Literacy 95
      Level 6 of ESQ – Emotional Regulation 97
      Level 7 of ESQ – Emotional Resilience 100
      Level 8 of ESQ – Self-Motivation 102
      Level 9 of ESQ – Optimistic Outlook 103
      Level 10 of ESQ – Empathy and Rapport 104
      Level 11 of ESQ – Social Awareness 106
      Level 12 of ESQ – Social Intelligence 106
   Understanding Your Values 107
   Ego Maturity 111

6 Individual Development in Action 119
   The Complete Intervention 120

7 Collective Development in Theory 127
   We're Not Taught How to Communicate 129
      Perspective Taking 132
   We Don't Appreciate Difference 134
      Survival Not Sophistication 137
   We Don't Appreciate How Values Impact Relationships 139

8 Collective Development in Practice 143
   Values Revisited 145
   Team Development 148
      A Level 1 Pre-Team – Talented Individuals 150
      A Level 2 Team – Battling Experts 150
      A Level 3 Performing Team – Dependent Experts 150
      A Level 4 High Performing Team – Independent Achievers 151
      A Level 5 Best-in-Class Team – Interdependent Achievers 152
      A Level 6 World Class Team – Diverse Pluralists 153
      A Level 7 World Class Team – Integrated Pluralists 154
      A Level 8 World Leading Team – Broad Fellowships 154
      A Level 9 World Leading Team – Unified Fellowships 154
   Network Analysis 161
   Big Picture Thinking 163

9 Collective Development in Action ... 169

10 Behaviour and Systems Development in Theory ... 179
   Intrinsic and Extrinsic Motivation Theory   180
   Self-Determination Theory   184
      Autonomy   184
      Competency   184
      Relatedness   185
   Engagement Theory   187
   Systems Theory   191

11 Behaviour and Systems Development in Practice ... 199
   Designing Motivation and Engagement into the Solution   202
   Schools as DAOs and DDOs   203

12 Behaviour and Systems Development in Action ... 209
   A SEND Case Study   210

13 TKAT Case Study ... 221
   The Catalyst for Change   221
   The Development Journey   221
      Assessment   222
   Developmental Intervention   226
   Key Benefits Delivered   227
   TKAT CEO's Transformational Journey   227
   Coaching for the Senior Leadership Team (SLT)   228
   Leadership Development for Headteachers   229
      The Transformative Impact   230
   Future Plans   231

   Conclusion ... 233

   Index ... 236

About the Authors

Alan Watkins

Alan is the CEO and Founder of Complete, a consultancy that specialises in developing exceptional leadership through individual, team and organisational development.

Alan advises completely different businesses in totally different market sectors, in different geographies, and works with many different types of businesses from tech start-ups to FTSE 10 giants. He consults with them on how to grow their revenues, transform their strategy, step change their leadership capability and develop their culture. He is a disruptive thinker and a modern business innovator. He can take complex global concepts from multiple market sectors, integrate his own ideas with the wisdom of the crowd and come up with novel answers that have proven extremely helpful to the 100 different companies that constitute his client base.

Alan has written many books including *Lie-Ability: How Leaders Build and Break Trust with Simon Jones* (Routledge 2023), *Step Change: The Leader's Journey* (Routledge 2022), *Innovation Sucks! Time to Think Differently*, co-authored with Simon May (Routledge, 2021) and *HR (R)Evolution: Change the Workplace, Change the World*, co-authored with Nick Dalton (Routledge 2020). Alan is based in the UK and is a Visiting Professor at Kingston Business School, London, and also on the Board of the London Interdisciplinary School and the California Institute of Integral Studies.

www.complete-coherence.com

Matt Silver

Matt is Founder of The Glass House Leadership Lab, an educational coaching and co-consultancy group that believes the catalyst to system transformation is the personal development of leaders and learners.

He was previously a CEO and Head in outstanding Education Settings and MBA Director. His doctoral action research was based in curriculum, culture and system design using frameworks of human development. He is digitising the change management process with a deliberately developmental approach so that leaders can share common models, language and best practice. He is partnering with some of the largest Trusts and leadership trainers in the UK, such as the Institute of Education, UCL and The National College of Education to enhance leaders' journeys within and beyond their programmes to feed developmental practice back into their organisations by linking leadership to learning.

Matt has published a range of academic papers and chapters in international books including: *Self-Determination in Positive Education* (2021), *Pastoral Care in Education: New Directions for New Times* (2023) and *Mentoring and Coaching in Education* (2024).

www.glasshouselab.com

Acknowledgements

As children we are born with an innate curiosity, but sadly, by the time we reach adulthood many of us have lost this gift. Fortunately, as a kid, I spent a lot of time alone, exploring and imagining a world in which I wanted to live. This was the start of my education.

Then throughout my life I've been extremely fortunate to encounter many great teachers.

My mother taught me, by example, how to be compassionate. My father taught me humour and perspective. At school my history teacher, Mr Roebuck, inspired me with his passion for his subject. My rowing coach, Mr Blythe taught me the importance of leadership. At medical school Dr Hilton Davis taught me the beauty of child development and play. Dr Peter Nixon taught me to have the courage to challenge conventional thinking. Dr Anthony Vogelpoel taught me the importance of friendship and kindness. I could go on as I've met so many sages on my travels. But I'd like to specifically mention the great Ken Wilber who's been a mentor to me. His wisdom and brilliance have guided my own development. He is a gift to the world. Diane Hamilton whose wonderful countenance effortlessly integrates spiritual discipline with compassionate philosophy, and a wicked sense of the ridiculousness of it all. And most of all, Sarah, my wife, who has taught me about love – the greatest gift of all.

I'm also indebted to Karen McCreadie whose has, as always, been a skilful editor and has made this a much better and hopefully more useful book.

Finally, I'd like to acknowledge my co-author, Matt Silver, whose expansive mind and thoughtfulness was apparent at our very first meeting. It's been a pleasure writing with you. Finally, I want to thank you the reader for reading what we've written. Reading is a such a key skill in our development as human beings. If we can explore with child-like curiosity, we can reinvent the education system and create a better world for our children and grandchildren to inherit.

Alan Watkins

The inspiration, not just for this book but also my life's work in education and charity, has come from the sheer determination backed by incredible character that the young people with diverse needs have demonstrated to me on multiple levels. This has been in seemingly small steps that are truly significant to my first experience of rapid transformation. Two students who I witnessed take it into their own hands to grow have been the greatest teachers of all. The humbling of what I perceived to be challenges bare very little significance in the challenges they face on a moment-to-moment basis. Working alongside them has driven me to break down barriers both in education but also in myself and match their courage to try, fail and learn in many different ways. Thank you to my parents for involving me in Group 13 from such a young age and for being inspirational educators also.

Karen McCreadie, your patience in helping me make my thinking make sense represents to me what I wish my own school experience had been like. We cannot rush our young people through their journey, it is superficial.

I especially acknowledge my wife, Anna, as a catalyst to doing something to make sense of these experiences. She pushed me to do my Master's when during most of my school life I perceived myself to be just above average, and said "why not" when I considered my doctorate. She has been there to help me get back up when I have stumbled and together created three incredible children who provide me with an energy source every day.

When I thought my school was the biggest impact I could have on the education system, I met Complete and my co-author Alan. The support in my development from the team and especially Dave Hughes has allowed me to understand and connect the 'how' and 'why' of the knowledge we have and branch out our impact across leaders in education to transform their schools despite the many barriers we have written about. These leaders fuel my belief that the system can indeed be reinvented without waiting for the cavalry.

Matt Silver

Introduction

From the age of 4 to 16 years old we spend about 14,000 hours at school. What happens to us during these precious hours can define the outcome of our lives.

School helps establish our identity, plays a role in how confident we become and shapes what we believe to be true about ourselves. It can also help us develop our ability to make sense of the world, teach us what's important and how to differentiate between right and wrong. Hopefully, the learning we receive at school makes us more open and receptive to new ideas, develops our curiosity, allows us to understand the importance of fairness and teaches us how to set standards by which we can live. We can develop our ability to be happy and fulfilled and discover how to live a purposeful life. We can cultivate our interpersonal skills and make lifelong friends while figuring out how to be more inclusive and treat others with respect, kindness and compassion.

If these years go well, it can set the stage for a happy, healthy and successful life. If they go badly, we can end up suffering endless problems, powerless to change course, unable to recover from a downward spiral that damages us, those around us and ultimately society. In short, it's impossible to overestimate the importance of education for individuals, families and society. As Nelson Mandela said, "Education is the most powerful weapon which you can use to change the world."[1]

If we look around the world, there are a few countries whose education systems are working well for all stakeholders. But sadly, for most countries, it's difficult to escape the conclusion that their education systems are failing and failing badly. They're failing not because the people in the system are inept, incapable or unable to make things better. They're failing because the world has changed and is continuing to change, so fast, that this change has simply overtaken the system. The result is that most educational systems, like many other systems in society, are no longer fit for purpose.

It's time for a complete rethink.

The future of Britain, and most other countries in the world, depend on getting this major overhaul right. In fact, the survival of humanity itself depends on reinventing our education systems and making them work for the world we live in now.

Our education systems also need to develop much greater levels of change capability. They must be able to change themselves continually, at speed, with skill and evolve to meet the changing needs of society. Anything less ambitious will condemn future generations to a life of increasing failure. That's not a legacy we want to pass onto our children. They deserve better.

We could have written a book that chronicles the specific failures of our educational system. It would include a very long list of causes and symptoms. We could even suggest who and what is to blame, and there's been a rich and passionate debate in educational circles on this subject. But those discussions haven't moved us closer to a solution. What's needed is a more nuanced and sophisticated approach.

Instead of listing the failures, we will take you on a whistlestop tour through 'Seven Great Waves' of change in education systems (Figure 0.1). Starting from the inception of education, we will journey through the major waves of change, what strength in practice has emerged and reveal what is yet to come.

Each wave of the educational system correlates to the great waves of change in society. We will discover how these changes in the way society was thinking and the dominant 'world view' at that time has led us to this moment of inflexion. We'll look into the future and suggest how we can choose a different path forward, one that we believe should excite and empower all stakeholders and restore hope for our collective future.

The waves of societal, educational and cultural evolution have been extensively described by numerous academics over the last 50 years. Chief amongst them is Clare Graves, a psychology professor from New York in the 1950s. He and researchers inspired by his work defined six and subsequently eight colour-coded values levels or world views (Figure 0.2). Graves discovered that what we value matures over time as we develop. These evolutionary levels hold true whether you're an individual, a group, an educational system or a whole society. These value systems determine what we think about, what we consider important and direct the solutions we come up with for the problems we encounter. And each value system emerges to transcend and include the previous levels.

Graves' insightful work offers us a new way of looking at the education system we so badly need. So many of the issues we face are the consequence of an educational system that was designed to address the different needs and priorities of a different economic and social reality. When we understand how our value systems have evolved over the last 120 years and how this evolution has impacted education, we're better able to understand why we are experiencing so many problems. And, crucially, why we tend to hold on to things that worked at previous levels rather than allowing the system to develop further as the world changes.

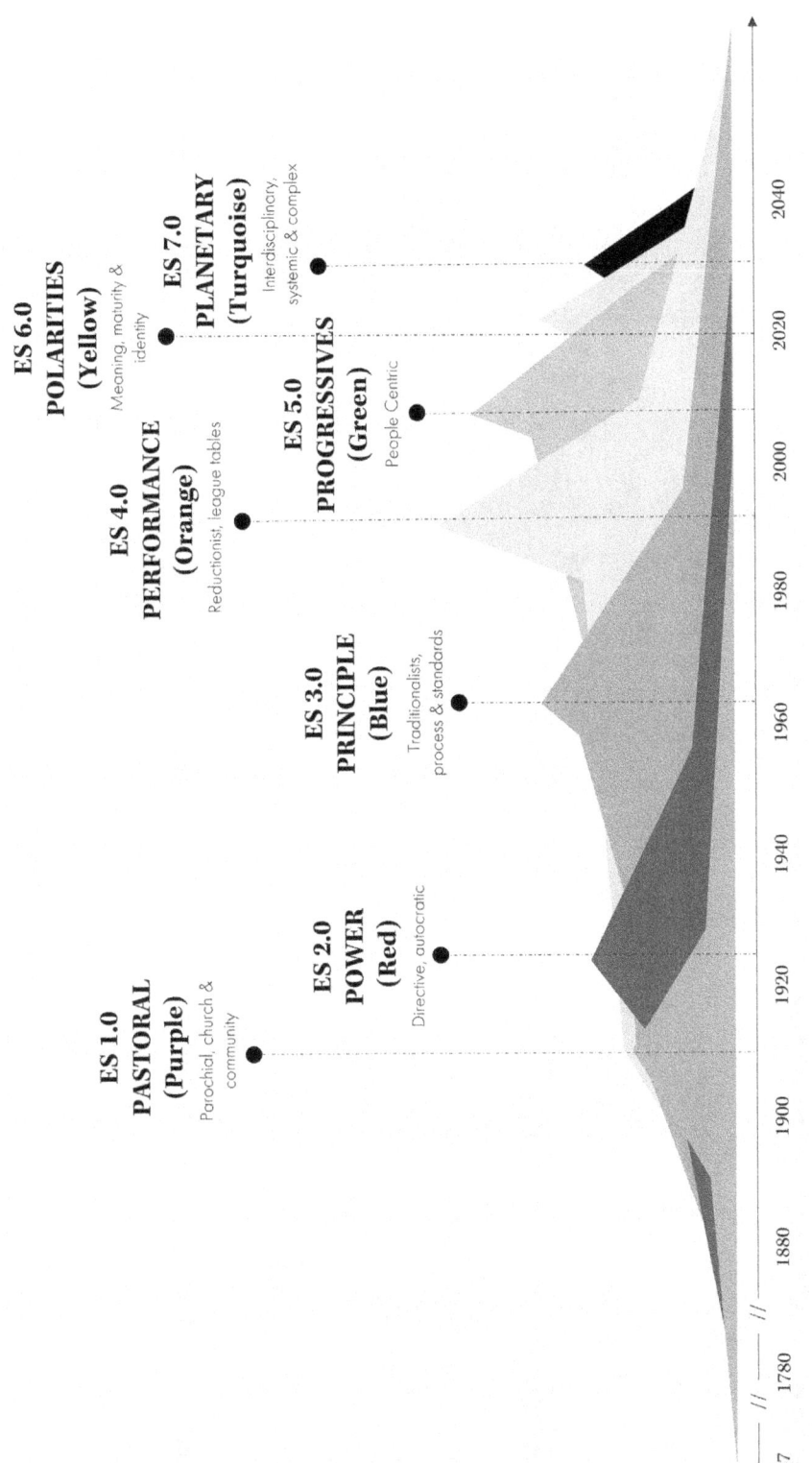

Figure 0.1 The Seven Great Waves of Change in Education

	WHAT'S VALUED	COMMON THOUGHTS	MOTIVATED BY	GOAL	WAY OF OPERATING
T	Systems balance	Consider everything, balance everything, take the long view, be of service	Evolution and the greater good	Unity	Transpersonal and compassionate
Y	Innovation	Innovate the future, be flexible and spontaneous, learn and take responsibility	Ideas and genuine transformation	Variety, novelty and an interesting life	Philosophical
G	Social connection	Include others, take people with you, do it together	Affiliation and sharing	Building a community	Personal touch
O	Wealth	Make it work, achieve the target, succeed	Winning and success	Wealth	Pragmatic and competitive
B	Order	Stick to the plan, be loyal and respectful, do the right thing	Principles and process	Salvation	Disciplined and adherent to the rules
R	Power	Go for it, work hard, play hard, take charge	Being number 1	Power and pleasure	Use their own authority
P	Belonging	Don't risk it, stay vigilant, work together, look after the group	Reassurance	Safety	Tribal
B	Survival	Get through the day, stay alive, I have what I need	Basic urges	None	Reactive, extremely short-term

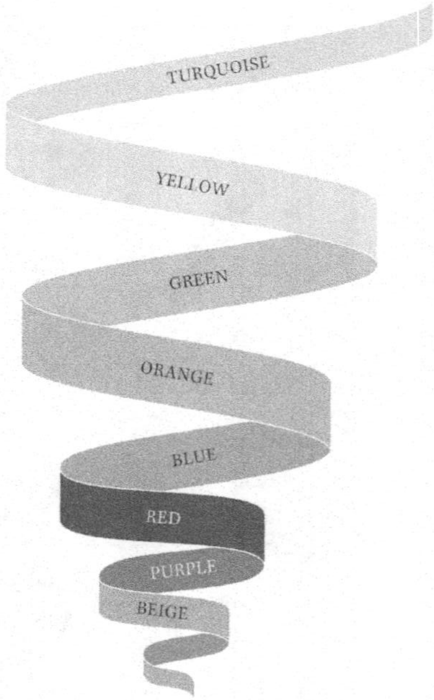

Figure 0.2 Eight Value Systems or World Views

As we evolve, our appreciation for the things we valued at earlier levels declines. Earlier concerns become less important as our focus shifts to more expansive and sophisticated issues. However, under pressure we can regress and fall back down the values spiral. For example, when Covid-19 hit, what was valued or considered important in education shifted. Some people advocated a back-to-basics approach, others put their teams or communities before themselves, others sought to innovate around delivery with the use of technology. We can see these shifts in values and what we collectively considered important through the course of educational history. Understanding this evolutionary dimension can help us to contextualise the challenges we face in the education system today and why they exist.

It's also worth noting that the focus switches from the individual to the collective and back again. As we grow up and mature through these levels, we also realise we can't skip a level. We can't bypass or jump to more advanced world views, we must evolve through every single level in turn. Think about this in terms of school maturity. Schools wishing to turn their performance around are operating at a very different values level to those innovating at the edge of what education can deliver. It is not possible to jump from turnaround to innovation, we must progress through the various value systems to ready the stakeholders for transformation.

Each wave delivers significant benefits to all stakeholders in the educational system and wider society. But eventually progress always falters resulting in a surge of negative and unintended consequences. As each level fails, new problems emerge. If those new problems are not understood in the context of value systems, it almost always triggers a surge of 'bring-backery' or a desire to go back to approaches that worked in the past.[2] But if understood, those new problems can trigger an evolutionary leap forward to the next values level even though such jumps can be uncomfortable for those involved.

When culture changes, chaos often ensues. We've seen this time and again in the educational system. The emergence of new cultural value systems often triggers a battle as stakeholders operating from different levels fight for control of the system itself.

The most widespread 'culture war' at present is the 'Trads vs. Progs' battle. The traditionalists want to go back to basics, advocating a more conservative, traditional approach to education which, they claim, works better. In contrast, the progressives argue that the world where this traditional approach worked no longer exists. They suggest that we must move forward and find a system that works for the world we live in today. These value waves provide us with a much-needed map to better understand the battle, reconcile the polarisation of opinion and outcomes, and make peace. As such it also offers a crucial blueprint to the future of education.

So far five waves have already emerged. As of 2024, the 'cutting edge' is the Progressive Wave, although a handful of thinkers have gone further in certain aspects of education. This progressive cutting edge includes a sizeable minority of people who've consolidated around a more inclusive, advanced, learner centred approach. These stakeholders have consciously designed solutions using a more sophisticated way of thinking than the majority who inhabit the leading-edge Performance Wave. Whilst there is nothing inherently better or worse about each level, each level does have strengths and weaknesses that are important to understand so that the right strength is applied to the right challenge in the right context and weaknesses can be mitigated. The Performance Wave is where most educationists currently reside. Those progressives, who've made it to the cutting edge, represent the next step in our evolutionary path. But we'll show that there's an urgent need to uncover the sixth great wave if we want to accelerate into the future and find real solutions that resolves this battle.

Let's Start at the Very Beginning

Education in England all began with St Augustine who arrived in 597 and founded the first grammar school, King's School in Canterbury, a year later. But it only taught Latin to priests or the 'sons of gentlefolk' to sing in the cathedral choir!

For the next 1,000 years education remained pastoral, parochial and rooted in the church or confined to a handful of rich families. Ecclesiastical and elite tribes jealously guarded their schooling to protect their position in society. Teaching the priests or the privileged, often in a foreign language, created a commonality of language for the elite and a glue for these two communities. The rest of the population was left to fend for themselves, illiterate and excluded from the evolutionary potential that education provides. In that regard, most of the population was still stuck in survival mode, living hand to mouth operating from the value system that precedes the Pastoral Wave of cultural development.

The word 'education' comes from two different Latin roots. Firstly, 'educare', which means to train or to mould, and "educere", meaning to lead out.[3] The church certainly sought to mould its priests and the privileged sought to maintain power so they could continue to lead out in society.

In medieval England, as towns prospered, the demand for more grammar schools grew. 'Free grammar schools,' i.e. free from church supervision, started to appear from 1150 onwards and began to teach other subjects. In theory they were open to all, tuition was free to those that couldn't afford to pay. But poor children rarely attended. When food, water and shelter are the main concerns in life there's rarely sufficient energy available for education. Even though it was education which could have best protected them from the vicissitudes of what was still a largely harsh and often cruel life. Education was a luxury that poor families simply couldn't afford.

Winchester College, founded in 1382, was the first school to at least attempt to teach the masses where 'scholars' were boys from poorer families. But that was only because so many people died during the Black Death leaving the church short of trained priests. Winchester was operating in exceptional circumstances, and this was certainly not the norm across the country.

Education for the masses was made harder still when Richard II outlawed education for 'serfs' in 1391. A serf was an agricultural labourer bound by the feudal system to work on their lord's estate. These men were viewed as valuable assets, and education posed a threat to the landowners. Such a conflict of interests is a theme that will be repeated time and again throughout the emergence of every one of seven great waves of education. At this point it was still very much education for the wealthy but little for everyone else.

Such elitism and disparity were of course, largely driven by the immediate demands of the economy. The children of the wealthy weren't needed in service or to plough the fields so they could be educated, whereas the children of the poor were vital breadwinners needed for family survival.

In the 18th century there was some teaching at church Sunday schools, but apart from this the only education poor children received was in the home where fathers would teach their sons their trade, whether that was blacksmith or farmer, and daughters would learn from their mother how to cook, sew, take care of the house and help raise younger children.

Eventually, some small village schools emerged, but these were as much about childcare, allowing both parents to work, than they were about education. In these, often informal schools, the teacher was almost always a woman who would focus on the basics, reading, writing and simple maths. The gender difference in access to education and provision of teaching between the rich and poor remains in many parts of the world today. The sons of wealthy families were always taught by men, and in the less formal village schools, poor children were taught by women who had a far lower status.

Sadly, there are still parts of the world where the lower status of women still prevents them from accessing school at all. For example, since taking control in 2021 the Taliban administration in Afghanistan have stopped female students attending anything above primary school. When they were last in power from 1996 to 2001, they banned female education and most female employment. But after returning to power in August 2021 the group had promised opportunities for girls' education and employment, but so far, such opportunities have not materialised.[4] The Taliban are harking back to a time where only boys were educated, and girls were expected to be nothing more than be good wives and mothers.

For whatever reason, patriarchy, misogyny, religious or cultural difference, male teachers are still often held in higher regard than their female counterparts.

The downside of this early Pastoral Wave is that the schooling provided was often poorly thought out. Educational outcomes were not considered and much of the focus would have been on the successful continuity of the family or tribe from which students were drawn. Such a stance was designed to maintain the status quo rather than drive progress. There was no need for change, society was not moving fast and so this pastoral approach sustained for more than 1,000 years.

What eventually caused education to change was the explosion of society with the birth of the Industrial Revolution.

The First Great Leap Forward

With the emergence of the 'factory system', the Pastoral Wave, characterised by a parochial approach to education, was no longer fit for purpose and the Power Wave swept in. Large workforces were needed and many of the apprentices, journeymen and master craftsmen who had previously taught their sons their trade were either put out of business or attracted by higher wages in the factory.

What we recognise as schooling today came out of the observations of a young Anglican chaplain, Andrew Bell. While stationed in India he noticed that the Hindu culture structured education and training around status. The top 5% of society included the industrial caste, the warrior and administrative caste and the super-elite Brahmins. This 5% trained for law, medicine, teaching and other professional occupations.[5] Interestingly, regardless of country, these professions still drive parental goals for young people today.

As for the other 95% of the population, they were divided into the menial caste and the 'untouchables'. People lived and died in the caste they were born into. Bell could see the benefit of such a system to provide enough of a workforce for the Industrial Revolution. Effectively, the elite and wealthy of society would take on the role of the top 5%, something they were doing anyway, and the rest of the population would be conditioned to accept their lot without question.

Although it didn't happen straight away, these observations led to compulsory schooling as we know it today. Bell suggested that "schooled ignorance was more useful than unschooled stupidity". In other words, if you took young children from their homes and got them used to long hours of monotonous, boring 'work', they would slip seamlessly into the long hours of monotonous, often dangerous work in the mills, factories and workplaces of industrialised Britain.

Across the Atlantic, wealthy industrialists such as Andrew Carnegie and John D. Rockefeller ploughed vast sums of money into 'education'. As late as 1915 Carnegie and Rockefeller were individually spending more than the entire US Government. Their motives may have been genuine, but the following excerpt from the first mission statement of Rockefeller's General Education Board, 1906, suggests something else:

> In our dreams . . . people yield themselves with perfect docility to our moulding hands. The present educational conventions fade from our minds and unhampered by tradition we work our own good will upon a grateful and responsive folk. We shall not try to make these people or any of their children into philosophers or men of learning or men of science. We have not to raise up from among them authors, educators, poets or men of letters. We shall not search for embryo great artists, painters, musicians, nor lawyers, doctors, preachers, politicians, statesmen, of whom we have ample supply. The task

we set before ourselves is very simple . . . we will organise children . . . and teach them to do in a perfect way the things their fathers and mothers are doing in an imperfect way.[6]

This educational philosophy is all about power. It could easily be argued that those with the power, be that wealthy industrialists, politicians or other wealthy families, used that power to influence who was educated and what was taught in order to make more money and gain more power. After all, Richard II had proven the effectiveness of this strategy as far back as 1391.

The Industrial Revolution lasted from around 1760 to 1840. For almost all that period, children were rarely educated. Instead, they worked in the same factories as their mothers, fathers and siblings. And the powerful actively lobbied to ensure that children could continue to be a cheap and sometimes free source of labour.

Although the first Factory Act was passed in 1802 in the UK, which required apprentices and children to receive some form of basic numeracy and literacy schooling, it wasn't mandatory so only the most enlightened factory owners observed it. Although schooling for children aged 7 to 11 expanded during the Industrial Revolution, it consisted of a mixture of 'petties' which were small schools linked to grammar schools, writing schools, private schools, Dames Schools, Charity Schools, Sunday Schools and Ragged Schools. In 1818, John Pounds, known as the crippled cobbler, set up a school and began teaching poor children reading, writing and arithmetic without charging a fee. Pounds was a progressive thinker of this wave, and there would eventually be over 200 'Ragged Schools' teaching hundreds of thousands of poor children in Britain.

It was only when a bill was introduced to extend the protection of children in mills, in 1833, making those protections mandatory and employing inspectors to enforce the new law, did things begin to change. The 1833 Factory Act stipulated that:

- No child workers under the age of 9 years old.
- Children 9–13 years old to work no more than nine hours a day.
- Children 13–18 years old to work no more than 12 hours a day.
- No child to work at night.
- Two hours schooling each day for children.
- Four factory inspectors appointed to enforce the Law[7]

Prior to these provisions, children as young as five years old had been apprenticed to mills, providing free labour to mill owners. This development was an important nod to the need for schooling and the beginnings of standard setting, albeit with a limited number of inspectors and minimal enforcement. In truth education became a tick box exercise where mill owners would get a female member of staff to babysit the children for a couple of hours so they could then get back to work.

The Emergence of the Principle Wave

Interestingly, in 1833 Parliament voted to allocate sums of money to the construction of schools for poor children. This was the first time the state had become involved in education in England and Wales, although such initiatives had been running in Scotland since the 17th century.

The emergence of inspectors and some very basic quality standards signalled the emergence of the Principle Wave. This wave was initially characterised by processes and rules, and although those rules were not nationwide, more schools started to appear to educate everyone.

At the start of the 19th century, 'National Schools' and 'British Schools' sought to standardise education. This was the first attempt at universal education in Britain. In 1868, the Taunton Report stratified educational needs according to social class – a viewpoint that still influences education today!

Essentially, the Taunton Report divided parents into three grades:

- First grade who wanted their children to be educated up to and beyond the age of 18, and who still wanted their children to be taught the Classics.

- Second grade who wanted their children to be educated up to the age of 16 who approved of a curriculum that included subjects that could be turned into practical use in business such as English, maths and science, as well as Latin.

- Third grade who wanted their children educated to the age of 14 who only wanted the practical education – no Classics.

In many ways these principles made sense. Education was still seen as a luxury that many poorer families simply couldn't afford. Parents needed their children to work. This version of the educational system acknowledged this reality and sought to strike a balance between education and economic and social need.

A year later in 1869, acting on the Taunton Report, the Endowment Schools Act allowed grammar schools to change the terms of the endowments to tackle the uneven distribution of schools in the country and for the first time, seek to address the severe lack of education for girls.

The following year in 1870, the government mandated the provision of elementary education for children aged 5–13 years old via the Elementary Education Act. Attendance became compulsory for boys and girls from 5–10 years old, thereafter until attainment of the 'educational standard'. This standard, stipulated by the Taunton Report ensured a minimum curriculum of the 3Rs (reading, writing and 'rithmetic). There were attendance exemptions for illness, children in employment and those living too far from the school. But exemptions were revoked in 1880 and enforced by School Attendance Officers.

By this point the prevailing wisdom was that universal education would help to keep Britain competitive. But there was still fear, especially amongst those still operating from the Power Wave that educating the working class might encourage them to revolt. Besides, if the working class became educated, there would be no one left to do the hard, dirty and often dangerous work required in their mills and factories or to tend to their land.

The Second Boer War which ended in 1902 also influenced the direction of education in the early 20th century. Although it didn't directly lead to immediate changes in educational policy, it did contribute to broader social, political and cultural shifts including an increased focus on health and well-being, nationalism and patriotism, military training, imperial education and social reform. The Boer War is why Physical Education (PE) exists as a subject in schools.

However, the downside of the Principle Wave, or what's called the Traditionalist approach in education, is excess process, which can lead to bureaucracy and rule-bound rigidity. An over-reliance on principles and process can also significantly inhibit progress. Rigidity can become draconian, especially when imposed by people who still have one foot in the Power Wave. In the education system, imposing rules and standards often meant embracing corporal punishment, where a teacher would deliberately inflict physical pain on a student to deter undesired behaviour. The 'spare the rod ruin the child' idea has its roots in the Power Wave where punishments were meted out on the factory production line from those in charge. It's the same approach applied to education against students who break the rules. Corporal punishment has been a hot topic for decades, but it was only outlawed in state schools in 1987 and 1998 in private schools.

When Gavin Williamson was the British Secretary of State for Education (2019–2021), he was known to extol the virtues of corporal punishment.[8] This backward looking, grasping of simplistic answers is common when people don't appreciate the evolutionary dimension of change and are making decisions based on the education they experienced as 'true' or 'worked for me'. It can be very tempting to assume that old solutions that worked 150 years ago can somehow be resurrected in the present to deliver similar results. But it never works. Firstly evolution doesn't go backwards. And secondly, despite plenty of 'anecdotal evidence' that corporal punishment builds character and maintains order, there is a distinct lack of empirical evidence as to the effectiveness of corporal punishment in schools.

A reliance on punishment in the Principle Wave brings into focus an important insight about the evolution of each of the educational waves and the value systems underpinning them. The solutions offered in each wave always match the values level of the individual or group suggesting them. Those operating from the Red values system in the Power Wave will argue that the imposition of authority will make the difference. Those operating from the Principle Wave, like Gavin

Williamson, are adamant that a 'back to basics' adherence to traditional values will work, and so on.

And all the values levels in the 1st tier (Purple–Green) believe that they are right and everyone else is wrong. This is why there is so much disagreement when it comes to what's wrong in the education system and how to fix it.

It's only when the individual or group evolves to the 2nd tier (Yellow and Turquoise) that they can appreciate that all the value systems have merit, and the trick is to gather all the good initiatives from each one and leave behind what doesn't work.

Going back to the history, by the start of the 20th century, schools lacked cash. They were often old unkempt buildings running an autocratic disciplinary model of education that even then was starting to look a little outdated.

One of the decisive moments in the Principle Wave was the Education Act of 1902. Often known as the Balfour Act, this Act established the Local Education Authorities (LEAs) as the primary source of authority on education in England. It gave them powers to raise local taxes to fund schools. All the church schools and endowed grammar schools, which formed the bulk of what might be described as an education system, now came under the supervision of 328 LEAs. The idea was that these LEAs would pay for teachers and the maintenance of schools, and it also led to the creation of over 1,000 new municipal or county secondary schools including 349 girls' schools. LEAs were responsible for the secular curriculum which now included science and languages. And in 1904 the Board of Education mandated a four-year subject-based course of English, geography, history, foreign language, mathematics, science, drawing, manual work, physical training and for girls and 'housewifery'. This was the first time that a broad curriculum was available for all.

The Root of the Performance Wave (Leading Edge)

It's interesting to note that the word curriculum comes from the Latin verb *currere*, meaning to run. The noun curriculum translates as 'racecourse', and whilst it may describe the subjects taught there can be little doubt that the inclusion of a curriculum still constitutes a race designed to determine winners and losers. These roots, laid down at the beginning of the 20th century, would blossom much later and form a major part of the Performance Wave, with all its competitive league tables, financial based incentives and reductionist approach to knowledge.

In France in 1905, for example, the first intelligence test emerged. Commissioned by the French government to develop an instrument that could identify intelligence levels in school children so those that needed extra help could get it. Psychologist Alfred Binet, together with his colleague Theodore Simon, created the Binet-Simon Intelligence Scale.[9] Initially used in the Principle Wave to identify capability and stratify resources, IQ testing was subsequently co-opted by forces, benign and malign, to push their own agenda, including by those in the Performance Wave to win the game of education.

During the first half of the 20th century, education gradually improved as the principles of education and the quality standards began to bite. Educational delivery became more consistent and more efficient. The school leaving age was progressively raised to 11 years old in 1893, 12 in 1899 and 14 in 1921.

The Butler Act, a 1944 update to the Education Act of 1902, created an educational landscape that is very much recognisable today. State education was now free for all children, separating primary schools (5–11 years old) and secondary schools (11–15 years old). LEAs also provided nursery provision, disability provision and boarding. And the compulsory school leaving age was increased once again, first to 15 and then 16 in 1973.

Secondary education, stratified in the Taunton Report (1868), was formalised in the 'Tripartite system', consisting of grammar schools, secondary modern schools and secondary technical schools. Selective entry to grammar schools was based on the Scholarship Exam, later known as the 11+. Much of this activity was still driven from the Principle Wave.

After World War II the seeds of the Performance Wave started to emerge more strongly. In this wave it's all about pragmatism, productivity and hitting targets. The idea of testing children, which started with the IQ tests of Binet and Simon, really came to the fore. The goal was to segment children based on ability and to assess those with intellectual disability. In 1951 national exams were introduced in England and Wales, the General Certificate of Education with its ordinary O level and its advanced A level testing became widespread.

Rewards, very much an Orange value system idea actioned in the Performance Wave, became a tool alongside punishment, which was a throwback from the more disciplinary days of the Principle Wave. The importance of rewards were baked into the system from the inception of primary schools. Star charts and team points were used in tandem with demerits, the 'naughty step', and detentions to motivate children to behave in the expected fashion.

But it didn't take long for the obvious flaw in Performance Wave thinking to become apparent. The rewards in the system were only available to those who did well in exams and were extrinsically driven. Children with all sorts of other abilities were left behind. Remember the tests were heavily biased toward linguistic and numerical ability, and if a child didn't fit into that particular box, they invariably lost interest as their own identities began to emerge. These children often felt punished by their failure and felt the pain of the loss of social standing that accompanied such failure. In truth there had been winners and losers since the first ever schools in 597. Often the winners were the elites and the children of the wealthy (regardless of academic prowess) and the losers were the poor, reinforcing the ever-widening equity gap. The testing regime of the Performance Wave brought these disparities to the forefront.

The merit of rigid testing around narrow capabilities and the subsequent reward and punishment based on results remain a passionate debate in education to this day.

The Emergence of the Progressive Wave

For those who did well in exams at school there were options. For those that didn't, the options were much more limited. It didn't matter if they just couldn't adapt to the process, struggled to perform on exam day if they failed to 'get their grades', doors closed. It was the polarising nature of a narrow performance-driven system that created the conditions for the Progressive Wave to emerge.

The Green value system underpinning the Progressive Wave in educational thinking started with Rudolph Steiner. Steiner was a pioneer, way ahead of his time, advocating for a much more holistic, progressive approach in the late 19th century. But this sort of thinking didn't really become widely established in society until the 1960s. The desire for a more inclusive approach was rooted in the civil rights movement. It was fuelled by a rise in feminist thinking, gay rights and an interest in sustainability. In the UK progressive thinking delivered the introduction of a School Health Service which instituted the provision of school meals, free milk, medical and dental care. Schools were becoming responsible for more than just teaching.

Although logical and necessary to meet social need, the Tripartite system that came out the Taunton Report was deeply unpopular and socially divisive. The inequity it created was felt most strongly by the progressives. Some LEAs, particularly those in Labour controlled constituencies with their more socialist ideology, started to abandon such educational segmentation in favour of a more inclusive mixed ability comprehensive education. By 1965 the Labour government was encouraging all LEAs to do the same, although it was not mandatory. As a result, some LEAs retained the more Traditional 11+ and grammar schools, particularly in Conservative constituencies, but most went fully comprehensive abandoning the 11+ and streaming children based on ability.

The Plowden Report of 1967 ushered in a new optimism in education, promoting new ways of teaching. This consolidated the emergence of progressivism which espoused humanistic and child-centric approaches. In many ways the 1960s was the era of experimentation and idealism, of individualised teaching and teachers responsible for the curriculum. By the 1970s education had become a political football with battle lines drawn between the Traditionalists (often Conservative Councils) and the Progressives (often Labour Councils) and the more pragmatic believers in a performance-based approach. Little has changed in this debate since. The same battle trenches exist, and the same arguments are being made. The OECD's Programme for International Student Assessment (PISA) tables, which assess the knowledge and skills of 15-year-old students in reading, mathematics and science, still dominate senior decision making.

Countries strive to be at the top of the global academic tables in the same way a 5-year-old can prize being at the top of the maths test on a Monday morning. We have reached an educational stalemate where collaboration is almost impossible. If our economies are based on the quality of our education system, and that system needs to win or be at the top of some league table, no one is encouraged to collaborate for fear of giving away secrets that could allow another system to leapfrog them on the league table. The result is a kind of 75-year war, leaving us in desperate need of a breakthrough and a complete overhaul of the entire system.

In the early years of this 75-year war throughout the 1970s and 1980s, there was a growing sense of declining standards and school discipline – sound familiar? In 1988, to move the battle lines, the Education Reform Act, otherwise known as the Baker Act, introduced a compulsory National Curriculum consisting of 14 subjects. Teachers were no longer in charge of the curriculum. But they were accountable for it through the introduction of compulsory assessments (SATS) at ages 7, 11, 14 and 16 (GCSE). League tables became the evidence of excellence and failure. This reductionist approach changed what many call 'quality teaching.' The obsession with performance caused many teachers who don't see test performance as the only important outcome to disengage.

The Baker Act also marked the beginning of a separate war, to wrestle control of schools away from LEAs and teachers to an alliance of parents and central government. The aim was to boost standards by creating a 'market' in education of competing schools. This is archetypal Performance Wave thinking. The whole idea was to introduce business performance principles into schools, even though many passionate advocates for such performance principles have suggested that the business obsession with results, and in particular financial results, has been completely over cooked. For example, Mark Carney, the ex-Governor of the Bank of England, wrote a book admitting that financial performance advocates like himself may have lost sight of the importance of social value in the single-minded pursuit of financial value.

Nevertheless, parents were encouraged to choose which school they wanted to send their children to. Schools with declining headcounts would have to improve or shut down. Market forces were to determine the future of education.

In 1992 The Education (Schools) Act established the Office of Standards in Education (Ofsted) to inspect schools on a six yearly cycle, having the power to name and shame schools based on performance.

The Baker Act also saw the introduction of City Academies and specialist schools. From the early 2000s academies were state schools outside LEA control with autonomy in budget control and curriculum and 'academisation' became policy in the next three government administrations. Specialist schools allowed schools to focus on differentiating areas of the curriculum while still observing the National Curriculum.

The obsession with endless testing, and Ofsted inspections is widely believed to have had a detrimental impact on students, teachers and school administrators.

Clearly some form of inspection has its place, particularly around student safeguarding, but education itself is definitive. It involves human beings and they tend to be messy and complex. Those at the cutting edge of educational thinking, the Progressives, realised there was an unintended negative impact of excessive performance focus very early on. So, they've been advocating for a move away from an obsession with performance-based ideas to a more holistic, diverse and inclusive value system approach.

The roots of the Progressive Wave of education are in the alternative schooling methods, such as Steiner, Dewey or Montessori, which have been around since the beginning of the 20th century (more on that in chapter 2). The Progressive Wave promoted these until they have become more widespread and accessible. Parents unwilling to subject their children to endless assessment explored home schooling. In 2021 Councils in England reported a 34% jump in the number of parents choosing to take their children out of school and teach them at home or create a Free School. This equates to 115,542 children across 152 local authorities.[10] And that's just in England. It is steadily rising post-Covid.

Instead of results at all costs, which is the primary goal of the Performance Wave, the Progressive Wave seeks a much more human centric, individualised approach. Such a motive is understandable. But paradoxically, the desire for inclusivity extolled by the Progressive Wave may be creating an even more fragmented education system as new battle lines have been drawn with the traditionalists along the 'woke and anti-woke agenda'.[11]

Glimmers of the Polarities Wave

To the best of our knowledge there is no education system that is currently operating at the Polarities Wave. There are not even any individual examples of schools or projects that have taken this step, never mind a system scaled at a national level.

There are however glimmers of this wave in the Finnish and Singapore education systems. Whilst these systems are often held in high regard for their progressive nature and innovation, supposedly reflected in their PISA outcomes, there are still many parts of their systems that are presenting challenges related to the downsides of the Progressive or Performance Waves, respectively. In Finland, for example, the disparity in rural-urban education still presents issues despite the Finnish reputation for equality and community connection. Critics of the system also see the homogeneous nature of the population as lacking diversity awareness for global skills compared to Singapore's more global approach. Singapore's outreach is also internal, that whilst competitive, creates a 'give away our best ideas' approach between schools so that schools are forced to evolve further and come up with even better ideas.

Where Finland is criticised for less standardised testing, Singapore is critiqued for too much. Each major exam divides students into schools based upon their academic results. This tension creates judgement and performance pressure where students and their parents are constantly competing to get into the best schools. Unsurprisingly, over-tuition is rife relentlessly driving toward narrow success markers which, in turn, drive greater inequality. This performance pressure excludes creativity and critical thinking and puts additional strain on teacher workload despite the strong focus on continuous professional development (CPD).

Investing in human capital appears to have not quite struck the right balance. Whilst Singapore has begun to emphasise a more holistic, digital and global approach to education, aiming to develop students intellectually, socially, emotionally and physically, the focus remains on readying for the future workforce. The talk may be more in keeping with the Polarities Wave, but the action is still a mix of the Performance and Progressive Waves. Whilst this future planning can be seen as positive, the downside is that the skill set is being determined by the pursuit of excellence – the hallmark of the Performance Wave. Singapore's former prime minister, Lee Kuan Yew, managed to demonstrate both the upside of the Progressive Wave and the downside of the Performance Wave within the same sentence when stating their strategy was "to develop Singapore's only available natural resource: its people".[12]

No Longer Fit for Purpose

Collectively these waves of educational thinking in the UK and around the world have sought to create a system that meets the needs of the population, business, industry and society at each moment in history. It's no longer working.

According to the Times Education Commission Report published in 2022, our education system is failing on all measures, from giving young people the intellectual and emotional tools they need as adults to providing businesses with the skills they need. According to the report, 75% of companies say they need to provide extra training in basic skills.[13]

Never mind the financial cost and disillusionment of endless failed initiatives, there is a huge social cost associated with low educational attainment including unemployment, poverty, homelessness, crime and poor health.[14]

When children don't get the education they need, society, not just the child, loses out. A study by UCLA in the US found that high school dropouts in California cost the Californian taxpayers $37–$56 billion per cohort.[15] A study at the University of Michigan found that students who attended a better-funded elementary school were 15% less likely to be arrested at age 30 than those who did not.[16] In 2012 The White House Council for Community Solutions reported that if America could persistently connect all young people as full participants in the US economy, the nation's balance sheet would expand in the order of around $5 *trillion* a year in taxes paid and direct costs avoided.[17] It's likely to be significantly more today.

Right now, because we don't view the progression of education (or much else) from an evolutionary perspective, we tend to move forward including the worst parts of each era, not the best.

Arguably, one of the worse elements of the educational system that still exists today and was kicked off by St Augustine in 598 is the effective apartheid in teaching. In the early days education was only accessible to a tiny, privileged minority, the sons of the wealthy. It would be over 700 years before education was made available to the less privileged. This educational exclusion is still widespread in many countries today, despite significant evidence of the societal benefits when educational inequality is overcome.

Take Finland, for example, there are no fee-paying schools in the country. All the schools are 100% publicly funded. Finland keeps all students in the same classroom and provides extra help to those that need it. Every student has equal access to free school meals, health care, psychological counselling and individual student guidance, regardless of socioeconomic background.[18]

As a result, people of different socio-economic backgrounds mix and become friends. They better understand a different way of life and are more empathetic and compassionate. If wealthy parents want to donate money to the school to help their child, then everyone in the school or class benefits not just their child. Not only does Finland have one of the best education systems in the world, but this approach helps to bake greater equality into the system.[19]

Whether an education system is responsive now and ready for the future largely comes down to its purpose. During the Pastoral and Power Waves education wasn't even about education. It was little more than childcare that allowed parents to work in the factories of an industrialised society. Later it became a box ticking exercise to comply with regulation that allowed the children to work in those same factories and contribute to the larger economy. When society doesn't really value education and sees it as childcare or an enabler for the workforce, then teachers' well-being doesn't matter either. Often a woman pulled from the factory floor to 'educate' the children was all that was required. What's even more alarming is that some are suggesting that AI may make teachers nothing more than babysitters once again.

George Bernard Shaw once said, "Those who can, do; those who can't, teach." It's still a sentiment that is banded about today. The phrase is a corruption of Aristotle's "those that know, do. Those that understand, teach." But that truth is left on the cutting room floor. When education was little more than childcare, then the job of teacher fell to those that were valued less, in this case women.

The fact that there are so many female teachers is even being blamed for the lack of discipline in modern school and the fact that boys are falling behind. Because somehow having a female teacher disadvantages boys. But this is just one of many unintended consequences born out of the fact that genuine education was neither wanted nor needed. And even though the purpose of education has changed, the status of teaching has sadly not improved a great deal.

Researchers at Brown University and the University at Albany compiled and analysed decades' worth of national data from more than a dozen sources about factors like teachers' morale, the perceived prestige of the profession and interest in entering the field to create an annual profile of the profession between 1970 and 2022. What they found was a job that's steadily declined in prestige and attractiveness.[20] It's hard to imagine the results would be much better in the UK.

We are now in the unenviable position where the National Curriculum is no longer fit for purpose, and teacher's delivering it know this but often lack the agency to change it or how they deliver it. The world does not need obedient people to slot into factory jobs, not least because there are fewer and fewer factory jobs to slot into. Mechanisation, roboticisation and technological transformation is completely upending the labour market. The education that children are leaving school with, is not equipping them to meet the needs of society today let alone navigate the risks and opportunities of tomorrow.

The instructional approach still reigns supreme through a standardised curriculum and teachers are simply expected to race through it. Lessons are no longer just dominated by the textbook, but also PowerPoint presentations and detailed lesson plans. Teachers receive a set of slides to match the curriculum content, in line with the learning outcomes that leads towards the test content, question type and outcomes. Lesson plans or 'learning plans' outline the lesson down to the last minute and become little more than a daily teacher drudgery. Whilst the lack of agency for learners has restricted creativity and curiosity, and therefore confidence, this is now mirrored in those who must deliver the right content at a frenetic pace. There is no space. How can a teacher feel confident or curious about their own subject if it is formatted and handed to them digitally? The energy a teacher turns up with is key to creating the right state, context and connection to motivate and engage the young people. Yet teachers are being funnelled into a performance system as much as learners and their connection with learners is suffering as a result. No wonder teacher morale is at an all-time low and the profession is struggling to attract and keep the best and brightest teachers.[21] It's hardly surprising that so many are lured away into other sectors, with less stress, more pay and less abuse!

If we don't' learn and build from the past, we're destined to repeat it. And we can certainly see history repeating itself now. Prior to the 1840 Grammar Schools Act, the state was not very active in education. It had largely been the preserve of the Church, religious charities or philanthropic individuals. But grammar schools were in crisis. The curriculum was considered too narrow to cater to the needs of the Industrial Revolution. The 1840 Act made it legal to use grammar school income for more than simply teaching classic languages and religion. The school curriculum opened to teach English reading, writing, maths, science and languages. As such the system adapted and provided the education that was needed at that time. As we wrestle with the realities of the 4th Industrial Revolution, we face the same urgent need to pivot and the space and resources to do it.

But we've done it before so we can do it again.

Notes

1. de Villiers W (2015) Mandela's belief that education can change the world is still a dream, The Conversation.
2. No Author (2016) Why 'bring-backery' should go back where it came from, The Guardian.
3. Craft M Ed (1984) Education for diversity, chapter in education and cultural pluralism, Routledge, London.
4. Barr H (2022) Taliban close girls' secondar schools in Afghanistan, again, Human Rights Watch.
5. Taylor Gatto J (2017) The underground history of American education, Oxford Scholars Press.
6. Taylor Gatto J (2009) Weapons of mass instruction, New Society Publishers, Gabriola Island, BC.
7. Watkins A, Dalton N (2020) The HR (r)evolution: change the workplace, change the world, Routledge, London.
8. Toynbee P (2021) While Williamson calls for discipline, our children's hopes crumble around them, The Guardian.
9. Cherry K (2020) Alfred Binet and the Simon-Binet intelligence scale, VeryWellMind.
10. Weale S (2021) Councils in England report 34% rise in elective home education, Guardian.
11. McDonagh M (2021) Inside the woke classroom: what are they teaching your children at school? The Telegraph.
12. Suryadinata L (2012) Southeast Asian personalities of Chinese descent vol 1: a biographical dictionary, ISEAS Publishing, Singapore.
13. Sylvester R (2022) Bringing out the best: how to transform education and unleash the potential of every child.
14. No Author (n.d.) Bad apples: the high social cost of educational failure, Ed100.
15. Belfield CR (2014) The costs of high school failure and school suspensions for the state of California, The Center for Civil Rights Remedies.
16. Baron EJ, Hyman JM, Vasquez BN (2022) Public school funding, school quality, and adult crime, National Bureau of Economic Research.
17. No Author (n.d.) Bad apples, Ed100.
18. Weale S (2019) Top of the class: labour seeks to emulate Finland's school system, The Guardian.
19. Moore M (2017) Why Finland has the best education, YouTube.
20. Peetz C (2022) The status of the teaching profession is at a 50-year low. what can we do about it? Education Week.
21. Allen B, Ford I, Hannay T (2023) Teacher recruitment and retention in 2023, Teachertapp.

PART ONE
The State of the Education System

1 Current Reality in Education

If we look at education in the UK and around the world, most systems are locked in an ideological battle with two profoundly different waves (Principle Wave and Performance Wave) smashing against each other, with pupils and teachers caught in the cross currents and undertows. The Principle Wave seeks to impose an adherence to the rules through a prescriptive path of learning. The Performance Wave advocates measuring the success of learning or knowledge transfer via an endless battery of tests to determine the performance of the learner and the system. This endless tug of war between the waves is counter-productive, draining resources and creating chaos.

If we want to reset the system, we must start by addressing the purpose of education. Many believe the purpose of education is 'learning'. In the UK we have a 'knowledge rich curriculum' and a focus on 'lifelong learning' with lots of discussions about the learning environment, learning styles and readiness to learn. Unsurprisingly, teachers tend to stick with traditional chalk and talk methods, and are often afraid to switch pedagogical approaches within sessions. In many ways, a focus on learning makes logical sense. Surely, education exists to teach children knowledge that will prepare them for adulthood and how to be a productive member of society. But what does a productive member of society really mean, especially when that society has changed dramatically since the education system emerged.

In the Power Wave, a productive member of society was someone who worked insanely long hours in a mill or factory, and that included children. Their education, if it existed at all, was designed to get them back to their machine faster. Or education was an apprentice style teaching from adult to child that allowed that child to work the machines. To that end education did prepare the child for adult life. But it wasn't education as we understand the term today.

Obviously, any modern educational system must teach children how to read, write and be capable of basic arithmetic. This minimum standard is as relevant today as it ever was. Such skills are necessary to enable children to make sense of the world around them and interact with others. But being a productive member of society today is very different to what was required during the Power Wave of the Industrial Revolution.

In 1904 while the Board of Education created the first standard curriculum available to all, there were no standards on how to teach each subject. It was left to the discretion of the teacher, which had advantages and disadvantages. The curriculum and how subjects should be taught wasn't formally updated and modernised until 1988 via the Education Reform Act, which introduced 14 compulsory subjects. This introduced a more prescriptive way these subjects should be taught, at the time, via textbooks that aligned with the 'essential knowledge'. However, the use of textbooks has been replaced by cheaper online resources,[1] the quality and financial intention behind which remain a concern, as does the use of even more prescriptive practice papers that further narrows what needs to be known to pass exams.

The laying out of rules on how subjects should be taught and the creation of a National Curriculum both emerged from the Principle Wave. It was embraced by the hyper-rational, pragmatic Performance Wave as a way to deliver better results and improved productivity. It also provided a way of assessing teachers against a set of criteria. Performance Wave advocates are driven to understand how things work and will often break a system down into its component parts. In education that meant deconstructing what knowledge children needed to learn into the relevant subject areas, and further distilling this into what would be covered in each subject.

Whilst the current version of the English National Curriculum (2013) states that schools should "promote the spiritual, moral, cultural, mental and physical development of pupils at the school and of society" and "prepare pupils at the school for the opportunities, responsibilities and experiences of later life",[2] *the* focus remains on academic outcomes. This reductionist thinking fed into another Performance urge – the desire to test, separate and rank individuals based on capability. Sadly, the performance system that was built, and rolled out to all schools, is far from perfect, with good evidence that many exam papers are being mis-marked.[3] Nevertheless, a National Curriculum and a standardised syllabus has allowed a testing regimen to flourish.

When we look at education through this lens of evolving waves underpinned by different value systems. the upside and downside of our current system make much more sense. The problems with the current system are not due to bad intentions or bad actors. Most educational innovations are created with the best intentions, and the National Curriculum is no exception. It made sense at the time. But it doesn't anymore. One of the unintended consequences of the Performance Wave, which is increasingly causing educational and societal problems, is the 'Cult of the Expert'.

In most primary school systems in the world, one teacher teaches everything to all the children in the class. But in secondary school, each subject is taught by a 'subject expert'. If that child goes on to university, they often experience a micro-specialisation with lectures from a super expert. The general philosophy and direction of travel is that we increasingly encounter someone who knows more and more about less and less.

At each level from secondary school onwards, it would be a stretch to say that the teachers were experts in their specific subject. This isn't an insult to teachers. We know many teachers wouldn't consider themselves experts in their area. That's not what's being asked of them. Their job is to teach a prescriptive package of information to their students, so that those students can regurgitate the material in an exam and demonstrate the successful transfer of knowledge.

But often the curriculum teachers follow is ten or more years old. The National Curriculum in England for example, hasn't been updated since 2014.[4] To illustrate, in economics Milton Friedman is still taught as good economic theory, even though his thinking has been discredited and is seen as wildly out of date. Freidman is largely to blame for the systemic maximisation of shareholder value that even the most ardent hard-nosed capitalists acknowledge has been an overreach and has been counterproductive to economic sustainability.

In addition, the narrowing of knowledge transfer around the topics that will show up in an exam means there is virtually no cross-fertilisation of subjects. Knowledge remains siloed. A history teacher is unlikely to know about the geographic constraints on a society throughout history and how this may have evolved. They wouldn't be expected to know about the progress of mathematical thinking throughout history or how changes in artistic opinion affected culture and the perception of historical facts. All these subtle subject interactions are largely ignored. Such richness in understanding is not available to most pupils simply because education isn't thought of as an interdisciplinary sport. Education is seen as a collection of independent knowledge villages that are disconnected with few if any connecting roads, bridle paths or walkways.

The Performance Wave's desire to stick with the Cult of the Expert when knowledge is constantly changing seems both naïve and futile. Things we thought were true, even ten years ago, especially in science, are no longer accurate. Back in 1981, before the 4th industrial revolution with its digital acceleration, AI (artificial intelligence), machine learning and large language models, futurist and inventor R. Buckminster Fuller proposed something called "the knowledge doubling curve". He'd noticed that the more knowledge we accumulate, the faster we create and accumulate even more knowledge.

For example, until 1900 human knowledge doubled every one hundred years or so. By 1945 the complete knowledge of mankind doubled every 25 years. By 1982 knowledge was doubling every 12–13 months.[5] IBM predicted that knowledge would double every 11 hours.[6] No one has attempted to update this figure probably because it's now impossibly complex, but it's safe to assume it's even faster than that.[7]

And yet we're still teaching children about a world that existed when the National Curriculum was created in 1988 or at best 2014. Besides, do children really need to know that the stratosphere is the second layer of the atmosphere of

Earth, located above the troposphere and below the mesosphere. Or what the capital of Nigeria is? They may need to know if they plan to specialise in climate science or want to backpack through Africa but does that piece of knowledge need to live in their mind at 14 years old? Is anyone made wiser or more capable because of that knowledge? It may be useful in a school quiz, but there are much more useful things for teenagers to know. Anyway, in the unlikely scenario that they do need to know such a specific piece of information, they have Google.

We are all now connected to the internet, the world's largest library via our smartphones 24 hours a day. Technological advances are obsoleting the National Curriculum. In addition, advances in AI are already making it impossible for teachers to tell the difference between an essay created by a student and one created by ChatGPT. In one study of students over 18 years old, 89% confessed to using AI to complete study tasks.[8]

We no longer need the simple transfer of information from one brain to another. The urgent requirement is for critical thinking, problem solving and teaching children how to assess the accuracy and validity of the tsunami of information they are privy to every day inside a system that is dedicated to development and not just learning.

Learning on its own is now relatively pointless. Learning must be applied and used for it to be relevant. Little wonder that most adults struggle to tell you anything they learned in school that they use every day except reading, writing and arithmetic!

We must guide students to use the vast reserves of knowledge that are available to them, to make their lives better and to better prepare them for a world that is immeasurably different to the one even their parents grew up in. In the teenage years, learners are shaped and distracted by information that is increasingly fake or polarising. No wonder youngsters today feel lost and 'mental health' problems are on the rise.

How Does the Current Reality Impact Young People?

Education today seems to be a very effective method for crushing pupil's spirit and natural curiosity, and this can lead to a host of negative consequences.

According to social psychologist Thomas Curran, many of our young people are in the grip of escalating perfectionism. This endless quest for perfection, used as an indicator of self-worth, has been increasing at an alarming rate over the last 25 years. And yet perfectionism conceals a host of psychological challenges, including depression, anxiety, anorexia, bulimia and suicide ideation. Rates of suicide in the US alone increased by 25% in the last two decades. And there are similar trends in Canada and the UK.[9]

Mental illness among young people is higher now than ever before, largely because of the collision between two converging trends. First, education became a constant litany of tests, exams, metrics, rankings and league tables. And these measures are used as the yardstick of success. Individuals and schools are now quantified, ranked and sorted based on a very narrow set of capabilities.

And as Curran reminds us, this measurement starts young. Young people in America's big city high schools take around 112 mandatory standardised tests between pre-kindergarten and the end of 12th grade. This means about nine exams a year, or roughly one every month. If the educational system doesn't serve that student's way of learning, that's a monthly reminder of what a failure they are.

Ever since the Performance Wave came to dominate education, testing has been so widespread and relentless that pupils are now brain washed. Many pupils define themselves in very narrow terms, based on grades and percentiles. Parents are often drawn into such metric obsession and often see their own children as worthwhile if they remain a 'straight-A' student. With the disintegration of other social markers, parents often live vicariously through their child's success.

In addition to perpetual measurement and ranking, social media is the other major disruptive trend that puts massive pressure on young people to be perfect. Data from the Pew Research Centre show, for example, that young people born in the US in the late 1980s are 20% more likely to report life goals that include being materially rich compared to their parents or grandparents. Young people borrow more and spend more of their income on image goods and status possession to be displayed on social media to present the illusion of perfection, not just in the real world but now also in the virtual world too.[10]

The convergence of these two trends is destroying self-worth and setting far too many children up for failure and low self-esteem. Children who are assessed and compared all the time either by an education system, society or their peers are constantly classed as winners or losers, and of course most of them fall into the latter category. Little wonder then that most children are feeling left behind, rendering them vulnerable to extremist behaviour. This is particularly true of disenfranchised young men, in search of a sense of belonging and purpose who are now at risk of grooming by misogynistic influencers like Andrew Tate. Tate's reach and sway over millions of young boys is so alarming that schools across the UK are having to work out how teachers can respond.[11]

Although some of his ideology is straightforward personal development, his attitude towards women is abhorrent. The idea being that if women were subjugated again and forced back into the home and out the workplace, it wouldn't matter that so many of the boys 'failed', they would still be able to get a good job. The same hate of 'the other' extends beyond incel (involuntarily celibate) communities who hate women but also people of colour in white nationalism.

Of course, these are the extremes, but they are having a significant impact. These modern examples of outdated attitudes suggest we must challenge such arcane unpleasantness otherwise their influence may grow. There are now millions of polarised or marginalised individuals, particularly young men who feel inadequate and left behind. And they *are* being left behind, but so are millions of young women who are also being unfairly judged and pigeon-holed based on an insanely narrow definition of capability (or beauty) that is measured by tests (or likes) that are supposed to prepare them for a world that no longer exists!

The idea that if a pupil can remember facts and repeat them under exam conditions, they are a winner and if not, they are a loser is preposterous. Besides, the exams are rigged to ensure that only 60% can pass each year! There are two types of grading: grading on a bell curve and grading to a standard. Grading on a bell curve is grading by position. In other words, a student's grade depends on where they are in relation to the other students taking the test, with the top x% getting an A, the next y% getting a B and so on. Grading to a standard is when every student that scores say, 80% or more gets an A, 70–79% gets a B and so on. Most large-scale exam systems like the English GCSE and A levels use elements of both. The GCSE & A levels are mainly standards based, but some element of grading to the bell curve is used to finalise the grade boundaries, because while exam difficulty may vary from year to year, the abilities of large entry cohorts do not change much. So, roughly, the same number of A grades or Level 1s, etc. are considered *deserved* each year. Everyone in education knows this, and yet the government still beats up the profession for falling standards, even though it is the government that implements and adjusts the standards!

And a move to continuous assessment didn't help either. Instead of being stressed for a few weeks before the exams, young people are now stressed all the time, with the corresponding impact on mental health and well-being. In addition, continuous assessment disproportionately favours girls, who tend to be more diligent than boys, thereby inadvertently increasing the risk of more boys failing in education. Continuous assessment is also an extrinsic motivational driver, applied from outside, and yet we already know from motivational theory that extrinsic drivers only have an impact on simple tasks over a short period of time and continuous assessment is neither (more on that in chapter 10).

There are also many types of human intelligence, so disproportionately favouring maths, English or science and under rewarding musical, visual-spatial or kinaesthetic/sporting capability, to name just a few, seems completely outdated given what we now know about the predictors of success and flourishing.

Even the minority of pupils that succeed in the system and are rewarded, are also being groomed towards perfectionism, with the corresponding pressure on mental health. We are living with a system that can potentially render all students' losers in the longer-term game of life.

In addition, there are thousands of children that are excluded from school in the UK every year. Of those that re-enter post exclusion, many are just going through the motions and remain disengaged and uninterested – patterns that often become entrenched if they subsequently seek to enter the workforce. These pupils have been conditioned to believe that they have no value and can expect nothing more than poorly paid positions or zero hours contracts, perpetuating or widening the poverty gap. They are the equivalent of the factory workers in the Industrial Revolution, having to endure poor conditions because they didn't believe they had a choice.

Ironically, those who are the so-called winners may not do much better. They are no more prepared for the world than their less academic peers. They may secure a university placement and gain their degree but that's no longer a guarantee of future success.

As the late Sir Ken Robinson pointed out, when Baby Boomers and Gen Xers went to school, they were kept there with a story that if they worked hard, did well and got a university degree, they would get a good job. But children today don't believe that anymore and they are right not to.[12] For many graduates all they have to show for their efforts is massive student debt, crushed dreams and a disenfranchised outlook.

Robinson also reminds us that the way schools were set up, baked in the idea that there were academic people and non-academic people into the system. Over time this was simplified into those who were smart and those who were not. As a result, millions and millions of bright, gifted children left school believing they were not.[13] We are seeing this bias to narrow academic success amplified in the cost-of-living crisis, as scarce resources in state schools are increasingly pulled away from non-academic pursuits, further diminishing the perceived value of those subjects.

No one is cutting funding to maths. In fact, if former UK Prime Minister Rishi Sunak got his way everyone in England would have been forced to study maths until 18 years old. Sunak said he wanted people to feel confident when it came to finances![14] Forget for a moment that there is a national shortage of maths teachers or that maths is not necessary for every profession or that not everyone has a brain that is wired for maths, maths does little to help students understand how money works. That's an entirely different topic normally completely missed out of the curriculum or covered as an afterthought as part of personal, social, health and economic education (PSHE).

Perhaps worst of all, for both the winners and the losers, school, and by association learning, is largely viewed as something to be endured, in the hope that it will improve the future. The educational system fosters a disillusionment with the very idea of learning. The reductionist bent of the Performance Wave breaks knowledge down into subjects, but in doing so the subjects are separated from each other and from life. This can make them sterile, abstract and boring. Is it any wonder that children are desperate to bring their learning to an end and get on with life?

Even if a student goes on to university, they instinctively breathe a sigh of relief when the learning is over, and they have the qualification. The 'winners and losers' end school or university with a poor impression of learning and little experience, if any of development, which can limit their prospects. If this isn't addressed, we perpetuate the incredibly low expectations subsequent generations may have of the educational system. Besides, we live in an accelerating world where learning and development can never be over. We need to inspire young people and adults to become insanely curious, and sustainably commit to lifelong learning and development, not just as buzzwords but as a way of life.

How Does the Current Reality Impact Educators?

Burnout and disillusionment.

Given the educational cultural wars between the Principle Wave and the Performance Wave, it's little wonder that teachers become highly focused on separate but interconnected issues including workload, pay, cut-backs, constant assessment and student behaviour.

A performance-obsessed system addicted to endless data collection and testing isn't just stressful for the students, it's terrible for the teachers too. Even if the knowledge transfer was a useful cornerstone of the educational system, massive class sizes make it virtually impossible to go back over material to make sure everyone has understood and further undermines classroom relationships.

Perhaps unsurprisingly, the latest workforce survey from the UK's Department for Education (DfE) found that of 40,000 teachers, almost 9% of the workforce, resigned from state schools in 2022, the highest number since DfE began publishing the data in 2011. And a further 4,000 retired.[15]

Of course, teachers leaving in their droves also puts additional pressure on the teachers left behind. Class sizes are expanding and it's inevitable that delivery, agency and relationships suffer, especially when the funding has been cut for classroom assistants to help in classes of mixed ability. Unfillable staff vacancies add even more pressure. Increasingly teachers are expected to work longer and longer hours, all while having to contend with poor public perception of their profession, a historical hangover from the days of teachers as child minders, certainly in the UK and US. Often the assumption is that teachers have it easy because they have so much time off. As a result, we are entrusting our society's future to a pool of demotivated, disenfranchised, under-resourced, under-paid, under-trained, under-developed albeit committed individuals trying their best inside a crumbling system. No wonder so many are resigning or thinking of a career change. It makes no sense that educators are valued so little when their role is to shape young minds in the present and build the future.

During 2022 and 2023 teachers in the UK, along with many other public sector workers, engaged in a series of strikes to demand fairer pay. According to the unions supporting the strike, high inflation and a cost-of-living crisis meant teachers were enduring a 20% cut in wages since 2010.[16]

But it's not just their pay that's so depressing for teachers; decades of underfunding have seen resources and budgets slashed, school buildings are often not fit for purpose and yet they are expected to provide world-class education. An estimated 700,000 children in England alone are being taught in unsafe or ageing school buildings which is negatively impacting the quality of their education. The UK's National Audit Office (NAO) report says the DfE has since 2021 assessed the risk of injury or death from a school building collapse as "very likely and critical". Teachers have expressed concerns about risks posed by sewage leaks and asbestos.[17]

The situation for those with special educational needs and disabilities (SEND) has additional hardships. The care given by staff facing some of the most challenging behaviour and learning needs in the sector is truly courageous. It is often done without recognition of the true progress these young people make against outcome metrics. Despite incredible efforts by employment and social groups such as Project Search and an understanding of the long-term financial impacts of a lack of early intervention and support into employment, there is still an almost complete lack of purpose and direction in the SEND agenda. Special needs provision is currently nothing short of immoral. It has been chronically underfunded, and many local educational authorities actively obfuscate their legal responsibilities and abandon parents, all while claiming to be engaged in 'parent partnerships'. The government and therefore budget holders are constantly moving the goal posts to avoid having to fund those that are already struggling with developmental delays or needing to access appropriate educational provision.

The profound lack of leadership at senior levels, the incredibly poor co-ordination at the local and national level and the shrinking budgets for anything outside maths, English and science is frankly shameful. Art, music and drama amongst others have been pushed to the margins creating what some have called a 'Creativity Crisis'.[18]

And, if the day-to-day life of a teacher wasn't stressful enough, Office for Standards in Education, Children's Services and Skills (Ofsted) inspections add to the pressure. Ofsted is notoriously rigid; it is a product of the Principle Wave and there's very little nuance. A school is given a very short, graded assessment of either grade 1 (outstanding), grade 2 (good), grade 3 (requires improvement) or grade 4 (inadequate). In March 2023 Ruth Perry, headteacher at Caversham Primary School in Reading for 13 years, killed herself following a report that downgraded her school from outstanding to inadequate.[19] Sadly, Perry is not the first person to take her own life because of draconian Ofsted assessments. Like so many ideas in education, Ofsted sounds logical. Its intention was to give parents a way to easily assess and compare schools in their area. But the reduction of the enormous complexity of what happens in a school, across so many pupils and so many subjects, into a single grade, effectively renders the report meaningless. It may be simple but it's profoundly unrealistic to imagine that everything in a school is outstanding all the time. Every school – the good, the bad and the ugly – are evolving. What is accurate today may not be accurate tomorrow, and yet these assessments impact student numbers and therefore funding.

Collectively this has exacerbated existing recruitment and retention problems. The National Association of Head Teachers has identified this as a "school leadership supply crisis", which has far-reaching consequences on the ability of the system to deliver the quality of education needed to 'right the ship' after the pandemic, let alone achieve the ambitious targets set by the government for 2030.[20]

Add student absenteeism (22.5% of pupils are persistently absent post-pandemic[21]) and disruptive behaviour into the mix and it's hardly surprising that teachers are seeking alternate employment options. According to the National Association of Schoolmasters Union of Women Teachers (NASUWT), physical and verbal abuse (from pupils and parents) and online harassment are now common in primary and secondary schools.[22]

How Does the Current Reality Impact Parents?

It creates confusion and stress.

The impact on parents very much depends on the parents and the geography. In England, families rank either three or six school preferences for their children. Local authorities then act as clearing houses using an algorithm to match applicants to schools on the basis of parental preferences, admission criteria and the availability of places. Enshrined in law since 1988, it was meant to give parents more choice, but it's just led to greater stress. According to a study by the Social Market Foundation, greater school choice has left parents feeling more "cynical, fatalistic and disempowered" than parents in Scotland, for example, where students are simply assigned a place in their nearest school unless their parents decide to apply to a different one.[23]

Because of the choice, parents are stressed about making the *right* choice, even more stressed when one child goes to one school and another child goes to another or when they must move house to access the school they want. And that's before the child sets foot on the premises.

Once in school, parents are worried about the quality of education, their child's academic performance, whether their child is falling behind and whether they would be notified if they were. If their child has learning difficulties, these concerns are amplified as cutbacks have meant delayed assessments, lower financial support for interventions and fewer classroom assistants. Every parent hopes that their child will develop socially, be happy and make friends, but there are also increased peer pressures and bullying to contend with. Today, social media gives bullies unfettered access to their targets 24/7. This access is also a concern when worrying about how to keep children safe.

Parents are often anxious about homework, whether there is too much or too little. Helicopter parenting doesn't help development, and we can see the downside of too much parental oversight in many of the Asian countries where 'Tiger Moms' have adopted an uber-performance driven approach to education. The term 'Tiger Mom' is used to describe a parenting style that is characterised by strictness, high expectations and an emphasis on academic and extracurricular achievement. Parents labelled as Tiger Moms are deeply involved in their children's lives, closely monitoring their academic performance and pushing them to excel in various activities, such as music, sports and other pursuits.

Critics of the approach say that it stops the child from being a child, increases stress, heightens pressure to succeed and potentially harms the child's emotional well-being.[24] In her memoir, *Battle Hymn of the Tiger Mother*, Amy Chua outlined the draconian methods she employed to raise her daughters and created some controversy. Chua it seemed was not interested in raising 'prizeless slackers'. She wanted prodigies, even if it meant nonstop, punishing labour. The book chronicles the author's constant demanding, wheedling, scolding and screaming around seemingly never-ending piano and violin sessions.[25] An endless series of extra-curricular activity on top of crushing amounts of homework is not always good for the individual or society.

This uber-performance Asian mindset has been instrumental in what Japan calls 'Karoshi', death from overwork. And as many as one million deaths in China can be attributed to the same philosophy.[26]

How Does the Current Reality Impact Society and the Economy?

Fosters inequality and low productivity.

If we look at the levels of educational attainment in the UK and internationally, the performance-obsessed systems have not necessarily delivered more rounded, compassionate, kind students that parents can be proud of, employers want in their organisations or contribute to better economic outcomes for society.

It may be true that the number of students achieving at least five GCSEs or equivalent increased from under 40% in the early 1990s to a high of 82% in 2012. And the number of people with a degree in the working-age population has more than doubled since 2000. But despite these rising qualifications, England stands out internationally for nearly non-existent improvements in skills when making comparisons across generations. In virtually all Organisation for Economic Cooperation and Development (OECD) countries, literacy and numeracy skills are substantially higher among young people aged 16–24 than among the older generation (aged 55–65). England is the exception to the rule: while its 55- to 65-year-olds perform relatively well, especially in literacy, young people in England have not improved on these skills at all. That has left England ranked 25th out of 32 countries in terms of the literacy skills of its young people.[27] And literacy is one of the basics schools focus on!

This is clearly concerning for businesses and employers who are not getting access to a labour supply that can meet their needs. According to a poll conducted by the CBI, more than 40% of employers reported being forced to pay for remedial training to bring school leavers' basic skills up to scratch. The survey of 566 employers also found that 42% were concerned about basic literacy standards while 35% were worried about numeracy among recent school leavers.[28]

There is little doubt this education shortfall is playing a role in the UK economy which has underperformed the most, compared to other similar economies after 2008. This has been exacerbated by the global financial crisis, Brexit and the pandemic.[29] But an education system that is no longer fit for purpose and is failing all the stakeholders is certainly not helping.

Every economy needs a skilled workforce. Currently, the UK's relatively high proportion of low-skilled adults means it performs well below average for both the OECD and the EU.[30]

And to make matters worse, despite decades of policy attention, there has been virtually no change in the 'disadvantage gap' in GCSE attainment over the past 20 years. Although GCSE attainment has increased over time, 16-year-olds who are eligible for free school meals are still around 27% less likely to earn good GCSEs than less disadvantaged peers. Children from disadvantaged backgrounds also make slower progress through secondary school. And these gaps get even wider when looking at more rigorous benchmarks for attainment. Pupils who were not eligible for free school meals are around three times as likely as their more disadvantaged peers to achieve above the expected level at age 11 and at GCSE. They were also three times more likely to attend one of the most selective higher education institutions.[31] The system clearly sustains societal inequality.

This inequality starts early in the current education system, and the gaps have certainly been exacerbated by endless cutbacks. This inequality also threatens social cohesion in many countries, including the UK. We need education systems that encourage social cohesion, which as the OECD suggests, "looks beyond the enrolment and achievement rates and takes into account the inclusiveness of the education system . . . to enhance the sense of belonging in a society and improve the quality of education for better prospects of upward mobility."[32] Without the opportunity of upward mobility that good education should provide, adults are too often resigned to poorly paying jobs and endless financial struggle and the mental health challenges this can bring. And without intervention the poor attainment and subsequent poverty cycle repeats across generations.

Finally, it's worth noting that education is suffering because it is a political football. In the last 20 years, there have been 15 Secretaries of Education in the UK, each in post for less than two years, and six from 2021 to 2023![33] This creates too much instability, resulting in endless course corrections as governments lurch from one quick fix, short term 'solution' to the next.

Education as a Wicked Problem for the 21st Century

The challenges we have outlined so far are by no means exhaustive, but they are a glimpse into the lived experiences and issues that face the various stakeholders in education. Education is certainly a wicked problem for the 21st century.

Current Reality in Education **35**

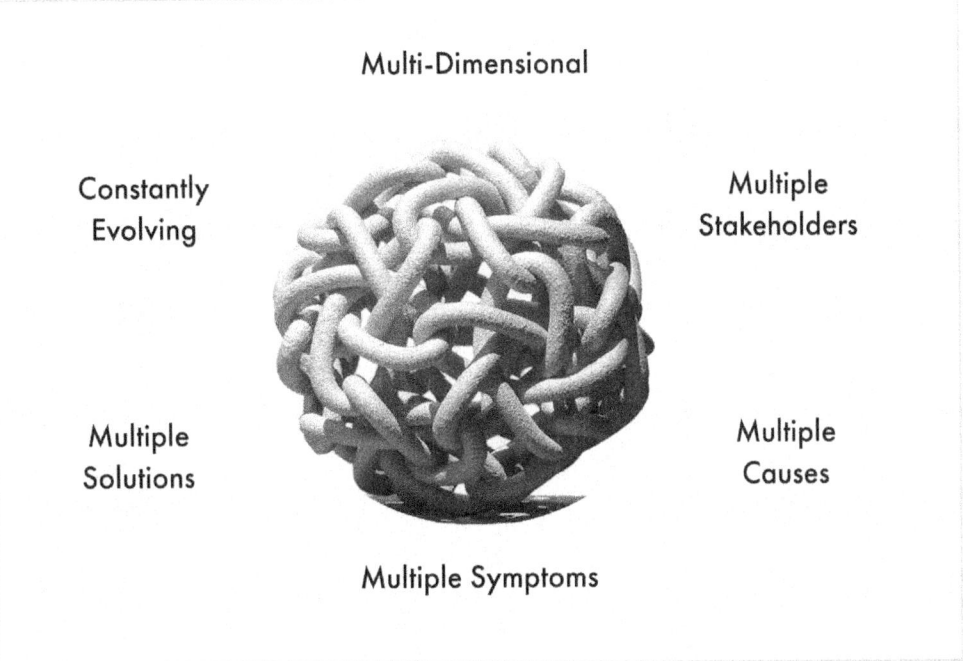

Figure 1.1 Definition of a Wicked Problem

The term 'wicked problem', originally coined by Professor Horst W J Rittel in 1967, was not used to suggest that the problem was somehow evil, although the consequences of these challenges can certainly appear so, but rather that there is a distinct difference between a 'tame' solvable problem and a 'wicked' intractable problem that is difficult or impossible to solve.[34]

A wicked problem has six key properties (Figure 1.1):

1. Multi-dimensional

2. Multiple stakeholders

3. Multiple causes

4. Multiple symptoms

5. Multiple solutions

6. Constantly evolving

Multi-Dimensional

All problems are multi-dimensional. Philosopher Ken Wilber was perhaps the first academic to clearly define the idea of the multi-dimensionality of life (Figure 1.2).

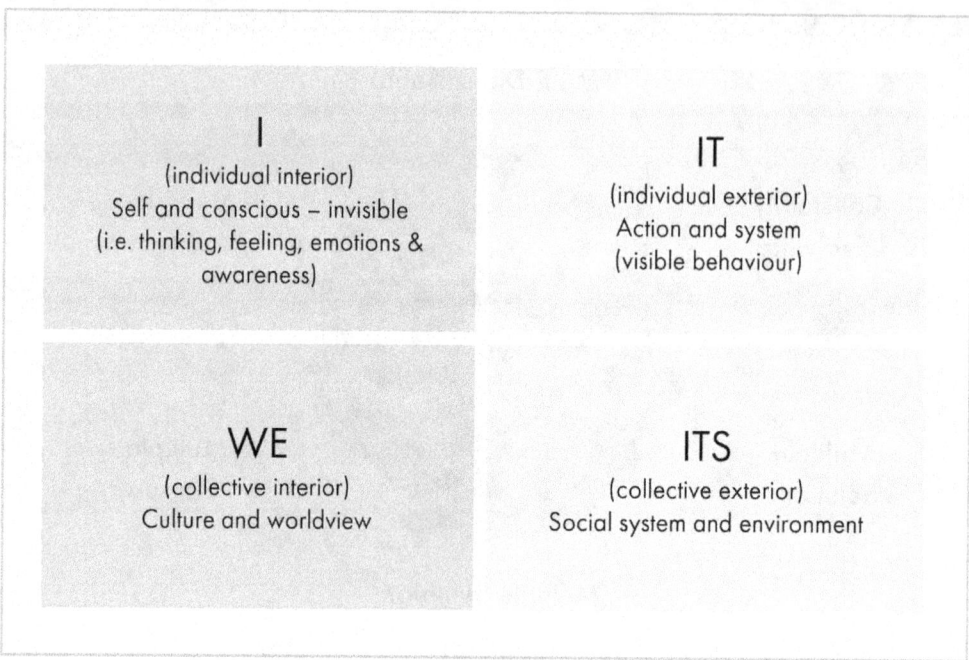

Figure 1.2 Original All Quadrants All Levels (AQAL) Model

He suggested that every aspect of human experience and every second of that experience occurs in more than one dimension. Therefore, all problems, wicked and otherwise, can be viewed from these dimensions.

He described these dimensions as the rational objective observable world of individual action ('IT'), as well as collective action and systems or processes ('ITS'). But he also pointed out that there were two interior dimensions: a subjective personal interior ('I') and an 'inside of the collective' dimension of interpersonal relating where all cultural norms exist ('WE').

When it comes to wicked problems, the common tendency is to exclusively look at behaviours ('IT') or systems, processes ('ITS') in the world of 'doing'. What are people doing about the problem? What systems and structures do we need to put in place? We ignore the interior subjective 'I' or 'being' and 'WE' or 'relating' dimensions.

We will unpack these dimensions in more depth in Part Two, but for now, just remember that wicked problems exist in all four dimensions: 'I', 'WE', 'IT' and 'ITS'. Each dimension has its own truths, its own values, its own perspectives. And all of them are incredibly significant. If we don't recognise the multi-dimensional nature of education as a wicked problem from the very start, then our attempts to solve it will continue to fail.

Multiple Stakeholders

Not only are wicked problems multi-dimensional, but they involve multiple stakeholders, each of which is multi-dimensional.

Wicked problems are wicked mainly because they involve people – usually a lot of people. Clearly there are a lot of people affected by the education system, including parents, students, teachers, business leaders, politicians, policy makers and researchers. Each stakeholder, as we discussed earlier, has a different experience, different hopes and aspirations, fears and concerns about the system. Each stakeholder sees the world in their own unique way and therefore has different ideas about the problems we face and how to tackle them. The relationships between stakeholders have also changed, and in education systems locked in the Performance Wave, many stakeholders are seen as something close to customers.

Each stakeholder group views the problem differently; they have different motives, opinions and objectives and will invariably stand behind a version of 'the truth' that suits their purpose, while simultaneously dismissing others' views on the problem and their solutions. If we can't define the problem or the definition varies wildly depending on the stakeholder we ask, then there can't be an accepted objective determination of the problem let alone an agreement about a quality solution.

Stakeholders' inability to effectively collaborate or even manage the differences of opinion from different people makes all attempts to improve education incredibly difficult. Until we mature as human beings and develop the ability to work skilfully with differences of opinion and drop the 'I'm right you're wrong' stance, we will forever struggle. Entrenched differences of opinion create factions and division that makes finding sustainable solutions nigh on impossible. Wicked problems always cut across many groups of people who can't easily be aligned on a narrative around the cause of the problem, let alone the solution.

Building sustainable solutions therefore comes down to skilful integration of multiple views and side-stepping superficial arguments on what's 'better' or 'worse'.

Multiple Causes

Not only are wicked problems multi-dimensional and involve multiple stakeholders, but they have multiple causes. And of course, the multiple stakeholders never agree about the multiple causes!

What causes the numerous problems in the education system? It really depends on whom you ask. When there are multiple causes, it becomes very difficult to separate those causes and identify those that are having the biggest impact. Plus, they are often so intertwined and interdependent it's impossible to know for certain what is causing the wicked problem. This is certainly true in education.

Of course, whatever the suggested cause is, this will undoubtedly influence the views on what constitutes the optimal solution. For example, a stakeholder group that believes that the teachers are to blame will propose solutions around teaching. Those who believe that government is to blame will propose a different set of solutions that involve policy change.

Ironically, it's often only when we've implemented a solution, which takes time, effort and money, that we more fully appreciate the real causes. Normally first implementations fail, nothing changes or perhaps the situation is made worse. Seeing an implementation failure as part of the solution to the wicked problem runs contrary to the way we've been taught to solve problems. Traditionally we've been told that to solve a problem we need to gather all the relevant information, analyse that information, and decide on the best course of action to solve the problem.

Such an approach doesn't work with wicked problems because we can't understand the problem without knowing its context, and we can't meaningfully search for all the information we need without first having some idea about what we think the cause is and therefore what we think the solution might be. In other words, for wicked problems, everything is back to front. Only when we have implemented solutions based on our best judgement and some informed assumption around cause do we fully appreciate the far-reaching interdependent complexity of the problem in the first place.

Plus, we're encouraged to avoid failure at all costs from an early age. And yet when it comes to solving wicked problems, we absolutely must be comfortable with failure so we can get closer to success. It's through the failure that we learn what we really need to learn. Paradoxically when it comes to wicked problems, failure can cause success, which may itself be one of the reasons we can't seem to solve them because we are so obsessed with success and perfection that the very notion of failure has become so unpalatable that we have simply stopped trying.

Multiple Symptoms

Not only are wicked problems multi-dimensional, involve multiple stakeholders and have multiple causes that are difficult to agree on, they also have multiple symptoms. It's often these multiple symptoms which muddy the water and prompt the multiple stakeholders to lurch in different directions as each seeks to address the symptoms that are particularly relevant to them, while ignoring other symptoms that seem less pertinent. To add to the complexity, many of the symptoms of one wicked problem are separate wicked problems in themselves.

If you think about poverty and poor education, for example, both are wicked problems, and each is a symptom of the other. Poverty can be a symptom of poor education because unless an individual can gain at least a basic education where they can read, write and count, then it becomes much harder to secure a well-paying job.

Conversely poor education can also be a symptom of poverty because if a child is continuously sent to school without food because the parents can't afford breakfast, then that child will probably not have the concentration necessary to attain a good education that could help lift them out of poverty. Plus, in many developing countries there may not be a school nearby or the children may be removed from school and sent out to work to supplement the family income because the family is so poor. Of course, those children then never get the education that could help them to break the poverty cycle.

Earlier we talked about the marginalisation of young men, left behind by a system they believe is now rigged against them. This phenomenon outlines multiple symptoms inherited from multiple causes. Declining behavioural standards in schools is also a symptom with multiple causes.

Wicked problems are incredibly challenging to handle because of the interdependencies between causes, symptoms and potential solutions. If our overall approach, from the beginning, is geared to multiple dimensions and interdependencies in virtually all realms, then we are much more likely to be able to spot – and address – these multiple complexities from the start.

Multiple Solutions

Clearly if a wicked problem is multi-dimensional, involves multiple stakeholders, has multiple causes that no one can agree on and displays multiple symptoms, then there will inevitably be multiple potential solutions.

If, for example, a stakeholder believes that poverty is caused by low educational attainment, then their conviction will influence their choice of potential solution. When sourcing a solution, they'll only look at education and how they can 'fix' education from their perspective. Of course, many different stakeholders have proposed many different solutions for fixing education. For example, school league tables were introduced in the UK to rank all schools against each other based on student results. The idea was that if performance was measured and ranked it would improve education, but as discussed, this solution is fraught with problems. School league tables don't improve student performance in the same way that health care waiting lists don't improve the performance of the health care profession. What waiting lists and league tables really do is allow those within the various systems to take their eye off the real objective to effectively manipulate the outward appearance of performance. This drift towards the 'gamification' of any metric has become a huge, time-consuming activity. But just because we can manipulate the data to look like performance is improving, either by refusing to add people to waiting lists until the very last minute or by lowering the level at which an exam or assessment pass is granted, does not mean that performance is *improving*. It just means it looks like it's improving.

Initiatives designed to improve performance have, in many cases, achieved the exact opposite, as people spend their time fixing or fudging the results rather than improving them. In education, the introduction of 'continual assessment' in schools is another 'solution' to raise educational attainment. And yet like so many 'solutions' to wicked problems, it just made matters worse. Clearly the idea was to ensure that children who didn't cope well with the intense stress of single tests or examinations were not unduly penalised. To some extent it was a valid idea, but a wicked problem is complex and interdependent, which means that any attempts to solve it often result in negative unintended consequences elsewhere. As a result, now all children are often stressed all the time, not just once at the end of the term or the end of the year!

Wicked problems don't exist in a vacuum. Because the causes, parameters and objectives vary, often the solutions end up exacerbating the problem or creating new additional problems. If we look again at education, is the objective to prove that something useful is taking place in school? Or, is it to cultivate our children's innate curiosity and work with what they know to develop a life-long passion for learning? Is the objective to impart information about the world or equip children with transferable life skills that will grow and develop as *they* grow and develop? A lot of what happens in modern education systems seems to be more focused on pouring information into children's heads and then rewarding them for regurgitating that information, rather than genuinely educating them and preparing them for the world we live in today or the world they will live in tomorrow.

Constantly Evolving

Ultimately whether a solution is 'good enough' or not will largely depend on the social context, who is making the assessment, and what the stakeholder's interdependent values and objectives are. The interconnected nature of all the causes and symptoms also means that binary 'right' and 'wrong' assessments are impossible. When it comes to making progress on wicked problems, we must look for that 'most workable solution for now'. Because the problem itself is constantly evolving, so must the solution.

The risk in doing this is that it leaves an enormous range of possible interventions, some of which can make things much better, some much worse. The goal is to develop much more complete answers that must embrace multiple purposes and integrate multiple perspectives, multiple areas of knowledge, multiple capabilities and multiple capacities if we're to improve the educational outlook for future generations. Opening up to multiple possibilities doesn't mean we must engage in some political fudge. Rather we must lay out a developmental pathway that can be invested in, and that can flex according to a world that is changing rapidly.

As we move forward with these evolving solutions, we must always remember that all the dimensions of all wicked problems, including the stakeholders tasked with solving the wicked problem, are constantly changing. Some stakeholders leave departments or lose power, particularly when there's a political regime change. The stakeholders themselves are also personally evolving as their understanding, views and opinions morph over time. In addition to evolving stakeholders, the causes of wicked problems are also constantly evolving. New causes are identified and new symptoms manifest.

Plus, each solution usually highlights a new, different and often conflicting aspect of the nature of the problem, so there is no end point. We will never reach a point where we can, for example, tick off 'education' as a task that has been solved and a wicked problem that has been eradicated. The problem-solving process, as well as the problem itself, is constantly shifting and evolving, so it only ends when we run out of resources, be that time, money, the desire to solve it or the extinction of humanity. Successive governments, for example, may shift their focus from one area to another because of their political persuasion, but the problems themselves are still there.

Trying to solve a wicked problem is often like trying to hit a moving target. Paradoxically solving wicked problems requires us to appreciate that all we can really do is constantly try. All we're ever able to do it to get a better or worse handle on a wicked challenge at a given point in time. Any solution therefore will probably be out of date or even obsolete by the time it's evaluated and implemented. And yet instead of attempting, failing and turning away from the problem, we need to attempt, fail and turn back to the problem armed with fresh insights and a new, better understanding of what we face.

There is no end because the landscape is evolving so quickly that it's impossible to know when we've 'finished' or been successful. The fact that there's no end is itself not a bad thing. Evolution has no end, and we still consider that to be a powerfully positive phenomenon. And just because there is no end does not mean we shouldn't bother.

The ultimate paradox is that if we are ever to really solve wicked problems: we need to accept that we will never solve wicked problems! We will only ever be able to solve and re-solve them repeatedly. This constant evolution is part of the very fabric of life. We don't need to fear it; we just need to embrace it with a more complete understanding of what we are truly up against.

Notes

1 Lennon B (2021) Why are English schools not using textbooks? educationblog.buckingham.ac.uk.
2 The National Curriculum in England: Key stages 1 and 2 framework document (2013) Department of Education.

3. Sherwood D (2023) Can GCSE and A Level exam grades be trusted? SecEd.
4. Department of Education (2014) National Curriculum for England.
5. Sorokin S (2019) Thriving in a world of "knowledge half-life", CIO.
6. IBM Global Technology Services (2006) The toxic terabyte: how data dumping threatens business efficiency.
7. Watkins A, Jones S (2023) Lie-ability: how leaders build and break trust, Routledge London.
8. Tangermann V (2023) 89% of college students admit to using ChatGPT for homework, study claims, The Byte.
9. Curran T (2018) Our dangerous obsession with perfectionism is getting worse, TED.
10. Ibid.
11. Evans A (2023) Andrew Tate: how schools are tackling his influence, BBC News.
12. Robinson K (2010) RSA animate: changing education paradigms, YouTube.
13. Ibid.
14. Francis S, Jeffreys B and Shearing H (2023) Rishi Sunak wants all pupils to study maths to age 18, BBC News.
15. Otte J (2023) 'The task is impossible': three teachers on why they are quitting, The Guardian.
16. Harris J (2023) I spoke to teachers preparing to strike. Their trauma was palpable, The Guardian.
17. Standley N, Evans A (2023) Estimated 700,000 pupils in unsafe or ageing schools in England, says watchdog, BBC News.
18. Weale S (2021) 'Creativity crisis' looms for English schools due to arts cuts, says Labour, The Guardian.
19. Sinmaz E (2023) Headteacher killed herself after news of low Ofsted rating, family says, The Guardian.
20. FED (2023) National Education Consultation Report 2023 Building forward together: Towards a long-term plan for education.
21. Education Committee (2023) Persistent absence and support for disadvantaged pupils – Report Summary UK Government.
22. NASUWT (n.d.) Risk assessment of violent and abusive behaviour (England).
23. Adams R (2022) Parents in England feel 'disempowered' by school choice, study finds, The Guardian.
24. Woo-Ming Park A (2023) Let's talk about the Tiger Mom, Psychology Today.
25. Wagele E (2011) The Tiger Mother controversy, Psychology Today.
26. Pfeffer, J (2018) Dying for a paycheck, HarperBusiness, New York.
27. Farquharson C, McNally S, Tahir I (2022), 'Education inequalities', IFS Deaton.
28. Cook C (2011) Business concerned by school leavers' skills, Financial Times.
29. FED (2023) National Education Consultation Report 2023 Building forward together: towards a long-term plan for education
30. Ibid.
31. Farquharson C, McNally S, Tahir I (2022), 'Education inequalities', IFS Deaton.
32. FED (2023) National Education Consultation Report 2023.
33. Ibid.
34. Watkins A, Wilber K (2015) Wicked & wise: how to solve the world's toughest problems. Urbane Publications, Kent.

2 Glimmers of Change

Fixing the educational system is difficult because, like all wicked problems, the issues are constantly evolving. Fortunately, there are three basic phases that apply to the evolution of anything, whether that's a new product, a new idea or a new education system.

- Emergence
- Differentiation
- Integration

Everything starts with emergence. Things seem to spontaneously appear – new recruits, a new genetic variation, ChatGPT, different thinking about education. It's not that these things arise from nothing and nowhere. Rather they break through from the substrate of what previously existed and then they appear in our awareness.

Once something appears, there's a lot of work to do. In the second phase of evolution this means differentiating the new from the old. The dimension, quality or feature of the new thing must be sufficiently different from what's gone before in order to add substantial new value compared to what already existed. If the difference isn't great enough, then evolution will delete it. However, if the new thing is too radically different from what already exists, it won't make sense or it will be impossible for it to align or integrate with what already exists.

The ability to differentiate the new from the old matures as we move from the Power Wave through the Principle Wave into the Performance Wave. The deconstruction of education into a set curriculum, with multiple subjects that must be learnt is an example of differentiation or what some call reductionism.

We also see this reductionist deconstruction in modern scientific medicine. Our understanding of the human body has advanced significantly over the last 150 years. For most of that time, scientists and physicians have been unravelling the complexity of the human body by systematically reducing it to ever smaller parts for study and analysis. This reductionism has been incredibly successful. Differentiating smaller and smaller parts has shed new light on how the human body works. It has generated an enormous amount of new information, spawned whole new areas of medical research and created a new language to articulate the myriad of discoveries being made.

A by-product of this differentiation is that it's become impossible to keep pace with all the new data and discoveries on health or human anatomy. As a result, each part of the human body developed its own expert. Each expert is a separate 'ologist'. These ologists now publish increasingly sophisticated insights in their own specialist journals or attend specialist conferences to share increasingly finer details about their specialism. Physicians often become not just specialists but super-specialists, contributing to the Cult of the Expert we mentioned earlier.

The differentiation phase of evolution, while necessary, often creates unintended consequences. In medicine, for example, we have largely mastered the emergence part of the evolutionary process, we are skilled at the differentiation element, but we have a long way to go to master integration. In fact 'integrated care' and 'interdisciplinary research' have only really emerged in the last 20–30 years as a concept, let alone matured as a practice. This is made even more challenging because the stakeholders involved must have knowledge of multiple fields which is rare, *and* they must be mature enough to build bridges between them.

In education the unintended consequences of breaking learning down into subject areas and requiring teachers to teach a standard set of facts around those subjects has resulted in knowledge being separated from life. Many subjects have become sterile, less relevant and even more boring.

Relevance to life is just one critical aspect of a flourishing educational system. Another is to ensure WHAT is being taught and HOW it is being taught is interesting to WHO is being taught. A few years ago, Alan was asked to give a keynote to an educational conference in Kauai. Unusually for an educational conference there were children present. In a session taught by a teacher from an alternative education school in America, ten children were asked what interested them. This was the start point of the lesson. The teacher asked the children, who ranged from six years old to 14 years old, if they had any questions. Of all the questions the children had, the one asked by an eight-year-old was chosen as the most interesting, and funny. The question the lesson started with was: Do fish fart?

What followed was a true masterclass in engaging the audience, while conducting a detailed exploration of the topic that embraced maths, physics, biology and chemistry. The teacher discussed what bacteria produced gas in the intestines of a fish, the chemical make-up of the gas, how it was possible to see a gaseous bubble in a liquid and how to measure the size of that bubble. It was hilarious. And because it was a question that the children wanted to know the answer to, they understood the concepts and remembered so much more and could even generalise the information to their own lives. This is what good education should look like – building bridges that learners can use to explore the world, armed with tools that help them make sense of their experiences and add value.

Such new thinking is what is required to solve the wicked problem of education. If we can integrate the very best of the differentiated thinking that has emerged over the years, then we have a real chance of architecting a workable solution for education based around emerging patterns. Here are some examples.

John Dewey

John Dewey (1859–1952) was an influential American philosopher, psychologist and educational reformer who made significant contributions to education. Despite starting his working life as a teacher, Dewey moved into academia after only three years, and his ideas and theories, collectively known as "progressive education", revolutionised the way education was approached in the 20th century. A man clearly ahead of his time, Dewey advocated for seven key elements to be included in education for the first time:

1. **Experiential Learning:** Dewey emphasised the importance of learning through experience. He believed that students should actively engage with the material, rather than passively receive information from teachers. Experiences and hands-on activities were seen as central to the learning process, allowing students to understand and internalise concepts better.

2. **Learning by Doing:** Dewey advocated for a curriculum that focused on practical and real-world applications. He believed that students should learn by doing, solving problems and participating in meaningful activities. This approach aimed to bridge the gap between theory and practice, and prepare students for active participation in society.

3. **Child-Centred Education:** Dewey emphasised the individual needs, interests and experiences of students. He believed that education should be tailored to each child's developmental stage and that teachers should adapt their teaching methods accordingly. This child-centred approach sought to foster a love of learning and encourage students' natural curiosity.

4. **Democracy in Education:** Dewey saw education as a fundamental component of a democratic society. He argued that schools should be reflective of democratic principles, promoting active citizenship, critical thinking and social responsibility. He believed that education should not only prepare students for the workforce but also equip them to be informed and engaged members of society.

5. **Social Interaction and Collaboration:** Dewey emphasised the importance of social interaction in the learning process. He believed that students should work together in cooperative learning environments, fostering communication and collaboration skills. Dewey saw schools as microcosms of society, where students learn to interact and engage with others from diverse backgrounds.

6. **Continuous Learning:** Dewey's approach to education focused on lifelong learning rather than simply acquiring knowledge for passing exams. He believed that education should be a dynamic and ongoing process that extends beyond the classroom and throughout a person's life.

7. **Integration of Subjects:** Dewey advocated for an interdisciplinary approach to education. Instead of compartmentalising subjects, he promoted an integrated curriculum where different disciplines are interconnected, allowing students to see the relevance and interconnectedness of various knowledge areas (like farting fish).

Dewey was one of the most prominent American scholars in the first half of the 20th century, and despite being over 100 years old, his insights are as relevant today as they were then. His ideas have had a profound and lasting impact on educational philosophy and practice.

Jean Piaget

Jean Piaget (1896–1980) was a Swiss psychologist known for his groundbreaking work in developmental psychology and cognitive theory. Piaget placed great importance on the education of children, declaring in 1934 that "only education is capable of saving our societies from possible collapse, whether violent, or gradual". His work significantly impacted the field of education, and his ideas have been instrumental in shaping modern educational practices.

The core of Piaget's theory is that children are born with a basic mental structure, which makes future learning and the accumulation of knowledge possible. Piaget was the first to separate learning from development and suggested that development was the progressive reorganisation of these mental structures. A process facilitated by biological maturation, as well as environmental factors.

His key contributions to education were:

- **Theory of Cognitive Development:** Piaget's most influential contribution to education is his theory of cognitive development. He proposed that children go through distinct stages of cognitive development, each characterised by different ways of thinking and understanding the world. These stages include the sensorimotor stage, preoperational stage, concrete operational stage, and formal operational stage. Educators use this theory to understand students' cognitive abilities and design appropriate learning experiences based on their developmental level.

- **Constructivism:** Piaget's theory is considered constructivist because it suggests that learners actively construct knowledge based on their experiences and interactions with the environment. According to Piaget, learning is not a passive absorption of information but an active process of constructing mental models and understanding. This idea has influenced modern teaching methods that emphasise hands-on learning, problem-solving and critical thinking.

- **Student-Centred Learning:** Piaget's constructivist approach to education places the learner at the centre of the learning process. He believed that education should be tailored to individual students' needs and interests, allowing them to explore and discover knowledge on their own. This student-centred approach encourages active engagement and fosters a deeper understanding of concepts.

- **Scaffolding and Zone of Proximal Development:** While Piaget's work primarily focused on the development of children, his ideas have also been applied to the education of learners of all ages. Educators use the concept of scaffolding, a term introduced by soviet psychologist Lev Vygotsky, to provide appropriate support and guidance to students as they tackle tasks that are just beyond their current level of understanding, in what is known as the Zone of Proximal Development (ZPD). This helps learners develop their skills and knowledge with the help of a knowledgeable instructor or peers.

- **Discovery Learning:** Piaget advocated for discovery learning, where students actively explore and experiment to construct their own knowledge. Instead of simply being told information, learners are encouraged to observe, hypothesise and test their ideas. Discovery learning promotes a deeper understanding of concepts and encourages students to become independent and self-directed learners.

- **Importance of Play:** Piaget recognised the significance of play in children's cognitive and social development (something completely dismissed by the Tiger mom). He believed that play is not merely a pastime but a critical mechanism through which children learn and develop problem-solving, language, and social skills. This insight has led to the integration of play-based learning in early childhood education.

His ideas have had a lasting impact on educational philosophy and pedagogy, shaping how educators understand and facilitate learning processes. Again, it's very hard to argue against any of Piaget's ideas and insight and yet they do not represent the norm in mainstream education, certainly not in the UK or the US. In many cases, what is experienced in schools is the exact opposite!

Howard Gardner

The next luminary in the field of education is probably Howard Gardner, an American developmental psychologist and the John F. and Elisabeth A. Hobbs Research Professor of Cognition and Education at Harvard University. He is best known for his Theory of Multiple Intelligences. Gardner states our "educational system is heavily biased towards linguistic modes intelligence and assessment and, to a somewhat lesser degree, toward logical modes as well".[1] We still see this bias in school today. And it's why Sir Ken Robinson said that millions of bright, gifted children left school believing they were not smart.[2]

Essentially the curriculum is too narrow and doesn't account for different types of intelligence. Initially Gardner identified eight different intelligences to articulate a broad range of potential in children and adults.

1. Linguistic Intelligence (word smart)
2. Mathematical Intelligence (numbers smart)
3. Spatial Intelligence (picture smart)
4. Kinesthetic Intelligence (body smart)
5. Musical Intelligence (music smart)
6. Interpersonal Intelligence (people smart)
7. Intrapersonal Intelligence (self-smart)
8. Naturalistic Intelligence (nature smart)

According to Gardner the first two are highly prized in our education system. The next three are often associated with 'the arts', the next two are personal intelligences and the final one is a new addition – nature smart. Gardner has considered adding more intelligences, existential/spiritual Intelligence (ultimate issues smart) and Pedagogical (teaching smart) and Digital (digital smart), but the jury is out on whether they will make his definitive list. We must also be wary of falling into the trap that creativity can only exist in certain subjects. In fact, it is often the merging of these intelligences, that allows creative thinking to emerge in what we would consider 'standard' subjects.

Gardner's work has had a significant impact on education. His theory challenges the traditional view of intelligence as a single, general ability and instead proposes that there are multiple types of intelligences and that they can integrate with each other.

Unsurprisingly Gardner's theory promotes individualised instruction and a personalised approach to teaching and learning. By acknowledging that students have different types of intelligence, educators can tailor their teaching methods to cater to various learning styles, preferences and strengths, whether they are genetic or nurtured. This can lead to a more inclusive, effective and textured learning environment. By recognising broader definitions of intelligence, schools and educators can place a greater emphasis on developing and supporting a variety of talents, not just those traditionally assessed by standardised tests.

Essentially, Howard Gardner's work brought a more inclusive and personalised approach to education. By recognising and valuing the diverse talents and abilities of students, educators can create learning environments that cater to individual strengths and foster creativity, critical thinking and lifelong growth. At least, that's the theory, but again, in practice his insights have never been baked into the mainstream experience.

Montessori, Steiner and International Baccalaureate (IB)

It's not just individual contributions that have emerged to inform education and advance its evolution. The differentiation process in education is well established, and this differentiation has already resulted in new integrations such as Montessori, Steiner or International Baccalaureate. These approaches represent new education methodologies.

A Montessori school, for example, is an educational approach that follows the principles and methods developed by Dr Maria Montessori, an Italian physician and educator. The Montessori method differs from traditional educational settings in several ways:

- **Child-Centred Learning:** Montessori schools prioritise the needs and interests of individual students. The curriculum is designed to meet the developmental needs of each child, allowing them to learn at their own pace and follow their natural curiosity.

- **Mixed-Age Classrooms:** In Montessori classrooms, students of different ages (usually spanning three years) are grouped together. This multi-age setup allows younger children to learn from older peers and older children to reinforce their learning by helping younger ones. It promotes cooperation, collaboration and a sense of community.

- **Prepared Environment:** Montessori classrooms are carefully prepared to encourage independent learning and exploration. The environment is filled with developmentally appropriate materials that are accessible to students. These materials are designed to be self-correcting, allowing children to learn through hands-on experiences.

- **Self-Directed Learning:** Montessori education emphasises self-directed learning, where students choose activities that interest them and work on them independently. Teachers act as guides, observing and providing support when needed, but the primary responsibility for learning lies with the student.

- **Focus on Practical Life Skills:** Montessori education places a strong emphasis on teaching practical life skills, such as cleaning, budgeting and preparing food.

These activities not only help children become more independent but also develop their fine motor skills and concentration.

- **Absence of Traditional Grading and Testing:** Montessori schools generally avoid traditional grading and testing systems. Instead, progress is assessed through careful observation and documentation of each child's development and accomplishments.

- **Respect for the Child:** Montessori educators view children as competent individuals capable of directing their learning. They respect each child's unique qualities, interests and learning styles, fostering a positive and supportive learning environment.

- **Emphasis on Peace Education:** Montessori education often includes peace education, promoting empathy, conflict resolution skills and a sense of global citizenship. The focus is on cultivating peaceful and compassionate individuals who can contribute to a harmonious society.

- **Limited Use of Technology:** Montessori education generally limits the use of technology in early childhood settings. Instead, the focus is on hands-on, sensorial experiences to enhance learning.

But even within this, much improved system, there is a wide range of Montessori schools and the implementation of the Montessori method can vary. Some schools may adhere more closely to Montessori principles, while others may incorporate elements of the approach alongside other educational methods.

A Steiner school is a different approach to Montessori and is based on the philosophy and teachings of Rudolf Steiner, an Austrian philosopher and social reformer. In Steiner schools the focus is on:

- **Holistic Education:** Steiner believed in the holistic development of students, addressing their intellectual, emotional, physical and spiritual needs. The curriculum is designed to nurture the whole child, fostering creativity, imagination and critical thinking alongside academic knowledge.

- **Developmentally Appropriate Curriculum:** Steiner schools emphasise age-appropriate education that aligns with the developmental stages of children. The curriculum is structured to support the natural progression of a child's physical, emotional and cognitive abilities at each stage of development.

- **Arts-Integrated Learning:** Steiner education places a strong emphasis on the arts, including music, painting, drama and handcrafts. These artistic activities are integrated into the academic curriculum to enhance learning and stimulate creativity.

- **Main Lesson Blocks:** Steiner schools use a unique approach called main lesson blocks, where students have an extended period (usually two hours) each morning devoted to in-depth exploration of a single subject. These blocks can last for several weeks, allowing for deep immersion and understanding of the material.

- **Role of the Teacher:** Steiner teachers, often referred to as 'class teachers', ideally stay with the same group of students for several years, developing a strong relationship and understanding of each child's individual needs and learning style. The teacher is seen as a guide and mentor rather than an authority figure.

- **Minimal Use of Technology:** Steiner schools typically limit the use of technology in the early years, aiming to foster creative play, imagination and real-world experiences. In later grades, technology may be introduced in a limited and intentional manner.

- **Delayed Introduction of Formal Academics:** Steiner schools prioritise a play-based and experiential approach in the early years. Formal academics, such as reading and writing, are introduced later, generally around the age of seven, after a foundation of social and emotional development has been established.

- **Cultivation of Imagination:** Steiner education values the cultivation of a child's imagination and creativity. Fairy tales, myths and storytelling are often used as a means to engage children's imaginations and stimulate their curiosity about the world.

- **Community Involvement:** Steiner schools emphasise the importance of community and cooperation. Parents are encouraged to be actively involved in the school, and a sense of community is fostered among students, teachers and families.

Overall, a Steiner school provides a unique and alternative approach to mainstream education, centred on the holistic development of the child and fostering a love of learning that extends beyond academic achievement. It places a strong emphasis on creativity, arts and the individuality of each student. It's often referred to as a Waldorf education after the first school Steiner established in 1919 at the Waldorf-Astoria factory in Germany.

In addition to Montessori and Steiner, the International Baccalaureate (IB) has become relatively widespread in Europe as an alternative approach to education. The IB is internationally recognised and offers a distinctive approach to education for students aged 3 to 19. It's designed to develop students who are knowledgeable, caring, open-minded and well-rounded global citizens. Again, there are key differences and unique features of the International Baccalaureate compared to traditional educational systems:

- **International Focus:** The IB program has a strong international focus, promoting an understanding of different cultures and global issues. It aims to develop students who are internationally minded and can communicate and collaborate effectively with people from diverse backgrounds.

- **Learner Profile:** The IB program emphasises the development of the whole person through its Learner Profile attributes. These attributes include being inquirers, knowledgeable, thinkers, communicators, principled, open-minded, caring, risk-takers, balanced and reflective. The Learner Profile guides students' personal, social and academic development.

- **Holistic Education:** The IB program takes a holistic approach to education, considering the intellectual, personal, emotional and social growth of students. It aims to nurture students who are not only academically competent but also emotionally and ethically aware.

- **Curricular Framework:** The IB program offers four educational programs: the Primary Years Programme (PYP) for ages 3–12, the Middle Years Programme (MYP) for ages 11–16, the Diploma Programme (DP) for ages 16–19, and the Career-related Programme (CP) for ages 16–19. Each program has a well-defined curriculum and assessment framework designed to meet the needs of students at different stages of development.

- **Inquiry-Based Learning:** Inquiry-based learning is a fundamental aspect of the IB program. Students are encouraged to explore and inquire into real-world issues and topics, fostering critical thinking, problem-solving skills and a deeper understanding of concepts.

- **Creativity, Activity, Service (CAS):** The DP and CP programs include a component called CAS, which requires students to engage in a range of extracurricular activities that promote creativity, physical fitness and community service. CAS encourages students to become active and responsible members of their communities.

- **Theory of Knowledge (TOK):** The DP program includes a unique course called Theory of Knowledge, which explores the nature of knowledge and how we acquire it. TOK encourages students to question the basis of knowledge and consider the ways in which different disciplines approach understanding.

- **External Assessment:** The IB program employs rigorous external assessment methods, including examinations, which are moderated internationally. This ensures consistent standards and recognition of the program's academic rigor globally.

- **Emphasis on Language Learning:** The IB program places a strong emphasis on language learning, fostering multilingualism and intercultural understanding. Students are typically required to study at least two languages throughout their IB education.

The IB program's emphasis on critical thinking, community service and language learning sets it apart from traditional educational systems. IB also offer state-of-the-art home-schooling options where students from all over the world join a virtual classroom.

The point here is that there are already several examples of great education being offered around the world. But the excellence lives in pockets, it's not joined up and it's certainly not available to all. The rare exception to this might be Finland.

Finland's Education System

As mentioned in the introduction, Finland's education system is often hailed as one of the best in the world. What makes it different and almost certainly contributes to its impressive track record are:

- **Focus on Equality:** Finland's education system is known for its commitment to equity and equality. There are no private schools, and all students, regardless of their socioeconomic background, have access to free, high-quality education. The system aims to reduce disparities in educational outcomes and provide equal opportunities for all students.

- **Minimal Standardised Testing:** Unlike many other countries, Finland places minimal emphasis on standardised testing. There are no high-stakes tests or exams until the end of secondary school. Instead, assessment is largely based on teacher-led evaluations, continuous assessment and individualised feedback.

- **High-Quality Teachers:** Finland places a strong emphasis on teacher professionalism and requires rigorous training for teachers. All teachers are required to have a master's degree, and teaching is a highly respected profession in Finnish society. This focus on teacher quality is considered a crucial factor in the success of the education system.

- **Teacher Autonomy:** Teachers in Finland have a high degree of autonomy in their classrooms. They have the freedom to design their own curricula and tailor their teaching methods to meet the individual needs of their students.

- **Play-Based Early Education:** Finnish early education is play-based and emphasises learning through play and hands-on experiences. Formal academics are introduced gradually, and the focus is on fostering creativity, social skills and emotional development in young children.

- **Shorter School Days and Less Homework:** Finnish schools have shorter school days and less homework compared to many other countries. This approach is intended to reduce stress and promote a healthy work–life balance for students.

- **Emphasis on Well-Being:** Finland values the well-being of students and places a strong emphasis on promoting physical and mental health. Physical education and outdoor activities are integrated into the curriculum, and there is a focus on providing support for students' emotional and social needs.

- **Collaborative Learning:** Finnish classrooms promote collaborative learning and teamwork. Students are encouraged to work together and share ideas, fostering a cooperative and supportive learning environment.

- **Integrated Special Education:** Special education is integrated into mainstream classrooms in Finland, rather than being separated. This inclusive approach aims to support the needs of all students and create an environment of respect and understanding.

And what makes Finland so special and so outstanding is that, as a country, it has managed to take the best of the best and integrate it back into a country wide system. And whilst they remain open to policy advice from international organisations like OECD and the EU, the Finnish system has remained relatively immune to the GERM virus. GERM has emerged since the 1980s and has increasingly become adopted as an educational reform orthodoxy within many education systems throughout the world, including in the US, England, Australia and some transition countries.

Since the 1980s, at least five globally common features of education policies and reform principles (standardisation of education, focus on core subjects, the search for low-risk ways of reaching learning goals, the use of corporate management models and test-based accountability policies) have been employed to try to improve the quality of education and fix the apparent problems in public education systems. None have been adopted in Finland in the way they have been adopted by many other countries including the UK. Instead, the Finnish system places high confidence in teachers and principals as high professionals, encourages teachers and students to experiment, putting curiosity, imagination and creativity at the heart of learning and pursues happiness of learning and cultivating development of the whole child.[3] And these unique features have contributed to Finland's reputation for having one of the most successful and equitable education systems in the world. Their focus is on improving the learning environment, so learners are nurtured.

When it comes to education, a great deal has emerged. Differentiation has allowed us to better understand what works and what doesn't. But without the third phase of evolution, namely integration, we get the fragmentation and even dis-integration we see in the UK education system and beyond. Fragmentation of the educational system means excellence is available to some but not to everyone. It is easy to argue that the current education system, available to the majority, has already fragmented and disintegrated – another symptom of a wicked problems.

We believe it's time to integrate all the wisdom and best 'parts' of all the myriad of educational innovations to design and build a more complete educational system for today and tomorrow. One that understands the pressing issues we face and is greater than the sum of the parts.

When we don't appreciate the three-steps of evolution, then we don't really understand the complexity of the world. This means our ability to handle that complexity is severely limited and any system can easily become a mess.

If this complexity is mis-managed, the wicked problem of education seems to defy solution, which is roughly where we are right now. Wicked problems are simply the product of our evolution – they are a product of our escalating complexity. Our ability to understand that escalating complexity and find a framework to untangle and comprehend that complexity is the part we've not yet mastered. The good news is wicked problems are solvable, they just need a more sophisticated approach and a far greater understanding of how to effectively navigate human interactions and find common ground from which to orchestrate workable answers in real time. If we can understand the complexity and reach a new level of integration, then new and beautiful things emerge and the whole magnificent evolutionary process begins again.

In May 2023, the OECD Schools+ Network was launched with representatives from some 40 countries, 25 organisations, over 160 schools experts, leading thinkers and innovators. The aim to get schools and educators, who are already innovating together, to seek better and create more joined up solutions that help everyone. There's already a deep understanding of what is termed 'broken' in education and a deeper understanding of what works. What's missing is a map to connect the two and duplicate and even improve on the pockets of excellence that already exist.[4]

As Carl Ward, Chair of the Foundation of Education Development (FED), said in his open to the 2023 FED Report:

> It's time to stop tinkering around the edges making incremental changes which don't make a jot of difference on the big issues and start thinking about what we want the next evolution of our education system to look like . . . Education must evolve over time, like everything else. As John Dewey said, "if we teach today's students as we taught them yesterday, we rob them of tomorrow.[5]

Notes

1 Gardner HE (1993) Multiple intelligences: the theory in practice Basic Books, New York.
2 Robinson K (2010) RSA Animate: changing education paradigms, YouTube.
3 Sahlberg P (2012) Global educational reform movement is here! Pasisahlberg.com.
4 OECD Schools+ https://www.oecd.org/education/school/oecdschoolsnetwork.htm.
5 FED (2023) National Education Consultation Report 2023 Building forward together: Towards a long-term plan for education.

PART TWO
Diagnosis and Treatment

3 Awareness Before Change

When most of us encounter a problem, we often instantly flip into solutions mode. What can we do? What needs to be changed? How can I move this forward? But this conditioned reflex, to act before thinking, can be counterproductive and may be a significant reason why the problems in education have become so entrenched.

We need to pause. In the space of no action, we take the opportunity to think very deeply to make sure we better understand the problems we are seeking to solve. Awareness is the first step toward change but just being aware of the problem doesn't mean we are clear about the solution.

In education there's already, as outlined in Part One, a thorough appreciation of the many problems that need solutions in the education system. Most stakeholders are acutely aware of the breadth and depth of these problems. What's missing however is an appreciation of the architecture that creates those problems and keeps them in place.

We've already shared a framework for understanding how the values of all the stakeholders in the system evolve. This values evolution framework gives us a better understanding of what's happened and is continuing to happen in the education system. When we can see the underlying framework or theoretical scaffolding, that underpins our experiences in the real world, it's far easier to appreciate the task ahead.

Instead of getting into discussions or arguments about who is to blame we can see that the outputs are just the logical consequence of a series of values-based inputs that were relevant at that time. And when we can see that framework, or theoretical scaffolding, we have a map that can ensure the education system we design today is relevant for today as well as the future.

Dewey was right, "if we teach today's students as we taught them yesterday, we rob them of tomorrow." And right now, we are certainly robbing them of tomorrow.

In addition to understanding the evolution of stakeholder motivations through the values frame, we also considered the three meta-steps of evolution using the EDI frame. EDI stands for emerge, differentiate and integrate. Everything from the chair you sit on, to the page you're reading went through a process of emergence, differentiation and integration. The education system is no different.

There are now countless examples of brilliant insight that have emerged that could, if applied, make our education system world leading. There's also been some exceptional differentiations around education methods, with new adaptations from previous models. The issue we have is that we are failing to successfully integrate all that's emerged and been differentiated into a coherent new approach fit for the 21st century.

And the third meta-frame we touched on was to describe the topography of wicked problems. Anyone who's paying even the slightest attention to education will immediately recognise that the failure of the education system is a wicked problem. It's multi-dimensional, has multiple stakeholders, multiple causes, multiple symptoms, multiple solutions and is constantly evolving. As a result, it is incredibly difficult to solve. This third framework enables you to see clearly why education is such an intractable challenge.

In Part Two we are going to offer a few more ways to dissect the problem to make solving the problem easier. Specifically, we'll dive more deeply into one of the wicked characteristics – the multi-dimensional nature of the education problems and how to tackle each dimension systematically.

To help us use Ken Wilber's AQAL model, Alan rotated it anti-clockwise and placed the leader, or in this case any number of educational stakeholders, at the centre looking forward into the rational objective world.[1] Standing at the centre of their world (Figure 3.1), the leader's attention is drawn to the front left, and the unbelievably long list of operational challenges that exist in every school. These issues seem so urgent and pressing that only the most resolute leaders have the discipline to look to the longer-term leadership issues in the front right quadrant. Most educational leaders feel so compelled to solve the operational issues, in the front left, that the rarely look over their right shoulder, to the myriad of cultural, people leadership issues that exist in every school in the interpersonal world of 'WE'. And even fewer leaders look over their left shoulder to the inner subjective world of 'I' and their personal performance.

When it comes to wicked problems, the default tendency is to focus obsessively on the operational, system and process issues in the world of 'IT'/'ITS' or 'doing'. If we notice the people issues at all, we think they may need a new 'IT' process to address them, rather than addressing the deeper, cultural or intersubjective dimension or 'relating'. And we almost never consider how our own maturity, resilience or quality of thinking in the inner world of 'being' would change outcomes.

But if educational leaders mature and the strength of the relationship bonds in their leadership teams improve, then the collective ability to solve the 'I', 'WE' and 'IT'/'ITS' problems in education are transformed. If that team then connects more effectively with staff below the leadership team, this helps them develop and strengthen their relationship bonds with colleagues and learners then real change right across the organisation becomes possible.

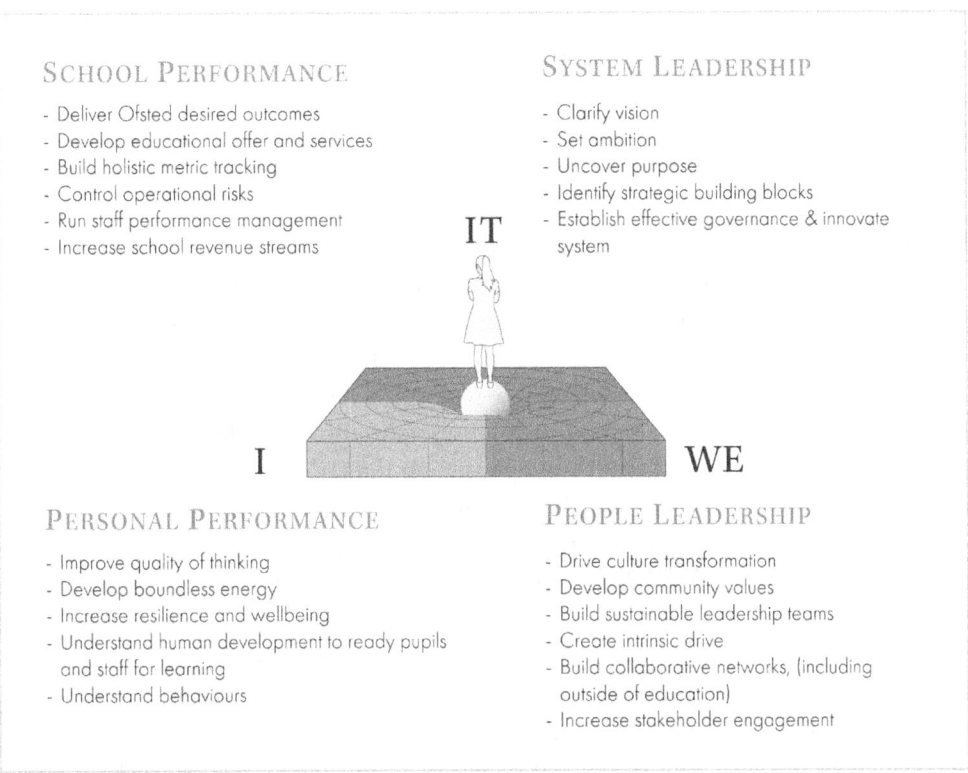

Figure 3.1 Complete Leadership Model Applied to Education

In essence, this is what the OECD is seeking to do with their OECD schools+ Network but it's not yet clear whether they fully appreciate all the 'I', 'WE' and 'IT'/'ITS' hurdles that are blocking progress and how a better understanding of the scaffolding of these problems and the right frameworks can create the space to help them to navigate the issues successfully. But at least the OECD recognise that there's a serious problem needing a more complete solution.

What's clear, from decades of failed attempts, is that the problems of education won't be solved in a silo. And they won't be solved unless we appreciate the multi-dimensional nature of the problems we face. We see this perpetual failure in business all the time. The executive team will fix the business process, but things don't improve because the 'WE' of culture is still broken. Or a business consultant may advocate redundancies to cut costs in the business which makes the business look better on paper, but with low morale and no one to do the work, then the business still fails. Removing cost may be right for profitability, but it can make the 'I' and 'WE' problems worse. This can create a potentially even more fatal problem than the redundancies were designed to solve.

Here's the kicker – you can't deal with the dimensionality of a problem if you don't even realise the problem has multiple dimensions to begin with. This four-quadrant framework clarifies that all the challenges, not just operational, must be addressed.

It's clear the education system won't be improved by piece-meal, disconnected interventions or by grand sweeping reforms. What's needed is multiple inclusive, comprehensive solutions that meet the needs of multiple stakeholders, today and tomorrow. Solutions that remove the symptoms and causes across all dimensions and are flexible enough to evolve as needs change.

Part Two explores the frameworks and scaffolding that you need to implement solutions in each dimension and walks you through examples so you can see how that solution works in real life. Ultimately, it's what changes on the ground, in schools, that matter. When there's a perennial disconnect between academic research, much of which is locked inside impenetrable scientific papers or written up in obscure journals, and what's happening on the ground, it's obvious that nothing will change anytime soon, without a more integrated approach.

But with a more complete, multi-dimensional approach, one that integrates the vast treasure trove of insights that have emerged in the last few decades from human physiology, neuroscience, emotional intelligence, behavioural science, child and adult development, plus AI, we could already be implementing solutions and honing their impact in real time.

The purpose of Part Two is to show how the right frameworks deliver real progress in real life and increase all stakeholders' ability to contribute to a better future. So whether you are a parent looking to make a more positive input into your child's education, or a teacher looking to get better results in the classroom or a head teacher looking to improve a school, or a policy maker, or leader looking to drive systemic change, your ability to see the connection between the multiplicity of causes and symptoms can be the difference that helps our educational system transform.

Once we have the right frameworks or scaffolding in place to understand the problem and the evolving solutions needed, we can get on with the job of delivering the developmental blueprint. By actively dismantling the ineffective aspects of the old architecture that were holding the dysfunction in place and building on the effective parts we salvage, something new and better can emerge in its place.

What we are suggesting is not a sticking plaster solution, but total reinvention. A move from a system built around knowledge to a system build around development supported by a proven map of development that applies to every stakeholder.

A Word on Change

Before we dive into the solutions needed to develop the 'I' dimension, it is also worth bearing in mind just how challenging change is. We are programmed for homeostasis or the maintenance of a state of steady internal, physical, chemical or social conditions. In other words, we are programmed to avoid change. Change is often perceived as a risk. This risk is often exaggerated because our understanding of change is limited. We are not taught how to develop change capability so we simple revert to throwing solutions at the wall to see what sticks. This has been the reality in the education system for decades. Our approach to change itself therefore needs to change!

All the educational stakeholders need to become students of change. The good news is there is already a framework for better management of change, thanks largely to the work of Joseph Campbell.

Campbell was the American professor of literature who introduced the world to the Hero's Journey – essentially a road map for change. By studying myths and stories from various cultures around the world, Campbell suggested the existence of what he originally referred to as a Monomyth, becoming known more commonly as the Hero's Journey, a universal pattern common to heroic tales in *every* culture. As well as drawing the reader's attention to the basic stages of this mythic change cycle, Campbell also explored the common variations in the Hero's Journey.

Campbell was the first person to identify the universal nature of individual and collective change while also giving us clearly identifiable signposts of that process. In essence, there are three general stages: "Departure" (sometimes called *Separation*), "Initiation", and "Return". Departure deals with the hero venturing forth on the quest, including the *call to adventure*. Initiation refers to the hero's adventures where he is tested along the way. And finally, the Return which follows the hero's journey home. Of course, the hero is now forever changed by the journey.

The basic research to his findings were thousands, possibly hundreds of thousands, of stories from multiple cultures and countries around the world. Whether fairy tales or mythology, they talk about the human condition and how it changes. Too often, we get attached to the surface story. In the case of education, the good story is the woeful headlines that populate the media or the stakeholder forums that lament the state of modern education. But in the telling and re-telling of the familiar story, it's too easy to miss the underlying meta-frame and message. And that's the gift that Campbell provided to the world. He brought the underlying meta-frame or scaffolding for successful change to the surface. When we can push past the surface story or headlines to better appreciate where we are in the change process and what lies ahead, change becomes less stressful and fraught, and we are more mentally prepared to embrace that change.

Campbell's map allows us to make sure we are on the right track and are not veering off course. This meta-frame is also an allegory of the human condition. Knowing that there will *always* be trials and tribulations is strangely comforting. Knowing there is always a way through can be liberating.

Campbell's initial path is however, over 70 years old. Figure 3.2 is an integrated, up-dated version that consists of 12 steps and four stages.

Standing on the shoulders of a giant (Campbell), adding in the phases gives more precision. There are three steps in each of the four stages of discover, decide, develop and deliver.

Figure 3.2 The Change Wheel

These four stages correspond to the stages of human development. First, we must discover and 'wake up' to our current situation and 'wake up' from the delusion of control and power. Next, we must decide to 'own up' to our own part in the situation as well as 'own up' to the parts of our nature that we may dislike or that are holding us back. As we move into the develop stage, we 'grow up' through the lessons we must learn and the introspection this often triggers. Once we reach the deliver stage we are called to 'show up' differently, armed with new insights, lessons and growth. We are literally a different person to the one who started the journey. When we 'wake up' and 'grow up', this evolution alone can make a dramatic difference to how we 'show up' as a change agent which, in turn, can help us develop still further. If we refuse to make this personal journey, then we simply stagnate and become obsolete. We must evolve. All of us.

Each cycle of change alters us in a new way as we become more sophisticated, more inclusive, creative and capable. As such, we become change warriors and can successfully harness and utilise the increasing complexity, intensity and disruption in education rather than be debilitated by it. If we want to succeed long term and build an enduring legacy, becoming brilliant at change is the only way. Something new is emerging all the time but with this enhanced change capability, change is not only possible but constantly planned for and successfully executed for the betterment of all the stakeholders.[2]

This change journey is extremely relevant as we assess the whole education system. There is no one blanket solution that is going to fix everything. Instead, there is going to have to be a rolling timetable of change across the board that is managed and implemented step by step.

Successful change always follows a path, but that path is rarely linear. As Goethe once said, "Progress has not followed a straight ascending line, but a spiral with rhythms of progress and retrogression, of evolution and dissolution".[3] Behavioural scientists have also confirmed Goethe's original insight. Progress is almost always followed by faltering progress, stagnation or regression.[4] But when we don't realise this, we assume the faltering progress, stagnation or regression we're experiencing is a sign that change isn't working and that we should return to the comfort zone. This is not true; the confusion is just the next step on the way to the following step. The key is to become familiar with the 12 steps so that you can self-diagnose and take the right action toward successful change.

Navigating change isn't easy. But no-one said it would be. Besides, easy isn't where the joy is. As Joseph Campbell once said: "Where we stumble there lies our treasure".

Hungarian psychologist Mihaly Csikszentmihalyi said something similar when he said:

Contrary to what we usually believe, the best moments in our lives, are not the passive, receptive, relaxing times – although such experiences can also be enjoyable, if we have worked hard to attain them. The best moments usually occur when a person's body or mind are stretched to its limits in a voluntary effort to accomplish something difficult and worthwhile. Optimal experience is thus something that we make happen.

This is true for all of us – it's the human experience.

Famous for his work on *'Flow'*, Csikszentmihalyi goes on to remind us that

such experiences are not necessarily pleasant at the time they occur . . . Getting control of life is never easy, and sometimes it can be definitely painful. But in the long run optimal experience adds up to a sense of mastery – or perhaps even better, a sense of participation in determining the content of life – that comes as close to what is usually meant by happiness as anything else we can conceivably imagine.

We need to reframe these challenging experiences as simply pitstops on our developmental journey and encourage all stakeholders from students to employers to turn away from the course of least resistance or distraction and embrace the challenge of individual and system change so we can develop resilience and tenacity – critical skills for a life well lived.

Notes

1 Watkins A (2021) Coherence: The science of exceptional leadership and performance, 2nd Edition, Kogan Page, London.
2 Watkins A (2022) Step change: the leader's journey, Routledge, London.
3 Phipps C (2012) Evolutionaries: unlocking the spiritual and cultural potential of science's greatest idea, HarperCollins, New York.
4 Prochaska JO, Norcross JC and Diclemente CC (1994) Changing for good, Avon Books, New York.

# Individual Development in Theory

When we work with leaders all over the world, we often ask them which leader has had the most positive influence on humanity in the last 100 years. The answer is always the same, whether we're asking leaders in Asia, North America, Australasia, Africa or Europe – Nelson Mandela. One of the most fascinating things about his life is that the 'doing' world wasn't available to him for 26 years. He was imprisoned on Robben Island. In addition, he engaged in very little 'relating', only chatting to a couple of inmates, a few guards and potentially the odd visitor. He spent 26 years of incarceration mainly focused on his own development, the maturation of his 'being'. Therefore, it shouldn't be any surprise that when he was finally released and able to do something in the world that he was an incredibly, mature, compassionate and charismatic individual who went on to have a massive impact on the world, South Africa specifically and virtually everyone he met. This reinforces the view that is consistent across thousands of books and articles – leadership is an inside-out game. In other words, it starts with the inner 'I' and who we are as human beings.

But for our own leadership to improve, we need more details. What exactly did Mandela develop within himself to ensure he became such an inspiration to millions? And can any of us develop the same things without having to spend 26 years in solitary confinement? Fortunately, the answer to this question is now well known, rooted ironically in educational research and studies on how children develop.

There have been many significant contributions to understanding child development. The early pioneers mapped the specific stages of child development that all of us go through. Academics in the field soon realised that development was not confined to children. And development didn't necessarily stop when we left school. They discovered that there are levels of development that adults can go through. And these levels are just as consistent as the levels of development that children go through. The definition of the levels of adult developmental is one of the most robust findings in scientific literature.

DOI: 10.4324/9781003530831-7

It builds on the research of Piaget[1] and Kohlberg[2] and extends the work of Jane Loevinger[3] to luminaries such as Ken Wilber, Robert Kegan, Eliot Jacques, Kurt Fischer, Susanne Cook-Greuter, William Torbert and Clare Graves. Each researcher describes the various levels of adult development from a different perspective.

Wilber, for example, looks at the evolution of awareness or consciousness of self. Cook-Greuter studied the development of ego maturity. Torbert defined what sort of "action logic" was available to adults as they developed and how these levels play out in business. His collaborations with Cook-Greuter have been especially insightful when looking at behaviour. Professor Clare Graves' described the evolution of value systems, which we've already briefly explored.

Collectively this work offers incredibly useful insight into how we can continue to mature as human beings, from our earliest days at school through young adulthood and for our entire lives. This work provides us with a developmental frame that can help us navigate the various stages of our lives and handle the challenges we encounter with more grace and understanding. It would not be an over statement to say that this research can change the world. And it can certainly help us transform the educational system and solve all the dimensions of this wicked problem – all whilst keeping the learners at the centre knowing that this golden thread of development runs into their future.

Even though this research grew out of child development, most teachers, and educators ironically, are unfamiliar with the idea of adult development. As such, incredible insights remain largely trapped on the shelves of academia, known only to a tiny minority of leaders and treasure hunters.

But any parent, or individual who's spent any time with a child will have noticed that children move through well-defined developmental stages. These stages impact a child's physical growth; the way a child thinks; how they develop socially and emotionally; their ability to understand right from wrong or their moral development. In fact, virtually all aspects of a child's life, including how they make sense of themselves and the world around them, can be tracked through these developmental levels. Given the transformational power of this research we believe it's worth explaining, via another whistle stop tour, the full development journey from infant to young adult, to mature adult and enlightened leader. The specific research findings are, on their own, unremarkable. But when they are put together, what emerges is the most dazzling array of insights that may just change your entire view of teaching and the very purpose of the educational system.

Once again, let's start at the very beginning. Initially, a baby has no appreciation of the fact that they exist separately from their parents or their environment. They are sensing and responding to their world, but they don't yet know they're alive. This is a pre-conscious level of development.

Then at around one year old the most incredible breakthrough occurs, and the first level of consciousness emerges. A baby bites its thumb and it hurts. But when they bite their blanket, it doesn't hurt. They repeat the experiment by putting their foot in their mouth. The baby can feel their gums and their foot. In contrast when the baby bites the table it can't feel the table. They start to realise they exist – 'I am the thing that hurts when I bite it'. This first level of awareness is rooted in physical sensations. At this level of development, all that matters are physical needs. Eat, sleep, bodily functions and repeat.

Once the baby has developed the ability to objectify their physical self as separate from others, the next level of development requires an infant to objectify something much more subtle – their emotional self.

Initially, a baby has little or no control over their own emotions – which is why parents experience what they call 'the terrible twos'. When the baby is hungry, they believe everyone in the world is hungry and we should all eat. They haven't yet developed the ability to see their emotions as separate from their parent's emotions. This is the point of maximum egocentricity.

Then around two to three years old something magical starts to emerge, and you can witness this in supermarkets across the world. A young child is having a tantrum, screaming in rage because their dad won't buy them a chocolate. They look at their dad totally baffled by the fact that he's not also crying at the lack of chocolates. Their '1,000-yard stare' testifies to the fact that the second level of development is beginning to emerge. They are beginning to realise that not only are they physically separate from their dad and others but they're also emotionally separate.

At this second level of development, children are emotionally, highly contagious because they only have the most rudimentary level of emotional regulation. They can easily spark each other into fits of laughter or floods of tears. They're also massively influenced by the mood of the adults around them, even though most of those adults are also largely unaware of their own emotions. This is part of the reason why adult carers are so influential at this age.

With the developing ability to objectify, first their physical existence, then their emotions, an infant's world begins to open-up and become two-dimensional (the physical world of 'IT' and the inner world of 'I'). An infant's emotions give depth to their experience, and at this stage their self-identity is based on how 'I' feel. At this basic level of awareness, children don't really understand how the world works. Their thinking is still magical, for example, a child of this age believes the clouds follow them.

Level 3 of child development changes everything. This third level blossoms around three to six years old, although it may start earlier. At this third level of development the child's ability to objectify extends beyond their own physicality and their own emotions to things 'out there' in the world. This third level is the emergence of the 'conceptual self'. The main thing that comes online is language. A child starts to use sounds, images, symbols to represent the concepts in the world around them. The world moves from two-dimensional (the physical and emotional self) to three-dimensional, for the first time.

During this developmental phase, children acquire words at a phenomenal rate, roughly six new words a day. This is why reading to children from a very young age is so powerful for their development. Children at this stage start to ask questions about what things are and label everything. This helps them navigate their world and a child starts to make sense of the world and themselves in it.

As a child starts to objectify and label things, cat, dog, ball and even their own emotions, their thinking moves from magical to mythical. This means they move from not knowing how the world works – "it must be magic" to creating a story or myth – to explain how things work. For example, emotions, previously simply felt and acted upon as impulses, are conceptually represented as feelings albeit simple ones such as 'happy', 'worried' or 'sad'. And a child begins to create a story to explain those feelings. A child starts to consciously appreciate that their feelings belong to them and may or may not be shared by others.

The child realises they can't boss the world around (magical), but someone can (mythical). This third level of development can be a little frightening, as a child realises that they are no longer in control of the world, someone else is. Worry or anxiety may appear for the first time. Concerns about being abandoned by their parents in play group or reception class at school is seen as separation anxiety. Such experiences need careful handling if we want to avoid mental health issues later in life and can influence many transitions to come.

Still largely operating from the first person perspective, a child at this level of development is still concerned primarily with 'me, my, mine and I'. They have some awareness about the fact that they may be feeling sad, but they still haven't been taught or developed much self-regulatory capability. They're still largely driven by their own egoic needs and desires. 'Mine' is a very strong concept in children at this stage. They tend to believe everything belongs to them. Everything is 'mine'. Which is why children at this age can't really be accused of theft. They don't understand the idea of possession. If everything is 'mine' they don't understand the problem when they pinch their brother's lunchbox.

If something goes wrong at this stage of development, then the child may continue to age but their inner maturity doesn't. This is why we can see adults stuck at this ego-centric level of development. Such adults often believe they're above the law, or the laws don't really apply to them. Kohlberg wrote beautifully about the development of morality and ethics which doesn't really kick in until late in level 3 and beyond.

Consider just one of the indictments against former US President Donald Trump over government documents including classified documents. His response to requests by the National Archive to return countless boxes of documents taken from the White House was that they were 'Mine', "the boxes are mine". When the US Department of Justice subpoenaed Trump for the return of the documents, he allegedly obstructed justice and sought to hide the boxes.[4] Why? Because "they are mine". Of course, they were never his, they belong to the US government. This is not the behaviour of a mature adult, it's the behaviour of someone stuck at level 3! But Trump is by no means the only one. Board rooms are littered with middle-aged men and women who regularly throw temper tantrums, engage in power battles or bully their colleagues in behaviour teachers wouldn't tolerate in a school yard.

Having begun to understand the world is full of things, dogs, cats, bats, balls, mummies and daddies as well as emotions, the next level of child development is concerned with the rules that govern such concepts. The three-dimensional world of language, symbols and concepts becomes much more solid, more concrete. At this fourth level of development, a child's identity is also more solid and this is called the 'concrete self'.

At level 4 the new rules that have emerged must be learnt and obeyed. A child begins to understand what's 'right' and 'wrong', 'good', 'bad', 'acceptable' and 'unacceptable'. They begin to conform and will rehearse various social scripts as a way of learning the social rules or ways of behaving. At play school or reception class, children are taught to share the toys, for example, as not all the toys are theirs. This is a crucial developmental stage because it's the foundation of relationship building and success in the 'WE' dimension and sets the stage for all future relationship dynamics as adults. The fourth level can overlap significantly with the third level, but the fourth level mainly blossoms from five years old, when most children start school, and continues until they are nine or ten years old.

As children become more well-established as individuals, they start to make friends. Their need to belong is now more social than physical. Children at this fourth level are very susceptible to peer pressure and herd mentality. Rationality and 'self-talk' also begin, largely for the first time. Children at level 4 become much more sophisticated at justifying their behaviour, good or bad. Their ability to objectify the world and themselves in it becomes much stronger.

Unfortunately, this is where the developmental journey ends for many people as they live out their days in this concrete three-dimensional world, with rules and regulations to be followed or ignored. There is a degree of self-consciousness, but life's largely concrete and materialistic. The game is to work out the rules, decide if they are going to conform (join the maths club) or rebel (be a Goth). Just getting through school can become the primary objective and this may be repeated when they start working. Many people seek to simply get through their shift. Work is something to be suffered and life happens outside of work – these are the rules many operate within, without even knowing whose rule they are or where they came from. The rule or recipe for life at this fourth stage of consciousness is Have/Do/Be. 'If I have an Xbox, I'll be able to play (do) with my friends and then I will be happy'. 'If I have an iPhone, like all my friends, I'll be able to message them (do) and I'll be popular.'

Most children experience the next level of development to some extent, simply as part of their physical development. This fifth level of development overlaps with the fourth level but when it occurs, the fifth level is present from the age of nine to fourteen years old.

One of the main things that happens physically at this age is the front part of our brains speed up. The nerve tracks myelinate. This means that the wiring in the executive part of our brain becomes insulated, enabling the messages to travel much faster. This produces a massive upgrade in cognitive capabilities. It's the human equivalent of going from analogue to digital.

With much faster brain speed we're able to think in abstract terms properly for the first time. Prior to this upgrade, most children think linearly and literally. Abstract thinking enables more sophisticated analysis, greater reasoning ability and a more advanced ability to objectify things. This means children can comprehend algebra. If this abstract thinking hasn't kicked in, then algebra wouldn't make sense. Fortunately, these new abstract cognitive capabilities coincide with changes to the high school or secondary school curriculum.

As level 5 thinking comes online, it becomes obvious that the rules of level 4 don't always work or make sense. The pre-teens that make it to level 5 start to understand that they're not the centre of the universe. They're aware that something's going on beyond themselves and they become less ego centric. Level 5 awareness is characterised by the emergence of the transpersonal self.

This transpersonal level of development is a pivotal moment in everyone's developmental journey. For the first time, we have the ability to pull back the veil and think about the nature of thought. What are thoughts? Where do thoughts come from? What determines what we think and what determines how well we think it?

In such questions there's great opportunity. We can begin to understand that the quality of our thinking isn't just dependant on our knowledge, experience or our access to data. It's entirely dependent on what level of development we are operating from.

At level 5, self-awareness reaches a new height. A child at this level will start to question the who and why of rulemaking. They often start rejecting the rules of their parents or teachers in favour of their peer group. Sadly, their peer groups, parents or teachers seldom operate from a more sophisticated level of development, so broader consultation rarely helps.

The battle of wills around rules and boundaries leads to classic teenage conflict, as youngsters everywhere start to realise that the rule book, given to them by their parents or teachers, is a work of fiction. Sometimes the battle for control, authority or obedience can be quite intense, particularly if parents and teachers have no sense that the questioning of the rules, and the defiance that often goes with it, is a normal developmental milestone, not a game of 'chicken'.

As they struggle to make sense of their role in the world, many teens become self-absorbed. This isn't the same as the egocentricity of infancy. It's an attempt to understand the complicated, abstract, social rules created by someone who they don't know or understand.

If as young adults, they don't get caught up in anti-social behaviour or drug-induced anaesthesia, they may realise that there's more to life than just fighting or following the rules and roles laid down by parents, teachers or society. A surge in curiosity about how the world really works means that teenagers think more. The ability to judge and criticise lands with a thump, and young people at this stage often become very critical, hyper-judgmental and intolerant of both themselves and others.

In this transpersonal turbulence, several abstract and existential questions arise, such as the meaning of life, who am I and how can I change the future of the planet? Some teens pour their hearts out on the pages of a diary as they try to process the complexity of a world they clearly no longer control. Some seek answers in the security of a club, gang or 'in-crowd' allegiance. Many try to deal with their struggle by getting 'wasted' with drugs and alcohol. Such behaviour is a distraction or anaesthetic to the pain of their struggle.

The bad news for teenagers is that regardless of who wins these teenage wars, as soon as they leave home, a much more powerful parent called 'society' imposes its own rules. Society tell these young adults they must get a job, find a flat, have a relationship, work hard, pay taxes and contribute to a society they barely understand. If they capitulate to this more powerful parent, the opportunity of the transpersonal moment recedes and they fall asleep, returning to the concrete world they left as a pre-teen, usually oblivious to their own regression. Falsely soothed by their obedience to a system they can't see. They have effectively taken the blue pill and returned to the Matrix.[5] To paraphrase Henry David Thoreau, they fall back into conformity, accept the rules and "lead lives of quiet desperation".

The more rebellious may refuse the blue pill, but with little or no understanding of development, they are unlikely to make it through the transpersonal swamp. They end up stuck in its nihilistic night, in limbo, feeling despondent and hopeless. We see this in young people all the time, especially if they've been marginalised in school or don't fit the cookie cutter box of 'academically bright'.

Most people never glimpse the opportunity of real development again in their lifetimes. The system has them, and they don't even know it.[6]

Years later a lucky few may glimpse again the opportunity of transpersonal salvation. Rarely by choice, usually because they're forced to by an incredibly painful event – usually in mid-life. This may be the loss of a job, the loss of a marriage, the loss of a loved one, the loss of purpose or the loss of self-esteem through a period of depression. Whilst this 'midlife crisis' is typically something that happens to an individual in their 30s or 40s, it can also happen in our mid-20s or after a significant disruption in our lives. The crisis can be a moment in time, or it can creep up on us and can last for months or years. It may be better described as a 'disease of meaning'.

The pain of this affliction, whether acute or festering, causes us to realise that we've been following a set of rules and playing a certain role on the implicit 'understanding' that our obedience to these rules would yield a certain reward. Only the health, wealth and happiness we were 'promised' has never materialised!

When troubled by the disease of meaning, we ask ourselves, 'What's the point?' We feel despondent because we've kept our side of the bargain. We've been a dutiful husband/wife, father/mother, leader, worker, friend and colleague and things still didn't work out. We feel cheated. We followed the rules, but the reward never arrived. Or, if it did, it wasn't nearly as good as we were led to believe! The disappointment is more profound now than it used to be because we've spent so much of our life living in the concrete world of false promises after we fell back into the Matrix and society's systems. Many people with the same symptoms resort to the same solutions to dull the pain. The same anaesthetics (drugs and alcohol) and the same distractions (workaholics, shopaholics, sexaholics or affairs, gym junkies, social media addicts). But the results are no better. They may soothe us temporarily, but they can't cure the disease of meaning.

The only real solution is to fully wake up and start to grow up. Start really developing ourselves as adults. Escape the transpersonal swamp and discover the life we were meant to live.

But if we are comfortable in the Matrix, in our slumber, and we agree that the 'World is run by the Man'[7] so it's better just to give up, there is no 'burning platform' or strong need for us to develop any further. This is the life that billions of people in the world now live. We look like an adult on the outside but we're still effectively operating from an individual interior level of a teenager, sometimes even younger. We have not unlocked the levels of adult development that are available to all. We've settled. We've surrendered. And in so doing we may never discover the promised land of our own potential, abiding happiness and fulfilment.

Most people leave school or university thinking that their learning or development is over. But by 15 years old, we've only achieved the most basic levels of development from baby to child to teen and physical adult. For most, the move from immature adult to mature adult has yet to happen, and yet maturity is where all the really good stuff comes online.

Society and the law consider 18-year-olds to be adults. An 18-year-old or even a 21-year-old is at most an adult in name only. An 18- or 21-year-old may look physically mature on the outside, but most are 'stuck' at 14 or even eight years old on the inside. There's no doubt they may have scaled various 'learning curves' at school, university, during apprenticeships or at work, but they're far from fully developed adults. They've not 'woken up' and developed much self-awareness and have certainly not 'grown up', matured or reached the levels of development available to them.

What's even more troubling, in the context of education, is that this explanation does not end with students, it describes the developmental journey we all must travel and that includes all the stakeholders involved in education. Far too many parents are tasked with developing independent, mature and productive adults when they themselves are yet to access the adult maturity levels. Instead, they too are operating from the developmental level of a 14-year-old. It would be easy to argue that parenting is regressing not developing. Just look at the rise in single parent families, predominantly single mothers. No one is talking about absent fathers.

All the negative headlines are reserved for single mothers, who stay and raise their children while the father disappears physically, emotionally and financially. How much did personal, social, health and economics (PSHE) really prepare any of us for relationships, never mind parenting?

The social media pressure to be perfect is also fuelling a superficial surface approach, rather than a deeper, inner maturity, that is stunting parental development. Parents, often with different values, are consumed about how to bring up their children to be 'just right'. We are bombarded with social media expectations to continually broadcast about our gifted children, putting unrealistic pressure on us as parents and the children themselves. In our collective failure to meet such unrealistic and misguided expectation, we often seek someone or something to blame. Often this ends up being the education system.

And what about the teachers. How is it even possible for individuals, regardless of how well they might be trained, to adequately prepare children for this accelerating world when they themselves haven't done the inner development to take them past the basic awareness level of a functioning 15-year-old? The same is true of all the stakeholders trying to find solutions. Education is, indeed, a wicked problem! Do we honestly expect all the educational stakeholders, who are themselves only developed to a teenage level of awareness, to be able to solve all aspects of this wicked problem? Not without development.

What's required is a concerted effort to elevate all stakeholders' internal capability to match the external complexity and sophistication of the world around us.

The Disconnect Between Learning and Development

Currently the educational system is built around the idea of learning. It is a learning or knowledge transfer system. The primary goal is for students to learn a set of facts and acquire knowledge that they will then be tested on. This is the central tenant of the National Curriculum.

Development, if it's considered at all, isn't really part of the thinking or the construction of the education system. Yet it's development that holds the key to unlocking the vast reservoir of human potential in children, teachers, leaders and all educational stakeholders.

If we put development, not learning, at the heart of the educational system, there's a massive opportunity to completely transform the entire system. With a focus on development, we can start to map, prepare and guide every stakeholder through the gradual unlocking of human potential.

As we've already discussed, rote learning and the regurgitation of information in an exam isn't preparing young people for today's world. It's not providing children with a meaningful education that sets them up for life. And it's certainly not delivering young adults with the attitude or abilities that they will need to succeed or even the abilities that employers are looking for. In addition, our obsession with learning isn't providing the next generation with the tools to evolve their capabilities, as the world changes.

Part of the problem is the lack of understanding of the critical difference between learning and development. Many assume that development automatically follows the acquisition of knowledge. But learning doesn't necessarily lead to any development. For learning to convert into development it's necessary to understand the levels of development that exist in children and adults.

To clarify the importance of this distinction, we can consider learning to be a 'horizontal' change and development as a 'vertical' change. Horizontal learning is the acquisition of skills, knowledge and experience. This is what teachers are trained to deliver. Clearly, every child needs to acquire some basic skills, knowledge and experience, but that's really only the start of the developmental journey and a tiny fraction of what they really need in the modern world.

'Horizontal' learning is very different from 'vertical' development. Horizontal learning is like pouring water into an empty glass, whereas vertical development expands the glass itself.[8] Professor Robert Kegan calls vertical development a "quantum shift in mental complexity, a transformation of the underlying operating system itself".[9] Such a transformation of our personal operating system enables new skills and capabilities to emerge as each new level of development is unlocked.

With these new capabilities our mind can operate much faster, we can process much greater levels of complexity and generate wiser, more compassionate and sophisticated solutions to the increasingly challenging problems we face. Someone who has unlocked more levels of potential and therefore capability can transform the outcomes in whatever part of the educational system they're working in.

Let's dig a little more precisely into vertical development. When we talk of developing increasingly sophisticated capabilities, what sort of capabilities are we really referring to? It's possible for a human being to develop hundreds of different capabilities. The question is which ones are crucial in the educational system? We believe there are five main capabilities that humans can seek to develop:

1. **Technical Capability:** This requires learning and content knowledge. This is what the current educational system has been built around. It's what teacher training is focused on – developing technical ability. But with the explosion of knowledge and the emergence of AI systems like ChatGPT, teachers and students are increasingly unable to differentiate themselves based on technical ability. And as AI becomes much more widely adopted, the technical capability that work and society requires from individuals will be increasingly provided by AI, not by human beings. We're already seeing a switch to generative AI models in the legal, medical and accounting professions and many other areas too. Educational systems that are built around technical capability are therefore setting children up to fail.

2. **Operational Capability:** Teachers need to develop this capability to plan and execute a lesson effectively. To run the classroom and manage the children in the classroom, a teacher needs operational capability. Students too need to foster operational capability so they can get the most out of self-managed learning, especially if they go on to university where this is essential. This capability is usually best developed and fine-tuned in the workplace.

3. **Strategic Capability:** Strategic capability is useful for everyone as they plan their life and make decisions about goals and how to achieve them, but it is crucial for head teachers and leaders within the educational system. This is the ability to make choices that accelerate the growth of an individual, team or a system. If head teachers are going to maintain the relevance of their school and create a compelling future that attracts and retains the best staff, they need this capability.

4. **Personal Capability:** This is the game changer for all stakeholders. Personal capability isn't about what information an individual knows. It's about the quality of their interpretation based on that information. There are many types of personal capability (and information). We will explore these in more detail, shortly, because they are the primary driver of the transformation that the educational system needs.

5. **Change Capability:** This could be conceived of as a subset of personal capability, but we call it out separately because it can be applied to the 'WE' and 'IT'/'ITS' domains just as readily as the 'I' domain of personal capability.

If we restrict our deeper exploration, for the moment, to personal capability, we discover that there are hundreds of ways an individual can develop. As we discussed in chapter 2, this has been known, since Howard Gardiner's Theory of Multiple Intelligences highlighted the fact that most education systems privilege linguistic and numeric intelligence over all other types of intelligence.[10] Today, these different 'intelligences' are thought of as 'lines of development'. Most of the lines of development that Gardiner spoke of were lines that enhance technical capability (verbal, mathematical, visuospatial, kinaesthetic, musical). There are different lines that transform personal capabilities. Five of these probably make the greatest differences to virtually all the stakeholders in the educational system (Figure 4.1). None of these five key lines of development are formally assessed in educational systems. When we assess these capabilities within the personal domain, we're assessing them in a very different, and often more fundamental, way than when such things are assessed in the technical domain.

For example, if physicality is assessed at all, in the current educational system, it's more to do with assessing sporting prowess, technical ability or potential in a specific sport. In contrast, assessing the sophistication of an individual's

Figure 4.1 Five Key Lines of Development for Personal Capability

physical development within the personal capability domain is about quantifying the amount of energy an individual has, and defining the quality of that energy. It's not about their physical prowess or capability in the gym. Assessing the amount and quality of energy someone has is a more fundamental way of assessing physicality than defining technical prowess. Doing so often triggers a deeper conversation about their ability to sense and regulate their energy levels. Assessing physicality in this way is relevant to all sports, and even non-sporting activity. If we're exhausted with no energy left, we can't perform in our sport or complete non-sporting activities like our maths homework.

The second line of development, within personal capability, that's central to all students and educational stakeholders is emotional and social intelligence (ESQ). Most schools are now aware of the importance of ESQ. But often the thinking around the topic remains theoretical or, ironically, cognitively driven. There's rarely any training to help children or teachers develop their emotional and social intelligence in the classroom and ESQ isn't usually integrated into lesson plans.

Part of the problem is that there are more than 200 different assessments in the marketplace that claim to quantify ESQ. We've reviewed all of them and more than 650 academic papers that explore such measures. We've analysed more than 2,400 individuals ESQ questions and more than 800 separate constructs that relate to ESQ. From all this research it's clear that there's a massive amount of confusion about how to accurately assess the 12 levels of ESQ. Most of the 200 assessments only address, at best, half of the 12 levels of ESQ, often in a random rather than sequential way. Also, many of these 200 questionnaires are contaminated with concepts, such as introversion, that have absolutely nothing to do with ESQ.

The third line of development, within personal capability, is cognitive sophistication. Since the 1988 Education Reform Act, when the compulsory National Curriculum was rolled out, most schools and local educational authorities bought into the idea of performance-based league tables. It's now compulsory to assess children's cognitive capability before they leave primary school using a 'standardised assessment test' (SAT) at age 11 at the end of Key Stage 2, in year 6. This SAT test was rolled out between 1991 and 1998 to assess the impact of the National Curriculum.

Originally the plan was for compulsory SATs at the end of Key Stage 1 for 7-year-olds, in year 2, and SATs in Key Stage 3 as well. But testing such young children is met with significant resistance from teachers and the National Union of Teachers (NUT). The NUT described SATs for seven-year-olds as "unfair and unworkable". Consequently, SATs in Key Stage 1 are now optional but are still taken by most learners. In 2008 the plan for Key Stage 3 SATs was also abolished as it was thought to cause way too much stress for children at this age. And in September 2017, following a consultation period, the government announced that Key Stage 1 SATs would be scrapped in the 2021–22 academic year to be replaced by a 'Reception Baseline Assessment' test, administered when children entered reception. This started in 2021.

SATs for 11-year-olds are used to assess both the school and each child's progress in English and maths to determine whether children have achieved the expected standard, fallen below it or exceeded it. All children are scored between 80 and 120, with 100 being the expected standard.

As mentioned in chapter 1, the government updated the National Curriculum in 2014. And this was reflected in an upgrade to the SATs in 2016 which introduced more differentiated tests in maths and English. English tests now assessed reading, spelling and grammar. Maths test assessed arithmetic and mathematical reasoning.

In 2016 the way SATs were scored was also changed, from reporting 'levels' of capability to a 'scaled score', although a child's raw SAT scores were also available. The idea of a scaled score was to enable comparison across years, presumably because the difficulty of questions may vary across years and the percentage of pupils achieving a certain level would also vary. In addition to the SATs results in English and maths, children may also be assessed by their teachers in English, maths and science. All this testing is then fed into National League Tables to enable schools to be compared against each other. And secondary schools use the Key Stage 2 SAT score to stream year 7 children in English and maths. However, most secondary schools use their own methods to stream pupils using Year 7 SATs, teacher assessments and other cognitive ability tests. Private schools are not required to use SATs, although approximately 20% do. And some authorities still use an '11+ exam' for admission into grammar schools – all without considering the context of the learner and the relevance of the progress they've made.

All this testing simply assesses technical capability in two subjects – English and maths. SATs don't assess the level of cognitive sophistication, which is relevant to all subjects. The understanding of cognitive sophistication and how it develops in children and adults, and how to assess it is now understood. And it is way beyond the blunt and biased IQ testing that has existed since 1905. But sadly, this understanding hasn't been taken up by educational systems, as most are still obsessed with knowledge and learning.

Although there is a growing appreciation that this endless testing isn't delivering and that simple knowledge transfer isn't preparing children from the world we live in, change on the ground is slow. There are plenty of educators who believe that instead of teaching knowledge and testing memory via exams, the system should be shifting what is taught from knowledge to capacities such as critical thinking, problem solving and teaching children how to differentiate fake news and content from reality. For example, the 4Cs: Creativity, Critical Reflection, Communication and Collaboration[11] or the 6Cs of 21st century living[12] which includes the four already mentioned and character and citizenship. There is little doubt these are far more important skills to learn in school if our young people are to be equipped for the world they will enter as employees. These skills are also far more important to them as they become partners and parents and seek to maintain friendships over the long term. These are developmental capabilities that help us in the 'I', 'WE' and 'IT'/'ITS' dimensions and cross many lines of development, not just cognitive.

The point here is that there is currently no real attention paid to the cognitive line of development beyond trying to measure knowledge transfer – which is *very* low hanging fruit on the cognitive tree. There is no sophistication about the levels of cognitive capability and no effort to expand those levels. And whilst there may be an appreciation that knowledge transfer is obsolete, in most schools there is no workable solution on how to develop creativity, critical thinking, communication or collaboration skills. Or how to develop character and create upstanding citizens. Instead, creativity is ticked off by 'the arts'. And the rest are largely ignored or left to the parents.

In addition to assessing an individual's physicality, their emotional and social intelligence and their cognitive development, we believe it's vital to also assess the evolution of their values and their ego maturity. Understanding the motivation of a child or an adult can transform their ability to progress in life. Motivation is a primary driving force for children and adults. How many times have we heard that children are 'bored' by school or staff are disengaged.

Similarly, one of the primary roles of education is to help children develop a healthy sense of identity and sense of self. This is exactly what assessing ego maturity can deliver.

It may seem counter-intuitive to suggest we assess all five 'internal' lines of development when there's already a massive cultural resistance to measurement in education. But if such assessment were to be developmental instead of reductionist, they would transform the quality of the educational system. Such an approach would enable teachers to have much greater autonomy and impact which correlates with the transformation of classroom outcomes. As such, the resistance to technical capability assessment may give way to an enthusiasm for personal capability assessment. Once teachers and educational leaders understand these five lines of development and the various levels of sophistication within each line, they appreciate that this can be one of the key levers to transform the entire educational system.

These lines of development are personal, so everyone is more engaged in addressing their own resistance which then creates a culture of development. They connect the dots and can see how their early experiences shape them as human beings and therefore how that then shapes their approach to learners. And, more importantly how they can self-author something better for themselves that ripples out far beyond the school gates.

The benefits of unlocking new levels of development are non-linear. Each line of the five key lines of development has a different number of available levels to be unlocked. Moving from one level to the next in any line of development isn't as easy each time. For example, development up the ego line is initially straightforward, and largely automatic as we grow from a child into an adult, but there are huge gains to be made if ego maturity is developed in the teen years into adulthood.[13] And huge losses if it is not. Unlike the physical development from child to adult, the maturity development from adult to mature adult is not an automatic process – it requires conscious effort and attention.

To develop we must first learn about development. But a theoretical understanding of development isn't the same as developing, in the same way as knowing there are four more levels in a computer game doesn't mean you can access those levels. To unlock levels beyond where we currently operate from requires hard work and often skilful guidance from a coach that knows how to facilitate that evolution.

The playbook to unlock our own potential changes depending on which lines of development we're talking about, in addition to which level we're talking about. For example, if children or adults want to gain greater mastery over their energy levels then they must first cultivate something called interoception, or body awareness. This means developing awareness of the different physiological signals their body generates. Then they must be able to accurately quantify how much energy they have. Fortunately, this can be precisely quantified using heart rate variability technology and various wearable devices. Having cultivated much better awareness of the amount of energy they have available, it's possible to then develop an awareness of the quality of their energy. Increasing the sophistication of their energy regulation goes way beyond simple platitudes about the importance of sleep and trite statements about relaxation techniques.

To help children mature in their physicality we should give children the tools to recognise and manage their energy.

Understanding the Mental Health Crisis

Similarly, if we want children to develop their emotional and social intelligence, we should teach them properly about the 12 levels of ESQ and massively expand their emotional literacy. Even in schools that are dedicated to working with children who have social, emotional and mental health (SEMH) needs, we rarely educate children about the thousands of possible emotions we can feel. And we don't equip children or teachers with the tools to self-regulate. No wonder there is a mental health crisis!

We urgently need to change the narrative on mental health in schools. This starts with acknowledging that the problem is not typically 'mental' and it's not 'health'.[14] Mental health is not mental because, in the most part, cognition is normal in the person who perceives they're suffering from a 'mental health' problem. The content of their consciousness may be darker, but the processes of cognition are intact. Schizophrenia is a 'mental' problem because normal cognitive processes are disordered. The problem is emotional not mental. They are not the same thing. And this misdiagnosis of the issue as 'mental' is causing stigma and many suggest that the stigma results in more suffering than the negative emotion, be it anxiety, overwhelm, stress or whatever.

Also, mental health is not a 'health' problem any more than being unable to read is a health problem. If we've never taught children to develop their ability to handle negative emotions, then it shouldn't surprise us that they are overwhelmed when life becomes complicated by difficult challenges.

Mental health, as we understand the term today, is essentially a failure of development. A failure of education. Just like failing to teach a child how to read or write, we've failed to teach children to be emotionally literate or regulate their emotions effectively. And we could completely change the mental health narrative by correctly identifying the problem – a failure of emotional development. If we help children develop their emotional and social intelligence, then we could largely eradicate the mental health epidemic.

Imagine the positive impact on children's emotional and mental state if emotional literacy and self-regulation were built into the National Curriculum and became central to the education system. Imagine the positive impact on behaviour and performance and the knock-on effect that would have on teachers, parents and eventually employers. Imagine the impact on relationships between children and between adults if developing emotional and social intelligence became a central part of the curriculum. Such a shift is supported by research such as the Harvard Study of Adult Development which has followed the lives of 724 men since 1938. This study proved that what makes a good life isn't money or fame, or an impressive job title, or even good health. It's the quality of our relationships.[15] Surely, we should be giving our children the knowledge and tools to be happy and healthy in themselves and with others, now and into the future.

By focusing on development rather than learning, we can massively expand personal 'I' capabilities for all stakeholders involved in education. Right now, this isn't even on the radar of educational reform because there's very little understanding around vertical adult development despite educators seeking what is best for the learner.

Notes

1. Piaget J (1972) The psychology of the child, Basic Books, New York.
2. Kohlberg, L (1981) The philosophy of moral development: moral stages and the idea of justice, Harper & Row, London.
3. Loevinger J, Le Xuan Hy (1996) Measuring ego development (personality & clinical psychology), Psychology Press.
4. Chait J (2023) Why was Trump so intent on keeping "my boxes"? New Yorker.
5. The Matrix (1999) The Wachowskis, Warner Bros.
6. Reich RB (2020) The system: who rigged it, how we fix it, Picador New York.
7. School of Rock (2003) Richard Linklater, Paramount Pictures.
8. Petrie N (2011) A white paper: future trends in leadership development, Center for Creative Leadership.
9. Kegan R, Laskow Lahey L (2016) An everyone culture: becoming a deliberately developmental organization, Harvard Business.
10. Gardner HE (1993) Multiple intelligences: the theory in practice basic books, New York.
11. Jefferson M, Anderson M (2017) Transforming schools: creativity, critical reflection, communication, Collaboration Bloomsbury, London.
12. Kristoffy J (2018) 21st century skills: the 6 C's, Right Track.
13. Watkins, A (2016) 4D leadership: competitive advantage through vertical leadership development, Kogan Page, London.
14. Watkins A (2020) Why HR should stop talking about mental health and act, HRD Connect.
15. Waldinger R (2015) What makes a good life? Life lessons from the longest study on happiness, TED Talk.

5 Individual Development in Practice

Whether you're a student looking to extract more value from your education, a teacher looking to improve the way you teach and cope better with the stresses of the job, or a leader or policy maker seeking to find systemic improvements, you must first look at yourself and how you can change if you want to alter system outcomes. In our experience many teachers are so pupil-centric they tend to look for things they can 'do' to or with the students rather than look at themselves first. Often to do so feels 'selfish'. But step-changing your capability can make a

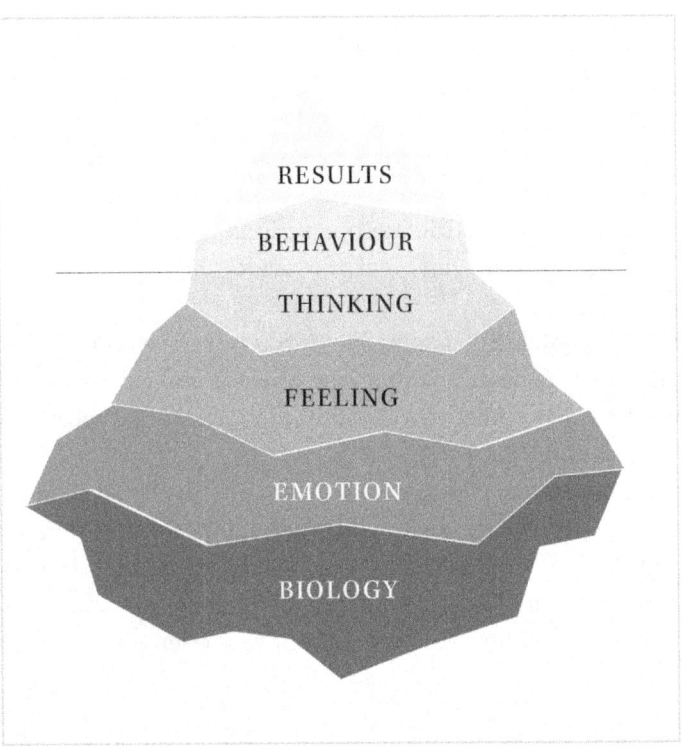

Figure 5.1 Integrated Performance Model

dramatic difference to educational outcomes. If we want to develop ourselves, we must understand, more precisely, how the human system works.

It's very clear that the results we achieve are down to what we do, our actions and our behaviour. Which is why we often focus on leadership behaviour or anti-social behaviour in schools.

But changing teachers' or pupils' behaviour is not easy. Why? Because visible behaviour is driven by things that aren't visible. These things sit below the surface. Like an iceberg where 80% of its mass is below the waterline. What's driving behaviour is below the waterline (Figure 5.1).

The first thing that determines what we do is thinking. What we think determines what we do.

If you're reading this and thinking, "What are these guys on about?", it's unlikely you're going to do anything different as a result of reading this book. But if you've made it this far, then you may be thinking that there might be some value in what we're saying. So, your behaviour – continuing to read the book or not – is determined by what you are thinking.

But our thoughts don't occur in a vacuum. Every thought we've ever had, what we think and how well we think it is determined by something more fundamental in the human system. And that's how we feel. How we feel changes what we think.

There is, of course, a reciprocal relationship between thinking and feeling. How we think changes how we feel; and how we feel changes how we think. But if thinking and feeling got into an arm wrestle, feeling would win every time. This is why feeling, rather than thinking, is really the primary determinant of what we do. We all know this instinctively.

A teacher may get to the end of the week and think 'I have to mark those last five essays'. But if she 'doesn't feel like it' – what wins? Thinking or feeling? Feeling wins – almost every time. Of course, it's possible to override our feelings with sheer will power, but feelings dictate our actions most of the time. This is especially true for children, who have yet to develop any sophisticated capacity to override their feelings.

So, if we want to change what someone thinks or how well they think it, then we need to change how they feel. But changing how we feel isn't enough because how we feel is determined by something even more fundamental in the human system, and that's raw emotion.

The reason it's so hard to change the way people feel is because we pay so little attention to our emotions and most people are emotionally illiterate. When asked how we feel, most of us don't really know. We say, 'I'm fine'. But we don't know whether we really feel fine, maybe we are 'OK' or 'relaxed' or even 'compliant', but most of us can't distinguish these emotions as separate entities. Effectively when we're asked how we feel, we're guessing. Most adults only experience about a dozen emotions on a regular basis. If we don't really know how we feel, because we're not paying attention to our emotions, then it's not surprising we can't change how we feel. Even if we were more aware of our emotions that still wouldn't be enough, because there's something even more fundamental driving our emotions. At the bottom of the iceberg, at the base of the human system, is physiology – all our biological reactions and processes.

Physiology is just data or information streams that each bodily system generates all the time. As you read these words, your body is taking care of a million little details that keep you alive – there is constant activity. Vast streams of data are being sent and received from one body system to another in the form of electrical signals, electromagnetic signals, chemical signals, pressure, sound and heat waves. And we don't have to think about any of it; the human body is the ultimate performance machine.

All of us experience this constant traffic of physiological information flowing around our body 24/7. But very few people understand its impact, and fewer still have learnt how to control the traffic and generate better quality outcomes. This is why the physical and emotion lines of development in the 'I' domain are so important. They give us far greater control of our system. If we develop the ability to manage our physiology, emotions and how we feel, we start to develop much greater control over our thinking and our consciousness. We can't think our way to better thinking, but we can get a better grip of our system which improves the biological and emotional context in which all thoughts emerge. With better thinking we make better choices and take more constructive action. All these levels are intimately connected, but the untapped potential exists in the bottom three levels, which have been largely ignored. Most schools favour approaches that predominantly focus on cognition.

We are suggesting that the fastest and most sustainable way to transform the education system is to help all the stakeholders embark on a developmental journey, transforming themselves, step changing their maturity, their ability to think faster and at a whole new level of sophistication.

Of the five key inner lines of development, the cognitive line requires less attention than the others, largely because the level of cognitive sophistication in most teachers and education leaders is good enough. Most are smart enough to drive the transformation required. What's preventing the transformation of education from happening has much more to do with the other lines of development. Teachers are exhausted, there is insufficient emotional regulation. Values and motivations are misunderstood and not leveraged or integrated. And we need to step change the levels of personal maturity to unlock the potential in the system.

Let's dig in a little and explore how to accelerate development in the other four lines of development that will help deliver the transformation: physical, emotions, values and ego maturity.

Developing Greater Physical and Emotional Intelligence

Developing a much more sophisticated awareness of, and ability to regulate, our energy levels and our emotional and social intelligence can be addressed together. The two phenomena – physiological energy and emotions – are intimately related.

The quickest way to understand this relationship is to use the metaphor that our bodies are like an orchestra. Each bodily system, like the heart, lungs, guts, muscles, etc., are equivalent to the different sections of that orchestra. We could consider the heart to be the string section and the guts to be the wind section, for example. Within each orchestral section we have different players. Thus, in the string section we have a violin, a cello and double bass. These could be the different physiological signals that the heart generates. Thus, the electrical signal of the heart is the violin; the electromagnetic signal of the heart could be the cello; the blood pressure waves would be the double bass.

The orchestra has many players, in the same way that our bodies create many physiological signals. This metaphor clarifies the difference between our physiological energy, our emotions and our feelings. The energy is the individual signals that each orchestra member creates. The emotion is the signals from all the 'energy-in-motion' or composite of the entire orchestra playing. And the feeling is the awareness of the tune the orchestra is playing.

Every child, every teacher and every educational stakeholder has an emotion every single second of every single day, because their 'orchestra' is always playing a tune. What most individuals don't have is a feeling. Simply because most adults and children are not aware of the tune their bodily systems are playing. They are not paying attention to these internal signals, they are paying attention to external signals whether it is the TV, a computer game, the screen on their smartphone, a spreadsheet or a social media feed. We're distracted by the noise outside and pay scant attention to the tune inside.

If we shift our attention to what's happening inside of us, some people can tune into the noise a single player in their orchestra is making. For example, some people may be aware that they're sweating. Others might notice their temperature or that they feel warm. Some people notice their posture when they're sitting or standing for long periods. Some are aware of some aspects of their breathing. But for most people such awareness is, at best, rudimentary and almost always transient.

There are, as we mentioned in the last chapter, 12 levels of emotional and social intelligence (Figure 5.2).

These levels embrace both the physical and the emotional lines of development. The 12 levels are divided into three sections. Every section starts with awareness because there is no change without awareness. Each section also describes a set of capabilities that come online as we unlock that developmental level.

Level I of ESQ – Energy Awareness

Teaching can be an exhausting experience. It's not just the responsibility of helping society's most precious resource, the next generation, it's also the amount of preparation that must now be done out of school hours to prepare each lesson. Teachers spend hours constructing lesson plans that can withstand the scrutiny of school inspectors, as well as hours spent marking homework. It's not

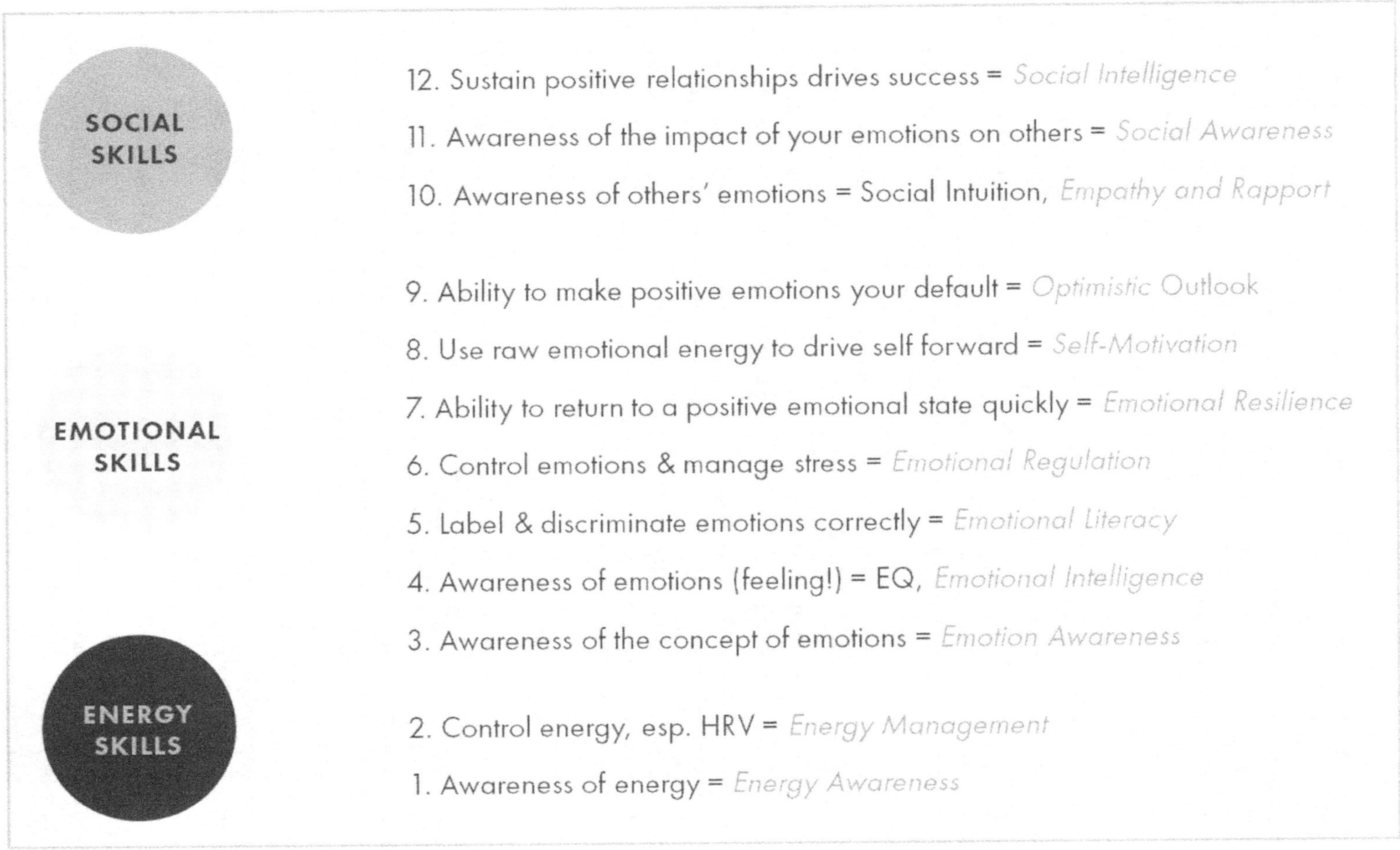

Individual Development in Practice 89

12. Sustain positive relationships drives success = *Social Intelligence*

11. Awareness of the impact of your emotions on others = *Social Awareness*

10. Awareness of others' emotions = Social Intuition, *Empathy and Rapport*

9. Ability to make positive emotions your default = *Optimistic Outlook*

8. Use raw emotional energy to drive self forward = *Self-Motivation*

7. Ability to return to a positive emotional state quickly = *Emotional Resilience*

6. Control emotions & manage stress = *Emotional Regulation*

5. Label & discriminate emotions correctly = *Emotional Literacy*

4. Awareness of emotions (feeling!) = EQ, *Emotional Intelligence*

3. Awareness of the concept of emotions = *Emotion Awareness*

2. Control energy, esp. HRV = *Energy Management*

1. Awareness of energy = *Energy Awareness*

SOCIAL SKILLS

EMOTIONAL SKILLS

ENERGY SKILLS

Figure 5.2 The 12 Levels of Emotional and Social Intelligence

surprising then that, in a survey of nearly 1,500 teachers, 58% say that they experience frequent job-related stress. This is nearly double that experienced by other workers in the comparison group. Also, 20% of teachers reported experiencing symptoms of depression. A quarter of teachers said they were likely to leave their job within a year. Teachers also reported the main stress in their job came from managing children's behaviour and a quarter said they even feared for their own physical safety.[1]

Accurately quantifying our energy levels is vital to ensuring we don't slip into a state of exhaustion. The best way to do this is to assess heart rate variability (HRV) for one to three days while at work. We've been measuring leaders' energy levels using HRV for more than 25 years. In our experience, teachers either massively over or underestimate how much energy they have, because like many people their awareness of their energy levels are wildly inaccurate. We are also not very perceptive about the different parts of our orchestra. Some people can only 'hear' one member or one section of the orchestra. For example, we may be very tuned into our heartbeat. Or we may be very sensitive to the rumblings, tone or spasms in our guts. Others, like yoga teachers, may be very aware of their posture.

Furthermore, most people have very little idea where their energy comes from and where it goes. It can be very helpful to make a list of all the things that boost our energy levels and all the things that drain our energy. We call this the *E-Bank* skill. Once we have identified the people, places, processes or things that boost or drain us, it's important to review our energy bank account so we can see the patterns that we are creating in our own lives. Once we can see these patterns in our E-Bank, we can set ourselves some goals for how to plug the leaks in our energy and amplify the deposits in our account. This is a big part of the work of ESQ level 1.

Level 2 of ESQ – Energy Management

Once we have greater awareness of our energy levels we need to cultivate a much greater control of our energy – the quantity and the quality. Here we can, again, use HRV to determine whether our energy management skills are working. We can also use HRV biofeedback to confirm whether we're able to improve the quality of our energy. Are we generating coherent or chaotic HRV.

When we've worked in schools, we've seen children very quickly pick up HRV biofeedback, using our Complete App to self-regulate. Using a sensor that clips on the child's earlobe, which is connected to a phone or iPad, the App has a breath pacer that the children follow to shift their heart rate from a 'red zone' chaotic signal into a 'green zone' coherent signal.

Often after a tumultuous experience at home or lunch break, children would come into the classroom and purposefully shift their energy from a state of physiological chaos into a coherent state. This meant they were in a much better energy state for the afternoon lessons and much less disruptive in class. Such proactive self-regulation was game changing for many teachers and the pupils themselves.

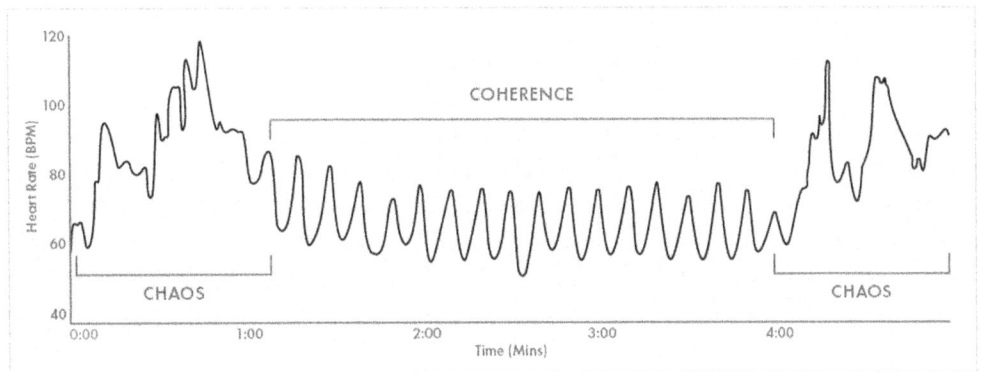

Figure 5.3 Rhythmic Even Breathing Creating a Coherent HRV Signal

Most children enjoyed seeing with their own eyes whether they were chaotic and 'in the red zone', or coherent and 'in the green zone'. Imagine live data to inform zones of regulation!

The skill that enabled them to shift from chaos to coherent was learning to control their breathing in a very specific way. There are 12 different aspects to our breathing that we can control. Rather than take a few 'deep breaths', which does very little to help brain function, we taught children to breathe rhythmically, evenly through the centre of their chest via the breath pacer on the App.

This BREATHE skill (**B**reathe **R**hythmically **E**venly **A**nd **T**hrough the **H**eart **E**very day) is a very effective way to plug the leaks in our energy account.[2] When our breathing is chaotic, our HRV signal is also chaotic and we lose energy very quickly. But when we use the BREATHE skill, we can plug the leaks in our energy because our HRV signal becomes much more coherent (Figure 5.3).

Developing coherence in the classroom enables pupils and teachers to maintain self-control even in highly charged situations. It prevents our brains from shutting down under pressure and allows us to think clearly. It's a highly effective skill for pupils to use in an exam, or for teachers to use when a school inspector is sitting in observing their lesson. The BREATHE skill stabilises our physiology, the bottom level of the performance iceberg. With a stable physiological platform, we can progress to the third level of emotional and social intelligence and start working directly with our emotions. This moves us from just dealing with the 'lead violin' in the body's orchestra (the electrical signal of the heart as seen in our HRV) and making sure it's playing coherently, to making sure the whole orchestra is playing coherently and 'in tune'.

Level 3 of ESQ – Emotional Awareness

The third level of emotional and social intelligence is focused on helping us to understand the nature of our emotions. This is vital because much of the confusion about mental health, and even emotions themselves, is because we've largely misunderstood emotions as an idea. This is particularly true in the way we educate young boys about emotions.

Boys are taught to 'toughen up' and suppress their emotions, or worse, deny their emotions even exist. We still hear this in adult leaders. Girls often talk to each other about how they feel, and it's much more socially acceptable for girls to express their emotions than it is for boys, yet women in leadership roles often reveal how they're influenced to adopt the 'male persona'. But neither boys nor girls are educated to understand the nature of emotions and the central role they play in our lives. It's hardly surprising then to hear adults say things like 'we need to take the emotions out of this'. Not only is this not possible, it's not advisable. Such comments reflect how much we misunderstand the nature of emotions, in all walks of life.

For example, emotions are what enable us to make decisions. In fact, if we were to summarise fifty years of academic research into the neuroscience of decision-making, it could be summed up with the single phrase 'all decisions are feelings justified by logic'.

Even the most hard-bitten neuroscientists would now acknowledge that 'rationality' doesn't exist without emotion.[3] Rather than suppress, deny or ignore our emotions, we should study them. We should understand what emotions are, how they work and clarify their purpose in our lives.

Essentially emotions are just composite physiological signals that are designed to provoke appropriate action. If we don't understand the emotional signal our bodies create, then we're more likely to take a wrong turn. If we don't hear the message of our emotion, we will keep making the same mistakes.

In summary, emotions are central to decision-making; they drive our behaviour, they underpin our motivation, they determine the clarity of our thinking, they can transform our ability to learn and they are central to all our relationships, our ability to manage change, our health and our quality of life. Emotions alter our ability to be present and enjoy the moment. They give our life meaning and purpose. They determine our sense of self and our identity. Emotions are so important to all aspects of our lives, there's a very strong case to make emotions a subject in school as important as maths or computing.

Level 4 of ESQ – Emotional Intelligence

Most of us have heard of the 'fight or flight' physiological response. In flight our system releases adrenaline, which gives us a boost of energy so we can run away! In contrast, when we fight, our body releases adrenaline's sister, noradrenaline, which readies the body for battle. If rather than psyching ourselves up to deal with a threat we freeze, play dead or faint, we are activating a very different physiological response.

All three responses are common before walking through the school gates or in the classroom. Most of us have experienced the flight response in an exam when we read the first question, or the freeze response when we panic because we don't know the answer. The fight response is equally prevalent in schools, as most children must learn to stand up for themselves or deal with bullying. Disruptive behaviour in class is often the consequence of triggering these defence reactions to threats.

All three physiological responses are equally prevalent in teachers. We recently had a design session with a well-being team in a school. We saw how the staff struggled to overcome unruly pupil behaviour simply because the pupils didn't feel safe and their physiology was triggered. Any conversation that the teachers wanted to have about trust building were a waste of time until these basic physiological threats were dealt with, and only then could psychological safety become established in the classroom. Now we encourage teachers to start every meeting with an emotional check-in before we try to achieve anything else. We must first deal with our physiology and emotions before we have any hope of having an effective meeting or lesson.

While most people have heard of adrenaline, which is seen as our 'accelerator fluid', very few people have heard of the brake fluid, which is a chemical called 'acetylcholine'. In general terms, heating our system up requires adrenaline, and cooling the system down requires acetylcholine. These chemicals are created by our autonomic nervous system (ANS), which determines our levels of activation, arousal or animation as well as our levels of relaxation.

Figure 5.4 Henry's Axis Underpins Performance

But contrary to popular belief, getting psyched up or being chilled under pressure doesn't determine the quality of our performance. Whether we perform well or fail is much more determined by our hormonal or 'neuroendocrine system' (NE). Our NE system underpins our emotional state, whereas the ANS determines the degree of our arousal.

If we put the ANS activation axis together with the NE emotional state axis, we get a much clearer picture of what underpins our ability to succeed (Figure 5.4). The relationship between these two profoundly important physiological systems was first described by James P. Henry, professor of physiology at the University of Southern California School of Medicine in Los Angeles.[4]

Level 4 emotional intelligence requires us to develop a sense of whether we are activated or relaxed, positive or negative. This very basic level of self-awareness is critical to our health and performance. If we are on the left-hand side of Henry's axis our body creates anabolic steroids that build us up, improve our health and our performance. If we're on the right-hand side of the axis our body pumps out catabolic hormones, particularly cortisol, which is the body's main stress hormone. This causes our system to go into a 'breakdown' state.

When our bodies produce too much cortisol, we get depressed. And when we get depressed, we produce high levels of cortisol. Cortisol creates low mood which creates more cortisol. It's a vicious cycle. Negative emotions massively impair our ability to learn, and persistently high cortisol levels can render us unable to make progress for months or even years.

In contrast, when we are on the positive side of the NE axis, our body produces a range of anabolic hormones, particularly dehydroepiandrosterone (DHEA). DHEA is known as the 'performance' or 'vitality hormone', and the body's natural antidote to cortisol. It's associated with more 'positive' emotions. When we experience positive emotions, we naturally produce more DHEA, which makes us feel better, which generates more DHEA. We create virtuous cycles. This is why, in sports, teams often have winning streaks, or losing streaks if they generate too much cortisol. It's why if children do well in their first exam, they might get 'on a roll' and outperform expectations on all their exams. If they do badly in the first exam, they might create cortisol-driven vicious cycles and bomb in all their exams.

The link between physiology and emotions doesn't just affect exam performance. If a child has a difficult home life or starts their day with conflict or bad news, before they even get to school, they simply won't be in a fit state to extract any value from the morning lessons. This goes for teachers too. If teachers have had a difficult journey to school, maybe they've been delayed by traffic or struggled to get their own children out the door, they may arrive in a less than optimum state to teach. If the teachers' and children's negative emotions at the beginning of the day are then compounded by a negative mood in the staff room or in the playground, then cortisol-driven impairment of learning and teaching can become endemic. Their emotional state can become a trait, leading to a negative emotional reaction even to the thought of school, creating further disengagement. But what if we design the learning environment to create peak experiences? Maybe we could create a positive response to the idea of going to school.

Clearly it's vital that children and adults know which quadrant of Henry's axis they are operating in. Are they on the positive or negative side of the axis. Is their system heated up or cooled down?

Level 5 of ESQ – Emotional Literacy

When we start helping school leadership teams to develop, we often ask them to spend five minutes writing down how many emotions they remember experiencing in the last week. Usually in a room of 20 adults, the answer on average is eight emotions, and often most of them are negative. Then we ask them to guess how many separate emotions it's possible to experience. Even the most ambitious don't guess more than 500 emotions. The truth is it's possible to experience roughly 34,000 different emotions.[5]

If teachers are only familiar with eight out of 34,000 emotions, they're basically emotionally illiterate. In fact, we've tested this question all over the world, and the results are always the same. Most adults are emotionally illiterate. Why? Because emotions are not a subject they studied at school. We never learn about them. We never learn to understand their role in our lives, and we certainly don't develop the ability to differentiate one emotion from another, or accurately label each emotion we do experience.

To help children and teachers develop their emotional literacy, we have loaded more than 2,000 emotions on the Complete App in what's called the 'Universe of Emotions'. Following the physiology of Henry's axis, we've identified whether every emotion is positive or negative, high energy or low energy. To avoid getting overwhelmed by 2,000 choices and to help children (and adults) build up their literacy, we can start with the four most basic emotions, the four Superclusters: Happy, Sad, Angry and Content. If we zoom in a little more, we can expand our literacy to the 16 Nebulae: the eight positive nebulae of Passionate, Amazed, Happy, Cheerful, Appreciated, Curious, Content and Relaxed; and the eight negative nebulae of Anxious, Angry, Tense, Stressed, Confused, Sad, Tired and Worthless. Once children and adults are familiar with these 16 and how they differ from each other in terms of energy and positivity, then they can explore the 64 galaxies in the Universe of Emotions (Figure 5.5).

Some schools have found it very useful to put this poster on every classroom wall, and maybe even the staff room wall, as a reminder that we all spend every moment of every day somewhere in the Universe of Emotions. The only question is: what planet are we on? It can be incredible useful to keep an 'E-Diary' by logging how we feel every day, using the Complete App and the Universe of Emotions. This shows us what planets we tend to gravitate towards when we're not paying attention, and how little 'navigational control' we may have on our own lives and

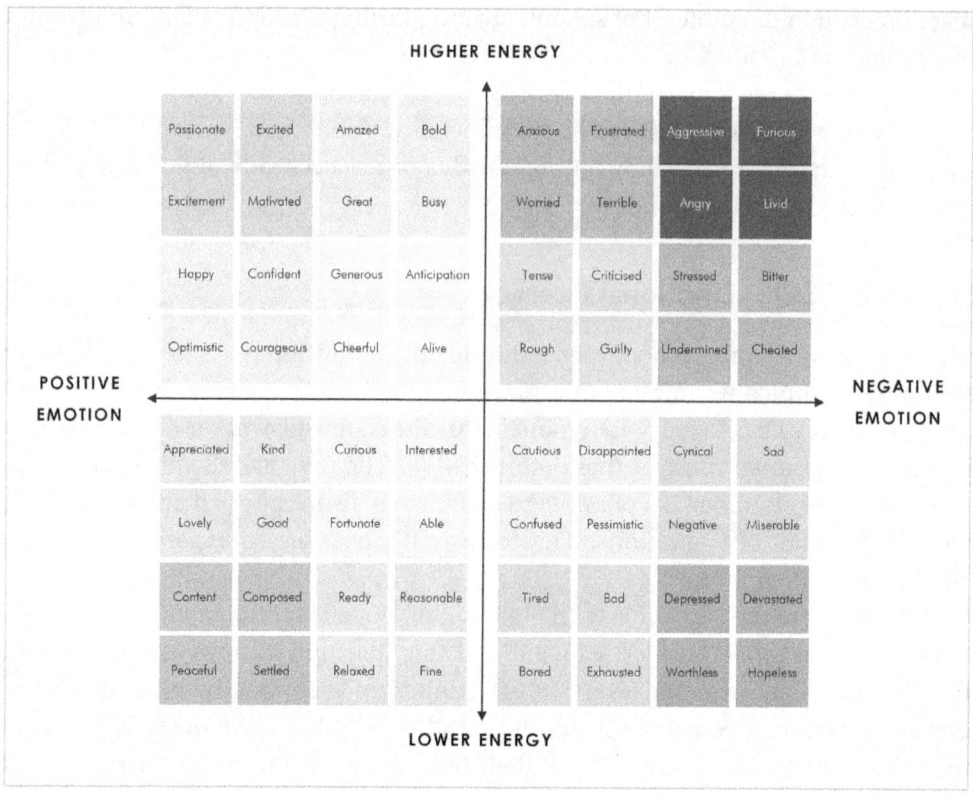

Figure 5.5 The 64 Galaxies in the 'Universe of Emotions'

how influenced we are by factors outside of us, rather than retaking control of our own emotional experience.

Obviously to be an effective learner or student, we need to be in the top left-hand galaxies in the Universe of Emotions. Between lessons, at break or at lunchtime we should be recovering in the bottom left-hand galaxies. Ideally, we should avoid spending too long in the top right-hand galaxies. But most of all we need to get out of the bottom right-hand galaxies if we are living there. The bottom right is the most dangerous place to be, for pupils and staff. These galaxies are pernicious. People operating from these galaxies mistakenly believe they're not in trouble because they are not agitated. But in the bottom-right galaxies we're still producing high levels of cortisol, and this is impairing our performance and ability to learn or teach. How many pupils and teachers are living on the planets of disengaged, detached, bored, apathy, inattentive, hopeless, helpless and many of the other unhelpful planets in this galaxy?

When someone is feeling angry, frustrated or anxious in the top-right, it is usually noticeable, and therefore action is more likely to be taken to shift to a better planet. But adults or children living in the bottom-right often go unnoticed. There is much talk in education about psychological safety, but we are not looking at the raw data and which emotions or planet we are stuck on every day.

Children who are stuck on the right-hand side will often experience well-being or 'mental health' issues, and attendance rates will often be very poor. As mentioned in chapter 1, since the global pandemic, school absence has risen dramatically. Now more than 20% of all children have missed more than 10% of their lessons. And the data are worse in more deprived areas, which will only compound social inequity over time.[6]

And it's not just the children who are not turning up. In the 2020/21 academic year, 68% of teachers took sickness absence with an average of 9.3 days per annum. This equates to more than 3.2 million days lost due to illness, a 56% rise since above pre-pandemic levels.[7] Even allowing for an average educator's salary of £33,000, this works out at £1,255 per year per person and a cost of £432 million to the system. Investing in this line of development clearly makes sense financially and socially.

Level 6 of ESQ – Emotional Regulation

Emotional awareness, at level 5, is necessary but insufficient to change outcomes. We must do something with our awareness and expanding emotional literacy. And that's to develop the ability to change how we feel on demand, every day.

When Matt was a headteacher, he introduced a 20-minute well-being session each morning focused on physiological and emotional self-regulation for children and staff. It was one of the best decisions he ever made. That and many other related interventions produced an 80% decline in negative behaviour incidents in a school with a population of complex needs and developmental delay. And this occurred despite significant initial resistance to using up 'valuable learning time'. Learners had the opportunity to check in on how they felt, let go of the challenges from the night before or during the morning transition into school and begin the day in a positive state. You can read more about Matt's experience in chapter 12.

Taking a little time at the start of the day to actively self-regulate also highlighted who may need additional support. Also, using the poster to create a common emotional literacy language with all stakeholders enabled everyone to share their experience and progress more easily with each other, starting with the leadership team.

This may seem like a relatively basic idea, but without first controlling our own emotional state, we can't even begin to address the wicked problems that are deeply embedded right across the education system.

Matt recalls how this simple initiative transformed student outcomes, even with the students who had severe learning difficulties. One young man struggled with very aggressive behaviour. Teachers had been sent to A&E with broken noses and many teacher's assistants were too petrified to work in the same room as this young man. There appeared to be no solution. When discussing this with his mother, she was naturally defensive and she claimed, "he's not like this at home".

Matt asked to visit his home to see if there was anything that could be learnt from that environment which could be transferred to the school. What he discovered was a normal suburban home where the young man was sitting quietly at a table with a glass of orange juice. This wasn't a behaviour they'd seen at school, where many cups had been thrown and shattered against a wall. The home visit went well and reminded Matt and his colleagues to drop their pre-conceived assumptions about what's possible and remember the vital part that the context plays in influencing emotional state. It reinforced the critical importance of staff first regulating their own emotions before trying to help others manage theirs. Emotions are contagious but leaders often set the climate.

There were many complexities to this young man's needs, but Matt and his staff worked on physiological and emotional self-regulation strategies, particularly at the transition points of the day. The strategies included reducing the sensory overload he felt at these key moments. The staff also worked on emotional self-regulation skills, which his mum was using to great effect at home. With these strategies in place, the changes were astonishing. The young man didn't become a perfect student, but the A&E visits stopped, and his difficult behaviours reduced dramatically. He was less prone to aggressive outbursts, more socially engaged and could even calm himself down at times.

It was so successful that these strategies were embedded into the rest of the school. Teachers practised and taught the techniques shared in this chapter as a foundation for all interactions. And, of course, these techniques aren't just confined to the school setting. They apply equally to public speaking, team discussions, learning how to drive a car. They've also been incredibly useful in the day-to-day interactions of the leadership team, creating a positive environment and a more stable emotional base that allows staff to deal with the many challenges they face more effectively. They understand that cleaning up the triggers of unwanted emotions helps prevent them from projecting their own experiences on to learners. Staff are now empowered to reshape their patterns of perception and their behaviour which sets the climate for trust, growth and challenge. We all recall which teachers we liked at school. Maybe the emotions that those teachers brought to the classroom and the climate they created was a big part of why we liked them?

One of the key skills of emotional regulation is to be able to sustain more helpful emotions once they appear. The difficulty most people have, if you ask them to maintain a positive emotional state, is they don't know how to. Simply because they've never been taught this skill at school and it continues into adult life, fuelling the cyclical nature of modelling. For most people trying to hold onto a helpful emotion is like trying to grasp a cloud.

To help we've developed a skill called MASTERY. The basic idea is that emotional states are subjective. This means we are the subject. The anger has got us. We haven't got it, it's got us. This is why people are so easily overwhelmed by their emotions, whether it's anger or excitement. To gain control over any emotion, it's necessary to objectify them. This is what's called a "subject to object" (S2O) move.

Rather than experience anger or excitement, we can learn to observe it. Next time you feel anything, see if you can sense what it is you're feeling. To help, the MASTERY skill provides a framework.

First, you can observe the 'basic features' of an emotion. Where are you feeling it in your body? What shape, size and colour is it? What's the temperature of that emotion? Does it have a sound? This is a fun exercise to do with children. You can print out a picture of a body and ask them to colour it in when they feel different emotions. The good news here is there is no right answers, so no-one can get the answer wrong. It's a great exercise to do in a classroom, to ask children and teachers to share how they experience different emotions. Not everyone experiences anger or excitement in the same way.

Once we've described the basic features of an emotion, we can then move onto observing the movement features. How does the emotion move through your body or off your body. The more detailed a description you create, the stronger the experience. Remember this is not a visualisation or an invention or an imagination. It's an observation. When you feel delighted, what is it that you are actually feeling? How is the energy moving through you.

Once we've described the movement features of an emotion, we can then move onto observing the special features. Does this emotion put a spring in your step, does it bring a tear to your eye. Does it make you want to punch the air, clench your fist or gnash your teeth?

The more detailed your observation of your emotion, the easier it is to hold onto that emotion for longer. You'll also find it easier to trigger that emotion or re-install it when you need it. Once you have a basic description, you can return to it many times and add more detailed observations until you've completely mastered the emotion. When you have mastered an emotion, you can turn it on when you need it because you are now very clear what you are trying to turn on. Just imagine being able to turn on confidence whenever you needed it and being able to sustain it for an hour. What a life changer that would be. Sustaining confidence is possible once you mastered that emotion, like any other that could help you.

To enhance your MASTERY ability even more, you can also use the PEP skill (Positive Energy Practice). The idea behind PEP is to identify the rituals and habits that you *already* engage in every day and tag them with a very specific emotion that you want to experience more often. You literally 'PEP up' that ritual.

For example, most people follow a specific 'getting up ritual' every day. So why not PEP it up by adding 30 seconds of appreciation into your ritual every morning. You can do the same with your shower ritual, adding gratitude to the experience because you are fortunate to have warm water in your home. Every day of your life could start with appreciation and gratitude. If you add in the PEP of feeling fresh when you brush your teeth and satisfied when you have your breakfast, you start to practice all these positive emotions without ever really needing to remember to practice. They just happen as part of your daily rituals. Again, this is a great conversation to have with staff and children in schools. Get people talking about their daily and weekly rituals and what can be added to them to make the practice sticky. It's fascinating how many rituals we engage in every day. There are so many rituals in our life, some academics have even gone as far as to question whether human beings have any free will left![8] We believe free will certainly exists but, ironically, you must be awake and aware to exercise it.

If you want to enhance your ability to regulate your emotions even further, you can add the Landscaping skill to the MASTERY and PEP skills. Landscaping is simply a way of more formally diarising the rehearsal of positive emotions throughout your day or week. When you look at your diary, you can often identify the possible tough moments of your week. Once you've done that you can deliberately diarise some positive emotions either before or after that tough meeting or experience to mitigate its potential negative impact on you.

Level 7 of ESQ – Emotional Resilience

With your newfound ability to control how you feel whenever you want, you've mastered the first six levels of emotional and social intelligence. The next step is to build your resilience. Resilience is simply the ability to quickly bounce back or even forward after a setback.

Resilience builds on the skills you may have already acquired as you've developed your emotional and social intelligence. Thus, without some emotional awareness you won't realise that you're experiencing a negative emotion. And without some emotional literacy, you may struggle to know whether you're trying to overcome anxiety or worry. They are not the same emotion and the antidote to each is slightly different. If you haven't developed the ability to distinguish these planets in the Universe of Emotions, you might struggle to get off the planet of worry, for example, because you think it's the planet of anxiety. The more adept you become at differentiating planets like anxiety, worry, concern and nervousness, the more skilful you'll be in escaping those planets and getting to a more helpful planet.

To get to a more helpful planet, and experience a positive emotion, you first need a sense of the planet you're trying to get to. For example, getting to the planet of confidence will be impossible if you have no idea what confidence is as a lived experience. This is why the MASTERY skill is key. It helps you objectify the planet of confidence, access it and sustain the experience.

But knowing what planet you may need to reach isn't enough. You also need to develop the ability to move from the unhelpful planet you're on to one that you may have mastered. Changing planets is a separate skill, called the SHIFT skill and it's vital to resilience. This SHIFT skill enables you to change how you feel whenever you want.

Most of the time how we feel is driven by something that happens outside of us. The sun comes out and suddenly we feel more cheerful. Or it starts raining and we feel frustrated. Or someone says something complimentary to us, and we feel appreciated. Conversely, a colleague says something that's unfairly critical and we feel judged. A letter arrives telling us we've won £1000, and we jump with excitement until we realise the letter is addressed to our neighbour. Then we feel deflated.

It's therefore not surprising that most people believe how they feel is down to other people or other things outside of them. If we feel bad, it must be someone else's fault. Our partner, our kids, our friends, our boss, our colleagues, maybe the government – someone. If someone else is to blame for how badly we feel, and we want to bounce back, it makes logical sense that it's down to the other person to make us feel better. Afterall it was them who made us feel bad in the first place.

The truth is no-one is making us feel bad. We are all the architects of our own emotion. We create the chemical signals, the pressure waves, the hormones, the heart rate changes the sounds waves of every single emotion we've ever experienced. If we stop blaming others for how we feel, then our lives will change forever. Our resilience depends on it and this resilience is essential for system evolution.

What's interesting about all this is we change how we feel all the time. The problem is we rarely do this deliberately and consciously. The SHIFT skill is the act of changing our emotion on purpose. SHIFT is an acronym that describes the steps of the process.

After we've noticed we may be on the wrong planet experiencing an unhelpful emotion

1. **S**top what we're doing and move our attention to the
2. **H**eart, which is where most people feel many of their positive emotions. Then
3. **I**nduce a positive emotion which we must
4. **F**eel, not just think a positive thought. We must experience the energy of the positive emotion, and if we do it well, we
5. **T**urn our brain back on, because it was shut down by the negative emotion we were experiencing prior to SHIFT-ing.

This simple skill has the added advantage of not just moving us to a more helpful planet but transforming our ability to solve problems.

Imagine one evening you're writing a school report. You've been at it for a couple of hours and you're stuck. You're on the planet of frustrated. You're not sure how to say what you want to say. What do you do to clear your mind? We've asked this question to teachers and educators all over the world. People use a range of techniques, which have survived for years because they work, but only sometimes. The techniques teachers offer are they:

1. Count to ten
2. Take a break

3. Go for a walk

4. Phone a friend

5. Have a coffee, tea, cigarette, chocolate, glass of wine

6. Sleep on it

7. Go for a run

8. Have a bath

We analysed why these techniques work sometimes, but not all the time. What we discovered is that they all involve the same four steps that are instrumental in their success:

1. Every technique involves you stopping what you're doing and shifting your attention to something else. It doesn't matter whether its coffee, wine, a friend or nature.

2. Every one of these techniques, when they work, induces a positive emotion. When they fail to work, it's because they induce a negative emotion.

3. And you must feel that positive emotion not just think positive. This is not an affirmation.

4. If you feel more positive, cortisol levels drop in your body and your brain turns back on. And the answer suddenly occurs to you on how to fix your school report.

The difference between all the above techniques and the SHIFT skill is that we've added an additional step. We've inserted a focus on the heart. This simple addition changes everything. It removes the hit and miss nature of all the previous techniques and makes sure that the induction of a positive emotion works. Focusing on the area around our heart makes it much more likely that we can induce a positive emotion. Also, it has the added benefit of not requiring us to look outside of ourselves for a positive stimulus. We can't rely on there always being a friend available, we may have run out of coffee, wine, cigarettes, or sunshine. But what we can learn to rely on is ourselves and our own heart for our positivity.

Level 8 of ESQ – Self-Motivation

If we practise the skills offered above, from the first 7 levels of emotional and social intelligence, we will completely transform our ability to self-regulate. We will also step change our resilience, our ability to handle challenging situations and our ability to think more clearly under pressure. Basically, we will have developed an advanced degree of control over our inner Universe of Emotions.

Level 8 takes this a step further and enables us to use our emotions to drive ourselves forward. Specifically, the skills at level 8 give us control over our motivation. Emotions and motivation both come from the same Latin origins; *'emotio'* and *'motio'*, both infer movement. Emotions move us and when we have control of our own emotion, we can use them to move ourselves. The key skill at level 8 is uncovering our personal purpose.[9]

Level 9 of ESQ – Optimistic Outlook

Level 9 is the final level of personal emotional development. By the time we reach this level we've developed massively. We're in control of our emotions. We can use them to motivate ourselves, and we have high levels of resilience. We're also now clear about our personal purpose and we're not the victim of others. The cherry on the personal emotion development cake is to be able to operate from the left-hand side of the Universe of Emotion most of the time. This doesn't mean we live on the delusional planet of *'happy-clappy'*, or we're stuck on the planet of *'idealism'*. Far from it, we operate with a degree of optimism because we know that no matter how tough things may be, or may become, we have the skills to deal with the challenges ahead.

This doesn't mean that it's wrong to live on the right-hand side of the Universe. All of us get blown off course and experience some less helpful planets. And sometimes it's entirely appropriately to experience anger, frustration or grief, for example. It's just that getting stuck on those planets doesn't serve us or others. Developing the ability to live on the left-hand side of the Universe of Emotions by choice improves our health and ability to perform to a much higher level, whatever we're doing.

We don't all live on the planet of optimism, we may choose to reside, as a start point every day, on the planet of 'upbeat', 'cheerful' or any of the 17,000 planets on the left-hand side. For example, 'appreciation' can be a very productive place to live. Appreciation has been shown to be a happiness booster. Psychologist Sonja Lyubomirsky from the University of California found that those who consciously counted their blessing – even just once a week – significantly increased their overall satisfaction with life over a six-week period.[10]

We've also found that being in a state of appreciation transforms people's ability to learn, at school and in life. Appreciation makes us more receptive to new information, more open to novel ideas, more likely to learn and develop. If we approach life thinking we already know everything we need to know, then we probably won't even listen.

Taking an optimistic approach to life and cultivating the trinity of positive emotions; optimism gratitude and appreciation can change our lives. In a social media obsessed world where cancel cultures and internet bullying are common and where many children live in fear of judgement, the simple act of self-appreciation can be a powerful antidote. Appreciation can boost confidence and enhance capability. One simple way to increase levels of appreciation is to write down all the things we appreciate about ourselves in the six main areas of life; mentally, emotionally, physically, socially, professionally and spiritually (or higher purpose if you prefer). We never have to show anyone this list. But if we write down what's definitely true regardless of whether we're having a good day or a bad day and then we look at this list, often, we'll discover our sense of appreciation starts to increase. When we look at the list, it's vital not to just acknowledge the statements as true, we must FEEL a sense of appreciation for the truth of the statements. Such a practice can boost our energy. It may help us access similar emotions such as valued, treasured, cherished, revered, blessed, thankful and many others. This is a particularly powerful practice for people living in very difficult circumstances. It helps demonstrate awareness and application, highlighting strengths and next steps.

Level 10 of ESQ – Empathy and Rapport

The first nine levels of the emotional and social intelligence journey focus on our personal 'I' energy and emotional skills. The last three levels focus on the social skills we need to transform our ability to relate to others in the 'WE' dimension which we will unpack in greater depth shortly. But for the sake of completeness, we'll finish the 12 levels of ESQ here.

Level 10 is about developing greater levels of empathy and rapport. Empathy is the ability to sense, understand and resonate with the feelings of others. It's not exclusive to humans. Research has shown that many animals such as chimps, dolphins, elephants, dogs, horses and some birds, bats and rats demonstrate prosocial behaviour. They will help or comfort distressed members of their group. Dogs, elephants and some primates are also known to empathise across species including with humans. But human empathy is significantly more advanced than other species. It's the sophistication of our empathy that differentiates us from other animals and much of this is based on our much more extensive emotional literacy.

Empathy is the ability to sense, understand and resonate with the feelings of others. Since emotions drive behaviour, the more we can understand how others feel, the more we can predict their behaviour and the more likely we are to be able to effectively motivate them. This understanding rarely shows up in behaviour management training or policy approaches and is largely considered 'soft' by those who are not yet able to apply it.

There are three types of empathy: cognitive, emotional and compassionate. Cognitive empathy is the ability to comprehend another person's thoughts and beliefs and their view of the world. It allows us to put ourselves in someone else's shoes and see the world from their perspective. Cognitive empathy also helps us comprehend what someone is going through, without necessarily sharing their emotional experience.

Emotional empathy is the ability to share and vicariously experience the emotions of another person. When we feel emotional empathy, we genuinely feel the same or very similar emotions as the person we are empathising with. This type of empathy involves mirror neurons, a type of brain cell that creates a similar emotion in us even though we're not doing the same thing as the other person. Emotional empathy creates a much greater level of intimacy and much stronger relationships bonds than cognitive empathy. Although, it can cause distress if we over-empathise with someone who is experiencing something distressing.

Compassionate empathy goes beyond just understanding what people think and believe (cognitive empathy) and beyond sharing what they feel (emotional empathy). It's defined by a motivation to alleviate someone else's suffering. This requires something more profound than just feeling what someone else feels. It requires an understanding of the cause of that person's feelings and a desire to act if they are distressed.

One of the most profound skills to develop at this level of social intelligence is the MAP skill. This skill enables us to connect much more deeply with people we speak to, and to do so quickly. We've seen this skill totally transform teachers' relationships with parents in a matter of minutes as well as children's relationships with each other. This skill and many of the earlier ones are described in detail in Alan's earlier book, *Coherence: The Science of Exceptional Leadership and Performance* (2nd Edition)[11] but essentially MAP is an acronym for the process we go through to ensure that we are really listening at a much deeper level than normal.

The steps are:

1. **M**ove your attention away from your own thinking and the noise in your head to your body and BREATHE through your heart area (not your stomach).

2. **A**ppreciate the speaker. This means find something you can genuinely appreciate about the person you're speaking to and try to radiate that positive regard towards them. If you do this well, they'll sense your encouragement. Generating a state of appreciation alters your biology and scientifically is what enables you to hear them at a much deeper level.

3. **P**lay back the underlying meaning. Once they have finished speaking, don't just precis or summarise what they said. Play back what you sensed they really meant beneath the words and the emotion of their transmission. What was their broadcast really all about, what's really going on for them right now?

The MAP skill goes way beyond what's often referred to as 'active listening'. In fact, when you're good at this skill you don't need to spend anywhere near as much energy as is normally required by 'actively listening' to someone's broadcast. The

MAP skill enables us to be significantly less distracted by the surface noise and the specific words being transmitted. It enables us to detect the deeper meaning and play that back. This skill significantly heightens our social intuition and helps build trust.

Level 11 of ESQ – Social Awareness

Emotions are contagious. The physiological signals that underpin them don't stop at the skin. We radiate our physiological and emotional energy out to all those around us. If we're in a bad mood, we can drain the energy of those we interact with. Conversely if we're in a good mood we can lift others' spirits. Even though most people are aware of this idea, few use it to benefit themselves or others.

In fact, most people don't even realise what a significant impact they're having on those around them. To help people better understand their impact on others, we've built a 'Team Energy Grid'. This is a 360-degree feedback tool where people rate the impact others are having on them using the Universe of Emotions. They rate the impact on good days and bad days. They also rate themselves. Even the simple act of reflecting on their own and other people's 'energetic footprint' is helpful. It spawns very rich conversations in schools and tees up the need to move to level 12 on the emotional and social intelligence journey.

Level 12 of ESQ – Social Intelligence

In many ways, all the previous 11 levels of development of our emotional and social intelligence culminate here. Level 12 is all about social intelligence. This is essentially our ability to build positive constructive relationships with anybody, even with people we may not like. Building sustainable relationships is one of the most advanced capabilities we can develop as human beings. It's central to our success, fulfilment and our health. We are social animals, it's what's made us incredibly successful as a species. We can consider social intelligence and relationship building as the 'final frontier' of our personal development. If we mature in the 'I' domain, the success of that maturation must be tested in the 'WE' domain.

Social intelligence is all about relationships and being able to consciously step in and out of 1st, 2nd or 3rd person perspectives is an advanced capability that most people don't possess. We will cover this in more detail in chapter 7 but it's the ability to control which perspective we're operating from, that's the game changer. It's the conscious awareness and deliberate shifting from one perspective to another. If you know which perspective you're in when you're in it, and you can also consciously shift perspectives then this is 4th person perspective taking – the ability to take a perspective on a perspective. This ability is strongly correlated with ego maturity which we will explain shortly.

Understanding Your Values

We started the book by taking a historical look at the education system through the lens of value systems or world views. This enabled us to better appreciate why we are where we are, and also understand that the problems we are experiencing are no-one's fault. They are the consequence of what society needed at each point in history, based on what that society valued at that time. The evolution of education has not always been fast, and it's not been a smooth journey, but evolution never is. The various systems that emerged did, at least, try to meet the changing educational needs of society.

As we explained in the introduction, the changing waves of values have been brilliantly defined by Professor Clare Graves and his values spiral. In the introduction we explored these value systems in relation to the evolving system of education. Now it's time to revisit the values spiral as an invaluable tool for helping us to better understand ourselves and what motivates us personally. What we value changes over time and follows the same path as the values spiral (Figure 5.6).

One of the gnarly characteristics of a wicked problem is that they involve multiple stakeholders. And those multiple stakeholders often have multiple ideas about the multiple causes, symptoms and potential solutions. We can see this in the education system where various stakeholder groups perpetually propose certain

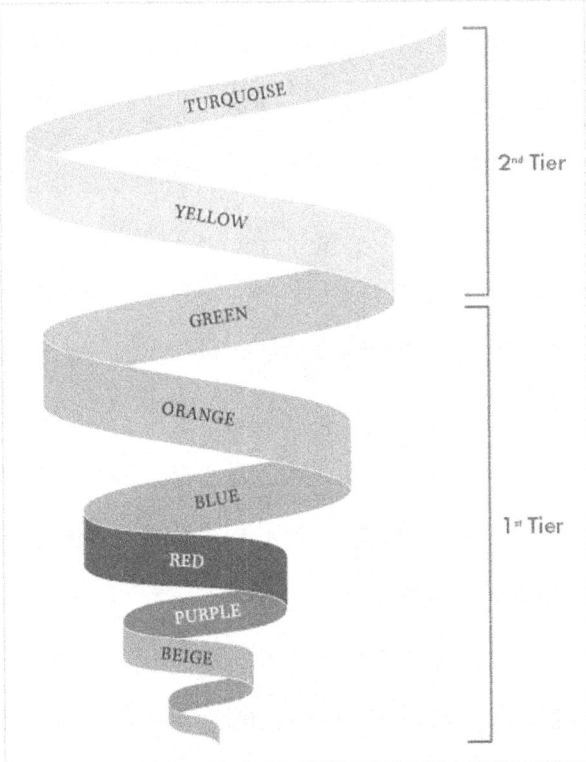

Figure 5.6 The Values Spiral

	PURPOSE OF EDUCATION	PREFERRED APPROACH TO LEARNING & TEACHING	QUALITIES TO ENHANCE IN EDUCATION	PROBLEMS CREATED BY EACH VALUE SYSTEM
T	To foster a more global consciousness and encourage spiritual growth	Emphasis on systems harmony, wellbeing and longevity for all	Evolution of harmonious systems that serve all stakeholders	Too philosophical and may not meet stakeholders where they are at
Y	To understand complexity and interconnectedness in systems	Emphasis on innovation, critical thinking & systems understanding	Quality of ideas, systemic thinking, critical analysis	Struggle with traditionalists, complicate things, too many changes at once
G	To promote equality, social justice and environmental awareness	Emphasis on learning together, collaboratively and empathically	Creativity, collaboration & community	Too woke, excess political correctness at expense of achievement
O	To gain knowledge, achieve success and outperform others	Competitive environment where individual success (grades) is the goal	Adaptability, pragmatism & freedom to work out answers	Excessive competitiveness, stress and burnout, ignore arts and culture
B	To instil moral, religious or specific values and societal standards	Structured and predictable timetable where hierarchy and rules are clear	Diplomatic, skills, rules to enable right answer to be discovered	Rigid adherence to the rules & oppressive compliance to structures, too traditional
R	A way to be the best, or gain power (knowledge is power)	Via personal authority and status, star charts & demerits commonly used	Fun, play, speed, novelty, self-expression	May be foster disruptive behaviour by indulging excessive individualism
P	To preserve cultural traditions and pass on ancestral knowledge	Through rituals and storytelling, in the oral tradition	Belonging, togetherness, honour, traditions	Resistance to change, might exclude people from outside culture
B	To acquire survival skills and meet immediate needs	Hands on	Meeting immediate needs	No long-term planning, inability to deal with complexities of system

Figure 5.7 How Each Value System Approaches Education

solutions to specific parts of the problem, that they believe are the most important, rather than suggest a way forward for the whole system. And which part they work on and consider important is determined by their own personal values.

Thus, stakeholders who operate from the Blue value system argue for a 'back to basics' approach and the importance of discipline in schools. They may also argue for the principles of fair pay for a fair day's work for teachers. In contrast, stakeholders who operate from the Orange value system suggest that schools must have measurement and metrics, otherwise how do we know if the school is improving. They would argue for more testing not less. They might also suggest the need for more of a 'market economy' for schools, where schools compete for the best teachers and the best pupils. They may advocate for economies of scale in multi-academy trusts with larger revenues to drive better outcomes. Individuals operating from the Green value system might make the case for pupil-centred learning, with a greater emphasis on well-being and a community approach. Individuals operating from a Yellow value system would take a more disruptive approach to the problems but critically would seek to integrate the best ideas from all of the other value systems. Individuals from a Turquoise perspective would align with the integrative approach of Yellow but would seek to balance all the forces in the system to enable the system to evolve as rapidly as possibly to meet the needs of all stakeholders.

The nature of the problem and the possible solutions they suggest change based on which value system each stakeholder operates from. Figure 5.7 provides a snapshot as to what is valued at each level and the likely problems that each level might provoke.

To make things even more challenging there is a distinct divide between the 1st tier value systems which are Beige to Green and 2nd tier which is Yellow and Turquoise. As mentioned in the introduction, all those operating from a values level in the 1st tier believe that they are right and everyone else is wrong. Those operating from the 2nd tier appreciate that every level brings value and therefore a healthy educational system should embrace the diversity of every level.

Currently more than 95% of the global population operate from the 1st tier. This often means that the stakeholders who are tasked with finding solutions can't even agree on the nature of the problem, never mind how to potentially solve it. And that won't change until everyone around the table understands value systems, where they operate from, and therefore what they value and how that is almost certainly different from the other stakeholders in the room. Those functioning from the 1st tier can still add massive value, but it is crucial they understand how they can do this rather than refusing to implement something because it's not their view.

Most of us don't understand our own motivations and which value system we operate from. Even if we do, we often get defensive about different suggestions because we mistakenly assume that if it comes from higher up the spiral it must be better. That makes us feel uncomfortable and likely to reject alternative ideas.

Higher up the spiral is more sophisticated but not better. A car is more sophisticated than a bicycle, but it isn't better than a bicycle. It depends on what we are trying to achieve. The Green value system feels this 'better worse, more or less sophisticated' conundrum more acutely than any other value system. People operating from Green values have often personally experienced pathological hierarchies. This is why they tend to see a values hierarchy as some sort of tyranny or oppression.

There is a real risk that the benefit of a values hierarchy is reduce to a flatland typology. If we do this, then we remove the very thing that drives progress and evolution. If all value systems are mere variations of each other, then we will never improve.

It's impossible to jump from one level such as Red to a level two rungs up such as Orange. We must develop from Red to Blue and into Orange. Every value level offers significant benefits that can be very useful in certain educational situations or environments. However, each level also has its own unique blind spots and it is

	UPSIDE	DOWNSIDE
Planetary (Turquoise)	Impact on context beyond school	Too abstract
Polarities (Yellow)	Big picture thinking	Over complicate things and hyper changeable
Progressive (Green)	Whole human development	Fears the potential of judgement
Performance (Orange)	Focused on outcome & effectiveness	A few narrow 'winners' disengage 'losers'
Principle (Blue)	Quality standards, structured	Inflexibility, doesn't evolve with the times
Power (Red)	Self-expression encouraged	Excess autonomy & Lack of fairness
Pastoral (Purple)	Safe Communities	Disorientation

Figure 5.8 Upside and Downside of Each Value System and Wave in the Context of Education

usually these blind spots that cause a problem which becomes the stimulus for the next level to emerge (Figure 5.8).

It makes sense therefore for all stakeholders, especially teachers, leaders and policy makers to understand which value system they operate from when they are planning change, executing change or managing others. If, as education system stakeholders, we develop an awareness of the assets and liabilities we bring to any discussion, it makes it far more likely that we will be able transform that system.

Once we realise that the pain in our current wave is less than the pain that awaits us, we will press on into the next wave of education, and we're more willing to commit to change. Doing this openly also models to other stakeholders that this is growth that benefits everyone. Each time we successfully evolve an aspect of education, the feeling of inspiring others makes the resistance to the next change that little bit easier and we gain the momentum for faster revolutions, shared processes and therefore system-wide evolution.

There are two key points to this process. The first is to recognise that this is a 'transcend and include' journey where we evolve upward without losing the upside of the earlier stages. The second is recognising the downsides, and the pain those downsides create is always mitigated by the upside of the next wave.

To this end we have developed the Complete Values Profile (CVP) which allows educational stakeholders to assess what they value and therefore what's driving their behaviour, their interpretation of the problem and the potential solutions they suggest. By taking the CVP, stakeholders can better understand themselves and those around them. It reveals what is driving them and allows them to acknowledge and appreciate difference, thereby helping to remove some of the personal angst and disagreements that so often occur when stakeholders are seeking robust and inclusive solutions to wicked problems.

Imagine the impact of such an assessment on the recruitment and retention crisis of teachers and leaders or the behaviour challenges of our learners if we were to accurately understand what drives our stakeholders and they were able to become conscious of how they are showing up and why.

Ego Maturity

The final line of development in the 'I' dimension that delivers an exponential return on investment is ego maturity, broadly defined as our sense of self, who we really are. Like values, ego maturity evolves, or at least it should through the course of normal human development. But like values, it can also get stuck.

The importance of knowing who we are, our understanding of our 'self' and how our identity and ego is formed and develops cannot be underestimated. Identity and identity politics are hugely important in today's educational system.

Our sense of self determines how well we make sense of and navigate the challenges of the world. To make sense of the world, we often relate it to who we are.

Thus, we constantly evaluate whether what we're experiencing is a threat to our survival; our point of view, our role or job; our social standing and our family. A strong and mature sense of self is vital to our health, our confidence, our resilience and our ability to make a positive contribution to the lives of others. A fractured or immature sense of self often impairs our health, our ability to contribute and can lead to significant suffering for others, particularly if we are in a position of responsibility or leadership.

Mature individuals can more effectively drive transformation because they can:

1. skilfully break down 'silo' structures
2. facilitate behaviour change
3. manage greater levels of complexity
4. step change stakeholder collaboration
5. align different stakeholder groups much faster
6. develop more powerful organisational cultures that embrace greater diversity
7. unlock the wisdom that diversity brings
8. be more innovative and disruptive in tough environments
9. drive greater levels of agility in a rapidly changing world
10. create more powerful and inspiring narratives.

Greater maturity allows us to let go of old boundaries or out-dated beliefs so that new ways can emerge, quietening the anxiety and the need for control. We become more comfortable sitting in discomfort. Change is no longer seen as a threat or a source of discomfort, it's welcomed and embraced.

Renowned authority on adult development theory, Susanne Cook-Greuter has spent 45 years researching ego maturity and how this plays out in organisations. Her work provides a practical explanation for why there are so many battles and 'political manoeuvring' in organisations. And these battles certainly occur at all levels of the education system. It explains why stakeholders keep coming up with the same set of answers to the same set of problems and why nothing seems to change. Bill Torbert, another well-known theorist in the area, has explored adult maturity from the perspective of what drives action. His 'Action Logic' describes how the various stages play out in organisations and his labels are normally recognisable to leaders. We have built on Torbert and Cook-Greuter's work along with many others to try to make the key levels more comprehensible.[12] There are twelve levels of maturity (Figure 5.9)

Maturity theory is increasingly understood as one of the most powerful maps for describing who we are. It's a much better predictor of human behaviour than personality tests, typologies or strength finders. It can certainly deliver a profoundly

TIER	LEVEL	NAME OF LEVEL	DEALING WITH	LEVEL OF THINKING
Tier 3	12	Illuminated	Reality	Post-post-conventional
Tier 3	11	Embodied	Reality	Post-post-conventional
Tier 3	10	Unitive	Reality	Post-post-conventional
Tier 3	09	Alchemist	Reality	Post-post-conventional
Tier 2	08	Integrator	Identity	Post-conventional
Tier 2	07	Pluralist	Identity	Post-conventional
Tier 2	06	Achiever	Identity	Conventional
Tier 2	05	Expert	Identity	Conventional
Tier 1	04	Conformist	Emotions	Conventional
Tier 1	03	Self-Protective	Emotions	Pre-conventional
Tier 1	02	Ego-centric	Emotions	Pre-conventional
Tier 1	01	Impulsive	Emotions	Pre-conventional

Figure 5.9 The 12 Levels of Maturity

insightful and practical framework for understanding much of the dysfunction witnessed in education.

We can now measure our own level of adult maturity and precisely define how we and everyone around us make sense of the world. The levels of emotional and social intelligence, discussed earlier, define how well we manage our emotions and relate to other people's emotions. The values assessment, which we also discussed earlier, defines what motivates each of us. In contrast, the maturity profile

TIER	LEVEL	NAME OF LEVEL	DEALING WITH	WAY OF OPERATING	KEY DRIVER	APPROACH TO THE GAME OF LIFE
Tier 3	12	Illuminated		Is a light and a reflection of the light of the greater grid	Radiance	No more games
	11	Embodied	Reality	Swims in and creates the ocean of boundless energy and particles	Magnetics	Be the game
	10	Unitive		Now understands the evolving nature of reality, and the oneness of all things	Harmony	Unite all games
	09	Alchemist		Experiences reality on a whole new level all answer are constructions	Transformation	Change the game
Tier 2	08	Integrator		Sees systems and thinks systemically, all answers are nested in systems	Disruption	Run the game
	07	Pluralist	Identity	Opens up to relationship with people and ideas all answers are contextual	Inclusion	Reframe the game
	06	Achiever		Sees the difference between knowledge and outcomes, believes in optimal answers	Success	Win the game
	05	Expert		Attached to own knowledge base, believes in one right answer	Prowess	Score points in the game
Tier 1	04	Conformist		Protects by conforming and securing sponsorship answers are what the collective agree on	Protect Role	Play the game
	03	Self-Protective	Emotions	Protect self by hiding emotions, defensive & blaming, answers are what maintains security	Protect Self	Stay in the game
	02	Ego-centric		Objectifies & justifies own emotions, answers are personal beliefs and opinions	Assert Self	Above the rules or makes the rules of the game
	01	Impulsive		Live in the moment, driven by own emotions	React in the moment	Follow the game

Figure 5.10 Details of the Different Maturity Levels

doesn't define 'WHAT' emotion or 'WHAT' motivation it answers the question 'WHO' is the person experiencing the anger, and the motivational drive. And 'WHO' we are is not a static thing that stops at the age of 18. Hopefully, we continue to grow up well beyond 18 years of age. Although sadly for many they stopped maturing much earlier in life.

If you want to read more on the detailed description of each level, you can find that in Alan's book *4D Leadership*,[13] but the key point in this context is that all the various developmental academics agree that most leaders and teachers in education operate from 'Achiever' or below. There are clearly leaders who have a more expansive perspective and greater maturity, but the current 'collective central' tendency,[14] is that 85% of leaders are hovering between Level 5 and Level 6.[15] And the effects of that are being painfully felt in the world today.

To develop our maturity, we need to know what level we're operating from right now. This is where the Complete Maturity Profile (CMP) comes in. Drawing on the best of the various developmental theories the CMP provides educational stakeholders, especially those tasked with finding and implementing solutions, with an accurate insight into their own maturity and that of their colleagues. Figure 5.10 provides a few brief details of what each level is about. The description of the higher levels may seem baffling, particularly if you've yet to really experience that level. Most people in the educational system, as we said, are operating from Level 6 or below.

The maturity model describes how we can evolve through three tiers. We've significantly adapted the terminology used by other developmental theorists to make it more user-friendly. Each new level unlocks new capabilities and each tier has four developmental sub-stages.

Understanding maturity helps stakeholders to better understand why all manner of people challenges exist. Maturity assessment provides a clear explanation for why people behave as they do, where they can regress to under pressure and where the greatest growth opportunities are for the individual and the team. As a result, the CMP explains why individual performance often falls short, why a team isn't working and most importantly, what to do about it.

A lot of leaders we've worked with see themselves at the centre of what they're trying to achieve, under pressure to know all and decide all. Matt worked with one Director of Strategy who, when he first began his coaching programme, felt wildly out of control. He was new to the educational trust's senior team and believed that others around him doubted his ability. How was he ever going to understand everything that was happening at scale, and manage the complexity of the strategy? He was an innovative headteacher a few years earlier, but with so many schools to oversee, he spent much of his time feeling like a failure. To him it felt like he'd gone from being the pick of the bunch to barely implementing the simplest of projects.

Using the ego maturity model, he instantly began to understand the Achiever narrative that he was operating with. Achievers like to predict, measure and explain the world. This enables them to see ahead, and they also like to look back in time to discover patterns, rules and laws at play. They notice and appreciate more pieces of the puzzle than Experts, and this is what enables them to succeed when Experts struggle.

But in his new role, it felt like this still wasn't enough. He reflected on how his Achiever narrative was holding him and the staff around him back. It also determined the staff's expectations of him and how they saw his role. He realised he needed to mature beyond a purely results and outcome-focused leader and implementer. He couldn't be the sole driving force and he realised he didn't have all the answers. He needed to completely change his approach. Instead of being at the centre driving things forward as the leader, he matured to listen to those in his team and seek to better understand them so he could better appreciate what they could add.

He started learning from them. Their views changed the way he saw the Trust's strategy. He made a public commitment to his team and explained where his drivers had come from in early childhood. His honesty, humility and vulnerability built a new level of trust in the team. The team also felt he was now listening to them much more deeply and they felt more valued. They got on board and implemented the changes with more gusto than he could ever have imagined. There was a rapid culture shift. And all because he'd had the courage to assess his own ego maturity.

All the assessments, tools, interventions and practices described in this chapter are designed to level up every individual. They define a developmental path for all stakeholders to follow. By investing in your own development, you can achieve vertical take-off. The new capabilities you unlock at your new level of maturity will spill out positively into all areas of your life. Being able to better manage your state will not only help you solve problems in the classroom or as an administrator or policy maker, but it will also improve your relationships and make family life more rewarding. Being able to protect your energy levels so you are not wiped out by the demands of your role, by gaining conscious control over your breathing to create a coherent HRV, is a practical skill that can be used to improve your performance and well-being at any given moment throughout the day.

In life, there's always a tendency to think that something 'out there' must change. But the only thing we can ever change is us. We are the ripple in the pond, and when we commit to vertical development, expand our interior 'I' dimension and embrace all the capabilities that go with that, we become, to paraphrase Gandhi – the change we wish to see in the world.

Notes

1 Will M (2023) What's happening to teacher stress levels, EDWeek.
2 Watkins A (2021) Coherence: The Science of Exceptional Leadership and Performance (2nd Edition) Kogan Page, London.

3 Damasio A (1999) The feeling of what happens: body, emotion and the making of consciousness, Vintage, London.
4 Henry, J P (1982) The relation of social to biological processes in disease, *Social Science and Medicine*, 16 (4), pp 369–80.
5 Goleman D, Dalai Lama (2004) Destructive emotions: and how can we overcome them, Bloomsbury, London.
6 Education Committee (2023) Persistent absence and support for disadvantaged pupils, Report Summary UK Government. Eyles A, Lillywhite E, Elliot Major L (2023) The rising tide of school absences in the post-pandemic era London School of Economics (LSE) Blog
7 Whittaker F (2023) Teacher sickness absence soars in wake of pandemic, Schoolsweek.
8 Sapolsky R (2023) Determined: life without free will, Vintage, London.
9 Watkins A (2021) Coherence: the science of exceptional leadership and performance, 2nd Edition, Kogan Page, London.
10 Wallis C (2005) The new science of happiness: what makes the human heart sing?, Time Magazine, 17 January.
11 Watkins A (2021) Coherence: the science of exceptional leadership and performance, 2nd Edition, Kogan Page, London.
12 Watkins A (2016) 4D Leadership: competitive advantage through vertical leadership development, Kogan Page, London.
13 Ibid.
14 Cook-Greuter SR (2004) Making the case for a developmental perspective, Industrial and Commercial Training 36 (7).
15 Rooke D, Torbert WR (2005) Seven transformations of leadership, Harvard Business Review, 1 April 2005.

Individual Development in Action

To give you a better sense of what individual development theory and practice look like in an educational setting, we're going to follow the developmental journey of a primary school head teacher we'll call Adam. Adam oversees 270 pupils. He has 62 staff members, including 25 teachers and 30 support staff in his school.

Adam was in his early 30s when we met him. His rise to head teacher had been rapid. He did a degree in economics, then went into teacher training and into teaching. He became an assistant head at 28, acting head not long after, and was promoted to head teacher as he turned 30. His progress had been accelerated by his design of the year 6 English and maths curricula that had transformed the school's Standardised Assessment Results (SATs) – making them the highest SATs in the region. He continually produced the best results in the local authority and was still teaching English and maths when we began working with him. However, he was conflicted by the knowledge that he wasn't really addressing the needs of the 'whole child'. One of his objectives was to build a broader curriculum. He was keen to establish a more balanced approach without losing the gains in English and maths, while taking his staff with him, because they saw the outcomes the school had achieved as a point of pride and didn't want to jeopardise them.

Although Adam's school had been deemed 'Outstanding' by Ofsted three years earlier, Adam was not complacent. He was expecting another visit shortly and was aware how quickly things can change despite their previous positive results. Adam was keen to plot a course so that the school could continue to develop. He wanted to take the school to the next level, but by his own admission didn't really know how to do that.

This indecision was even making him wonder if it was time to move on. Teacher retention is a major problem in education, including head teachers. Adam's situation was a reminder that retention isn't just relevant to teachers who are struggling, it's also an issue for those who are doing well. Given that many teachers discuss what other jobs they could do that 'pay more and have less stress', it's not surprising that retention is an issue across the entire system. Using the Change Wheel to define Adam's 'journey', he was at step 2, out of his comfort zone and experiencing the challenge of self-doubt. He was also at risk of getting stuck at step 3, resisting change, as he was beginning to avoid the whole discussion and just settle for what the central system perceived as 'good'.

The Complete Intervention

When we met Adam, the start point was to help him get a better handle on his energy and emotion. Adam felt he had most things under control but admitted he was under constant pressure. We asked him to wear a heart rate monitor for 24 hours, go about his day as normal, and send the unit back to us for analysis.

Adam's HRV analysis revealed he was pumping out way too much adrenaline than was good for him, almost certainly because he was under persistent pressure. Like so many people, Adam assumed he was handling the pressure well and it wasn't negatively impacting his physical, mental or emotional health. But that wasn't entirely true. He was more like the classic duck on a pond, serene above the surface but paddling furiously underneath, burning an incredible amount of energy to stay afloat and appear as though all was well.

Talking the HRV results through with Adam, it was clear that he wasn't particularly aware of his emotions and how his emotions were impacting his energy reserves throughout the day. Adam's first task was to use the Complete App to get a better sense of when his breathing was chaotic and how that felt. Then purposefully use the BREATHE skill and breath pacer in the App to regain control over his breath and ensure he could feel the difference between coherent breathing and chaotic breathing.

Most people instinctively know that breathing is important, not just to keep us alive but as a contributor to how we feel. For example, most of us have been angry or frustrated at some point and although we may not realise it, the first thing to 'go' is the control of our breathing. Most emotions involve a specific breathing pattern. For most negative emotions, our breathing pattern tends to be disordered or chaotic. Frustration, for example, often involves us involuntarily engaging in an unconscious series of mini breath holds or what is known as 'glottic stops'. If we replace this breath-holding with smooth, rhythmic even breathing using the BREATHE skill, then the frustration melts away. The same is true when we feel anxious or panicky. All these emotions involve some sort of disordered breathing pattern. If we use the BREATHE skill, these emotions also melt away. It's very difficult to sustain negative emotions in the face of rhythmic even breathing through our hearts.

Adam was surprised at how much of a difference this simple change in the way he was breathing had on his sense of control and the clarity of his thinking. He's now embedded the BREATHE skill into his daily life. He takes a few minutes each morning to make sure his breathing is coherent. He also uses the PEP and

	BOOSTS		DRAINS
1	Space to myself eating breakfast	1	Woken up by kids
2	Caught up on staff emails and safeguarding, feel good	2	Writing up yesterday's tricky meeting
3	Planned SEND parents meetings	3	Responding to parent's requests, felt like wasted time
4	Infant assembly	4	Chairing SLT session was draining
5	Taught maths lessons	5	Prep for governors meeting, too much paperwork
6	Met with parents on ADHD referral	6	End of day email volume
7	Parents open day, told story of school	7	Drive home
8	Meeting with business manager	8	Struggled to be present with my kids
9	Put one of kids to bed, created space	9	Vegetation in front of TV
10		10	

Figure 6.1 Adam's E-Bank

landscaping tools to ensure he's in the right emotional state before all his meetings. He's encouraged others to do the same. The staff have even baked the BREATHE skill into the culture of the school. There are a few minutes of coherent breathing in the classroom at the start of each day, and in assembly. Such a simple tool has essentially shifted the climate of the classrooms and the school.

We also asked Adam to keep a note of the events, situation and people that drained or boosted his energy levels (the E-Bank skill). Adam recorded several E-Banks to see if he could better identify where his energy was coming from and where it was going (Figure 6.1).

Adam recorded nine boosts and nine drains. We asked him to reflect on his two lists and what they revealed about his energy levels. We encouraged him to draw a conclusion from the pattern revealed by his lists. When reviewing several E-Banks he noticed that certain people and situations kept appearing on his drain list. It was like having a direct debit draining energy from his account. Similarly, he noticed that there were some people in his life, and certain situations, that could always boost his energy. These were the wonderful deposits that lifted his spirits.

Two energy drains in his account were red flags for Adam. The first was personal. He realised he was spending so most of his available energy at work. By the time he got home he was usually totally drained. This triggered some guilt, which compounded the energy drain. He concluded he wanted to be more present for his children and partner, so he began a new routine of parking five minutes' walk from the school. This created a fresh air buffer in the morning and evening which enabled him to plan what he wanted to achieve going in to school and similarly clear his mind on the way home. He used the PEP and the BREATHE skills in these buffer zones. The second red flag was how thinly spread he was across so many school operations. Up to that point the team had worked organically. Adam now realised he hadn't delegated the responsibility for the different elements of school activity across his leadership team well enough.

In addition to using the BREATHE, PEP, Landscaping and E-Bank skills, Adam also worked on improving his emotional regulation by practising MASTERY and by logging his emotions on the Complete App. In his first week Adam logged 10 different emotions, which is more than most beginners do. There are 2,145 emotions available to choose from on the Complete App. Most people only ever experience about a dozen emotions, or planets, around the stars of 'mad', 'bad', 'sad' and 'glad'! Within just a few weeks Adam's emotional range had quadrupled (Figure 6.2).

He also got better at the MAP skill, which enabled him to connect at a much deeper level with his staff and build empathy. With regular practice of all these skills, Adam's emotional and social intelligence improved dramatically. He became

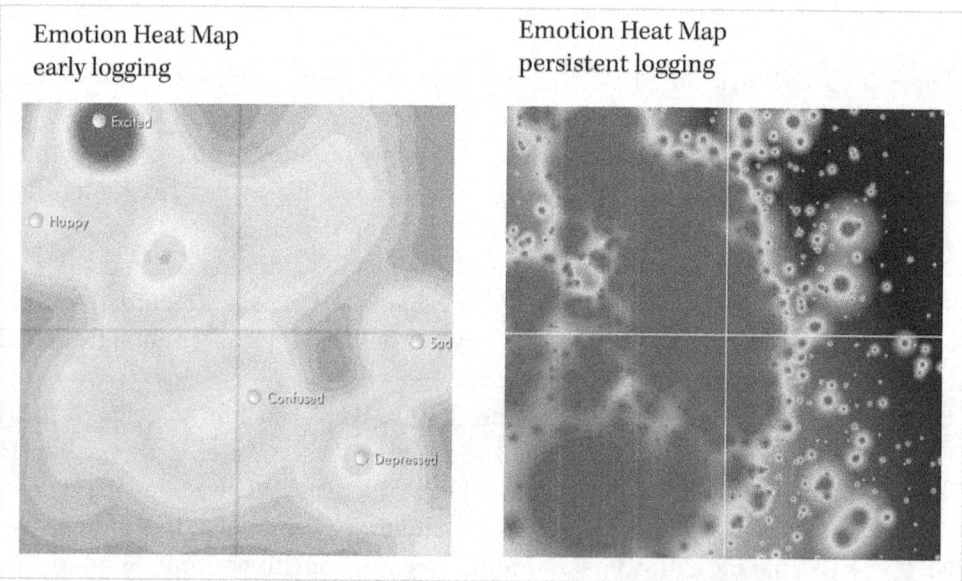

Figure 6.2 Expanding Emotional Literacy

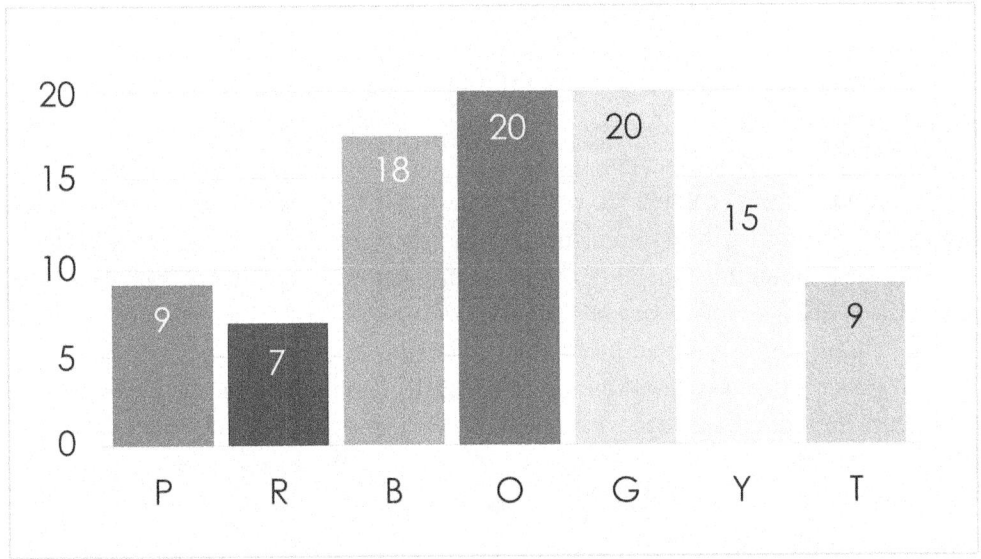

Figure 6.3 Adam's Values Profile

more conscious of his energy levels and how he could recharge himself and became more effective when interacting with his staff.

This increasing interpersonal capability aligned perfectly to Adam's value system, as defined by the Complete Values Profile (CVP). Adam's CVP revealed his centre of gravity was in the Green and Orange value systems (Figure 6.3).

People operating from Green and Orange values are motivated to find a more inclusive way of achieving success. They take a more sensitive, people-centric approach and are generally more emotionally intelligent, empathic and driven by a desire to help. But in their desire to be inclusive and reach a collective agreement, they can often get stuck trying to align multiple disparate views and end up creating an unhappy compromise rather than reaching a genuine consensus.

When we explained this to Adam, he could see the impact this world view had on his approach and how it was potentially holding him back. For example, he recognised he often overdid his desire to involve everyone. If the group he gathered got stuck, Adam would sometimes, in his frustration, push his view through and sell it as the consensus in the room, even when it wasn't. This was a subtle shift to a more Red autocratic stance and it would often demotivate others.

In the next team session, this issue was addressed, and the team collectively built a better way of interacting based on the value systems of the entire team. We also identified, based on the team's values, what aspect of the school each team member would be most motivated to take responsibility for. Adam was also able to restructure staff activities to give himself more time for strategic thinking. His role became more about leadership rather than management. He particularly enjoyed improving the school's governance processes, checking in with the team to ensure projects were on track, whilst personally adding some big picture thinking.

With these insights and some coaching, Adam started to mature and he moved from his Orange-Green value systems towards a more Yellow value system. He started to see the whole school more systemically, delegated more consistently and stopped rescuing others. He was also more effective in creating a culture that allowed everyone in the system, from students to teachers and support staff, to develop their potential too. This included the use of smart digital frameworks to allow the school to work more effectively.

By pushing past the forced inclusivity of Green, Adam became a better listener. He stopped making assumptions or jumping to conclusions, and the resistance to change he had experienced from others started to subside. His staff felt more heard and valued. We helped Adam to really explore his assumptions and reframe the conversations around what others wanted to achieve. This is essential to great change management.

One of the key moments in bringing the rest of his team on the journey was when Adam shared what had been driving him forward. When he'd personally left primary school, at the age of 11, he was unable to read. His sense of self was shrouded in shame. At that moment he'd made a personal commitment to ensure other children would not experience the same fate. Sharing his story and expressing such vulnerability required huge courage. His team and then his staff responded extremely positively, and this revelation gave them a much greater understanding of why Adam was so passionate and driven. His openness also modelled, to the team during their own journey, that vulnerability is not a sign of weakness, but a sign of strength.

Such courage breeds innovation, compassion and creativity and it helped to accelerate an incredible shift in culture. By understanding the arc of his own personal developmental journey Adam was able to create a much more powerful and inspiring Pluralist rather than Achiever narrative. He understood there was a more dynamic, exciting way to run the school. A way that was very different to what he'd previously believed and what he'd been taught and had been modelled to him in his educational training.

Adam now sees himself as more of an education and leadership coach, knowing when to use his tools from earlier value stages when appropriate. He adopted the idea we explained to him about how a school can become a deliberately developmental organisation (DDO). He's let go of the need to control everything and now includes others more, specifically facilitating their interaction. He's created an environment where everyone plays to their own strengths, driven by their personal values, as part of the DDO. His personal transformation means how others see him has completely changed. For example, the governors of the school used to consider that he was too protective and didn't engage with them in long-term thinking. Now they're co-designing five-year strategies, not one-year plans. The school is no longer dependent on Adam's ambition or passion. It's writing its own destiny and has become a shining light in the area for how a school system can be transformed.

Any school can follow the same journey. It starts with a better understanding of who you currently are. For any leader, including head teachers, there must be an acceptance that it's only possible to change anything by starting to change oneself. It is essential. The good news is that the effort is not arduous, in fact in can be liberating.

7 Collective Development in Theory

We human beings are social animals. Since the 1940s we've known that connecting with each other is a matter of life and death. It's as important to our survival as food, water and shelter. Science first realised this by noticing how high child mortality was in orphanages compared to children born into 'normal' families. Initially this was attributed to poor hygiene. But then Austrian psychoanalyst and physician Rene Spitz suggested that it wasn't contagion that was killing children, it was a lack of love. In 1958 British psychologist, psychiatrist and psychoanalyst, John Bowlby presented his watershed research on 'Attachment Theory'. He highlighted the profound importance of early childcare and the need for a baby to form a strong physical bond to at least one primary care giver. Quite simply if infants are unable to form early parental connections and feel loved and connected to at least one parent or carer, then their chances of surviving, let alone thriving, are significantly impaired. Bowlby documented how the scars of early neglect could run incredibly deep and were often extremely difficult to heal.

More recent research suggests that technology is providing a new potential threat to connection.[1] Physician Gabor Maté describes how technology acts as a distraction, or attention thief that is blurring human connection.[2] For very young children they can be ignored by their parents who are distracted by technology, or they are given the phone or tablet as a quick way to entertain the child without parental input. Whilst technology is not the only reason, it often reinforces the cycle of negative childhood experiences. A lack of attention in the early years of life means we are not receiving the basic care and connection required for our emotional development, interpersonal relationships and sense of self. This means we become fearful of the world around us, and this fear can lead to anxiety. If our parents or carers are not hearing our external cry, the cry can become internal and shows up later as symptoms of mental health and suicide ideation. This means rising numbers of young people are entering education in a state of anxiety and potentially addicted to the same technology as their parents. And if the ever-present technology is helping them to find meaning and a personal narrative rather than an engaged, ever-present parent, it's hardly surprising those individuals become fearful of school and opt to stay at home.

Interestingly, the central importance of relationships in our lives is coded into our DNA. Let's take a moment to step back to the inception of life on earth. The first living things on the planet were single celled bacteria. These bacteria had the planet to themselves for about a billion years. They spent all that time fighting for survival. One day it dawned on them that it was much more energy efficient to collaborate with each other than to kill each other. Obviously, a single bacterial cell didn't personally realise this, but evolution did. The consequence was these single-celled bacteria started to play nice. They did this by sharing some cytoplasmic DNA with their neighbour. This shared DNA was protected inside the cell by a newly formed membrane. This gave rise to the cell nucleus. Nucleation was the first great leap forward in evolution, and it took a billion years to happen.

Once bacteria were empowered by nucleation, war commenced again. Each nucleated cell tried to kill its neighbour to achieve an advantage. A second billion years passed until bacteria went "Doh, isn't it more energy efficient to collaborate than to kill?" The evolutionary penny dropped for a second time, and we experienced the second great leap forward. This time cells, possibly embarrassed by their stupidity and slowness off the mark, shared, and shared big. In fact, they joined forces giving rise to the birth of multicellular organisms.[3] Once cells crossed the multicellular threshold, the pace really picked up. And, as the story goes, five minutes to midnight on that metaphoric year depicting life on earth, human beings finally emerged.

In fact, we could argue that what makes human beings and bacteria the two most successful species on the planet is the same simple truth – cooperation. But here's the plot twist. If we look at both species, we discover that of the 11 trillion cells in the human body, 10 trillion of them are bacterial cells. We're only 10% human.[4] We're bacteria with a human coat. If we look at our DNA, humans have 30,000 genes in our body, but we also have 3 million bacteria genes within us. So, genetically speaking, we are only 1% human and 99% bacteria.

But within us we contain the secret of life on earth – it is always better to collaborate than to kill. We are collaborators. It's in our DNA. It's in our cells. And without love and connection we die.

The problem is we're still learning to play nice and much of humanity struggles with the concept. Just look around. We're still killing each other in Ukraine, and in the Middle East, and in many other parts of the world. If we're not killing each other, we're still engaged in the creation of excessive inequity. Greed and polarisation are widespread. Even when we try to get on with just one person and 'tie the knot', there's still a 50% divorce rate in many countries. When it comes to relationships it appears that many of us still have much to learn.

This is just as true in the educational system as anywhere else. In fact, we could argue that one of the key things that the education system should be delivering is a step change in human beings' ability to play nice.

Most parents worry if their children will make friends at school, particularly at the key transition moments as children move from kindergarten to primary, primary to secondary and secondary to university or work. A great deal of parental anxiety exists around their child's relationships. And there are lots of relationships to master. Children must make effective connections with friends, teachers, siblings in the family as well as with themselves.

When relationships go wrong in school, the price can be severe. Bullying, particularly online, has become a common problem in schools and is a major reason why the suicide statistics are so depressing, on many levels. A meta-analysis of studies published between 1996 and 2017, which examined the association between cyberbullying and self-harm, or suicidal behaviours in a population of over 150,000 children and young people under 25 years old, concluded that victims of cyberbullying are at a greater risk than nonvictims of both self-harm and suicidal behaviours. And, to a lesser extent, perpetrators of cyberbullying are at risk of suicidal behaviours and suicidal ideation when compared with non-perpetrators.[5] Clearly bullying hurts everyone involved. And whilst, most teachers are trained to be on the lookout for bullying, it can be very difficult to spot let alone fix, especially when so much of it happens online.

When we leave school or university and enter the world of work, our willingness to stay at a company and do our best work is often more about the quality of our relationship with the other people we work with than the salary we're paid or the corporate vision. We know good relationships and friendships mitigate the difficulties of life. As we said in chapter 4, the Harvard Study of Adult Development has proven that good relationships are what makes a good life.[6] Talking about the importance of relationships, Physician Dean Ornish said, "I'm not aware of any other factor in medicine – not diet, not smoking, not exercise, not stress, not genetics, not drugs, not surgery – that has a greater impact on our quality of life, incidence of illness, and premature death from all causes."[7] Human beings need quality connection as surely as we need air to breathe.

Even though we know the importance of relationships there are many reasons why we struggle. And unless we understand these it can be very hard to improve relationships. And without better relationships, we stand almost no chance of fixing the broken parts of the education system. Nothing is achieved alone; we must work together. But effective collaboration is tricky when we don't even understand the issues that conspire against us.

We're Not Taught How to Communicate

Let's explore the central building block of good relationships – communication. When we're growing up, we're not taught how to communicate properly. We're only ever taught half the formula. We train our children to broadcast, but we don't teach them how to receive messages. It's all transmission and no reception. Our obsession with broadcasting has been massively amplified by social media. We believe that we must broadcast our lives all the time on social channels. We should share pictures of our food, broadcast our thoughts and wax lyrical about our achievements. Many engage in performance activism rather than effective altruism. We even broadcast about our mental health problems, sometimes to a competitive degree, wearing our damage as a badge of honour, rather than exploring how to overcome the damage. We seek 'likes' for our broadcast in a desperate attempt to self-validate and create legitimacy.

Parents call their friends excitedly to celebrate their child's first word. But who rings up their friends when their child accurately receives a message, when their baby has understood the difference between a cat and a dog? We're much more interested in the outbound than the inbound. It's as though we believe our child's identity is only based on what comes out rather than what goes in.

Once reception starts to accelerate, around two years old, children start to question everything. Research by Harvard child psychologist Paul Harris suggests that a child asks about forty thousand questions between the age of two and five – that's a lot of questions.[8] Often, the relentless 'why' questioning becomes a tyranny, provoking many parents to tell their children to be quiet! Parents, and later teachers, correct a child's pronunciation, grammar and syntax. All of it is coaching transmission. But children rarely get coached in reception. Who asks their kids to 'play that back to me to make sure you've understood what I just said'. Parents and teachers are more likely to command their children to 'listen, will you' or accuse their children that they're 'not listening'. But they don't help the child by telling them how to listen.

Little wonder that children grow up into adults believing that 'listening' is simply 'waiting to speak'. To most people listening is the moment before they say something.

When we're in a meeting and the people around us are silent, we wrongly assume they're listening to our broadcast. They're not. What they're doing is thinking. Thinking about what they want to say next.

Teachers at the front of the class may believe that if the classroom is quiet the children are listening. Some may be listening. But some are day-dreaming, some are thinking about the game they will play later, some are wondering what dad made for lunch, some are thinking about whether Kirsty from Chemistry likes them or not. The whole notion of teaching is built on transmission. A teacher stands at the front of the class and transmits some information – it's even called 'chalk and talk'. There may be some questions to test instant reception within a class, but the main test of enduring reception is an exam or homework. A system that's built around knowledge transfer creates so much content to 'get through' it becomes impossible to do anything other than transmit and hope something is received.

None of this is deliberate, malicious, unprofessional or even intentional. It's just that most of us have never been taught *how* to listen. Consequently, our level of connectivity with others is often very superficial. We have, at best, heard the words people say, but we haven't really understood each other.

When someone starts broadcasting, we start thinking. It's automatic. Within a few seconds, their broadcast triggers our thinking. We switch off our reception and we start chasing our own thoughts. We have a dialogue with ourselves rather than a dialogue with the other person. In many conversations there's minimal reception. Both parties are often just broadcasting, almost independently, after having an internal dialogue with themselves! One person is talking, the other person's waiting to speak, and thinking about what they are going to say.

We see this in TV quiz shows, like *Family Fortunes*, where one member of a family will give an answer and it will be wrong and then the next member of the same family will give exactly the same answer. As soon as the question was asked the second team member stopped listening to the conversation and started to think about what they were going to say when asked the same question – so much so that they didn't hear their sister's answer and end up looking like an idiot on national TV!

We also see this in meetings. Part of the reason meetings go on for so long and little gets resolved is because no one is actually listening to each other. Everyone is just having a conversation with themselves: "I just said that!" "Did you? Oh I wasn't listening." We even say that to each other! And of course, the distraction of digital technology is not helping. When someone is looking at a screen, they don't even have to pretend they're not listening! How many times have we kept writing emails during a staff meeting?

Our default is set so strongly towards transmission, rather than reception, that it can be very difficult to stop someone from interrupting. Studies have shown that men interrupt more and are less likely than women to cede the floor when they are interrupted. Men speak more in meetings, and more powerful men speak even more.[9] Even if we're interrupting for legitimate reasons, to clarify the message, the interruption still breaks the transmission. When we do this, our actions often result in an elongation of the broadcast, because the broadcaster either gets thrown off track, or they repeat the broadcast from the start, or they say it in a new way as they realise their point may not be landing. The motivation for interrupting may be to reduce the length of the transmission but it often has the exact opposite effect.

When communication is so biased towards transmission, we not only impair reception capability but we also inhibit the possibility for deeper thought and reflection in the classroom. Quality thinking and critical reasoning requires deeper thought, better reflection and better reception. Without it, engagement and motivation are reduced, and disruptive behaviour or attention seeking increases.

Many people's understanding of how to improve their reception is so poor that they, like many schools in the UK's education system, buy into the idea of 'active listening'. Active listening focuses on the surface characteristics of a broadcast – the tone, the words and the body language of the transmission. Actively attending to these surface characteristics, so we can accurately summarise what's been said, means we don't sense the deeper content of the broadcast. We don't detect the thoughts, let alone the feelings, that sit beneath the words. And we certainly don't detect the real meaning behind what's being said. Our communication remains superficial and lacks substance. We have little sense of why this person is broadcasting this specific message at this time. What's going on for them. What beliefs and values are driving their broadcast. What's the real meaning of all this.

Perspective Taking

The success of our education system, like most complex systems, is dependent on whether the relationships between stakeholders is strong or dysfunctional. It's easier to change a process, a structure or create commercial or operational success than it is to improve a relationship, build a successful team or drive cultural change. Teams and cultures are bedevilled by the complexity of human interaction. Even though we as human beings are better at relationship building than most species, we still have a great deal to learn, and there are still many levels of sophistication we can develop in our ability to get on with each other. We only need to look around the world and witness the polarisation in many societies and the wars that are raging to know we need to up our game to have any hope of solving the wicked problems we face. In many ways, all wicked problems, like education, are relationship problems.[10]

And it's worth calling out the importance of perspective taking because it speaks to the anatomy of all relationships.

When we interact with others, most of us take one of two perspectives. They're called 1st and 3rd person perspectives. A 1st person perspective is characterised by the 'me, my, and I' subjective stance. People who show up to a meeting with strong opinions are often operating from a 1st person perspective. This perspective is powered by emotion, often passion or frustration. But the individual's emotion can overwhelm them and cause them to lose sight of the bigger picture. Their stance is deeply rooted in their experience, values and beliefs. They're unlikely to budge because they believe all their years of experience make their opinion right.

If we're not operating from a 1st person perspective, we're almost certainly operating from the much more dispassionate, but no less resolute, 3rd person perspective. This is characterised by the 'it's, they and them' objective stance. Individuals taking this stance are rooted in data, objective evidence and what they consider to be facts. According to this stance 'it's nothing personal . . . the facts tell a story'. This perspective is much loved by scientists, reporters, referees and chairs of meetings. People who operate from a 3rd person perspective believe they are simple witnesses without opinion.

Many meetings designed to solve a problem often go round in circles because the people in the meeting are operating from 1st and 3rd person perspectives without even realising it. To reach a decision, people need to flex. But without knowing about perspective-taking the need to flex often doesn't even surface in most people's minds.

People operating from a 1st person perspective find it difficult to flex because if they do, it feels like they are being asked to surrender their opinion and beliefs, which they can't bring themselves to do. People operating from a 3rd person perspective also find it difficult to flex because if they do it feels like they are being asked to surrender the facts or the truth, which they can't bring themselves to do. Both perspectives dig in and the meeting goes around in circles.

What often happens in these meetings is that someone makes a point (from the 1st or 3rd person perspective), the rest of the room ignores that point and someone else makes a new point. The new point is equally ignored. Several further new points are made like popcorn popping in a microwave. Such popcorn meetings can go on for a long time with little awareness of the lack of progress. People may claim to be listening, but they're often just stuck in a cycle of perpetual point making. No-one's really listening to each other. This, ironically, increases the likelihood that people then repeat their points over and over. Such popcorn meetings are an incredible waste of time and drain morale.

What's often missing, in ineffective meetings, is an awareness of 2nd person perspective taking. This is characterised by the 'we and us' relational stance. The 2nd person perspective is where relationships are built. But if stakeholders have no awareness of the fact that these three perspectives exist, they are unlikely to have any control over what perspective they're showing up from or why the meeting often seem to get stuck. When someone inhabits 2nd person perspective, either spontaneously or deliberately, they call out the shared view of the room, or they try to establish common ground. Developing the ability to step into 2nd person perspective taking can step change our ability to collaborate, and significantly improve the quality of our conversations as well as all our relationships.

To access 2nd person perspective taking, it can help to:

- make the other person feel heard
- identify joint benefits
- land all agreements
- cultivate good will and an appreciative attitude
- ask open ended questions
- acknowledge the validity of all views
- stop taking an 'I'm right, you're wrong' stance
- seek and call out anything that can be agreed upon.

The ability to take a 2nd person perspective is the foundation of all relationships.

We Don't Appreciate Difference

Few people have a sophisticated framework for understanding in what way they may be different from each other. Most schools and businesses think of diversity as a gender issue or something to do with ethnicity and skin colour. These things are important, but to assume that skin colour automatically gives you a different view of the world is, frankly, somewhat racist. In fact, it's getting stuck in 1st or 3rd person perspectives that often prevents those with diverse cultural narratives from hearing, and therefore understanding, how each other's views have been shaped, and what can be learned from each other. Similarly, just because a teacher is a woman rather than a man doesn't mean she has a different view of education. Diversity isn't just about colour or gender. It's about inner diversity as much as it is about visible, outer diversity.

Inner diversity is much more complex than outer diversity. And the source of greatest inner diversity is an individual's level of development, not their personality. When people clash it's because they have a difference of opinion, it's rarely because they have different personalities. And the thing that creates the biggest difference of opinion is their level of development.

Let's use age as a blunt proxy for level of development. The difference between the opinion of a six-year-old and the opinion of a 12-year-old is much greater than the difference between the personality of two six-year-olds. How a six-year-old and a 12-year-old make sense of the world is more diverse than the possible diversity of two six-year-olds.

If we want to understand diversity and become skilful at diffusing the tensions that arise from differences of opinion, we would be much better placed studying levels of development rather than studying personality, typologies or other forms of variation. If we study levels of development, we'll see that each new level of development is characterised by a step change in sophistication. As we mature to the next level of our development, new ways of understanding the world are unlocked leading to more sophisticated insights and ways of making sense of everything. For example, if we think values, beliefs, attitudes and opinions are all the same thing, then we're not very sophisticated. When we mature, we begin to understand how such concepts differ from each other. In fact, we start to realise that the ability to differentiate is itself a sign of maturity. And making sure we understand such differences is not just a 'nit picking' exercise or 'semantics', it's crucial to resolving some of the tensions that were present at the previous level of development.

Let's drop down one level from values and beliefs into the basic building blocks of diversity and culture. Let's look at the differences between thoughts, feelings and emotions. These three things are very different. You can test whether people understand the distinction between thoughts and feelings by asking someone how they feel. They will often tell you what they think. Why? Because they've not yet developed to the level where the difference between a thought and a feeling is obvious to them.

Figure 7.1 Composition of a Value and Belief

Thinking is a cognitive process that occurs in our head. Emotions are composite biological signals (energy-in-motion) that occur in our body. Feelings bridge the gap between thoughts and emotions. Feelings are the awareness in our mind of our energy in motion.

If we combine thoughts and feelings together in a cognitive cocktail, we create values and beliefs. Beliefs are thoughts wrapped in emotions. Values are feelings defined by thoughts or principles. They both contain thoughts and feelings, but in a different mix. Beliefs centre around thoughts, and values centre around feelings (Figure 7.1).

If we ask people what they believe, they'll usually describe a collection of thoughts that they've woven together, some of which are well enough crafted to be considered principles. These thoughts and principles are then infused, often unconsciously, with emotion until they become a solid belief. And, depending on the intensity of the emotional charge, their belief may be strong or weak. When woven together they develop a network of beliefs.

Values, in contrast, can be felt if you wander around the school. You can sense what a school values just by observing its cultural artefacts (symbols, rituals, customs, dogmas and metaphors), listening to the way people speak and tuning into the stories they tell about themselves. A school that values innovation feels different from a school that values collaboration. A school culture is more determined by its values than its beliefs because feelings are more powerful than thoughts in driving behaviour. If we want to transform the culture in a school or an organisation, we should focus more on values than beliefs, as they are more amenable to change and follow a well understood developmental, evolutionary path.

In relationships, liking someone, or not, often comes down to whether we share their values and beliefs. If we're not sure whether we like someone, it's usually because we don't know them well enough yet to determine whether we share values and beliefs. Before we've discovered someone's values and beliefs, we often guess what their values are and decide how closely they might align to our own.

We often instinctively reject anyone who doesn't align with our own values and beliefs, often because the difference is perceived as a threat.

Rejecting people who have different values to us is a problem for three reasons.

First, if we're going to solve the challenges we face in education and beyond we're going to have to work with stakeholders that have very different values to our own. Second, it's vital that we have stakeholders that hold different values because such diversity, if managed well, creates much better-quality answers for the school. Third, the more we understand how values and beliefs are created, the more we realise that our strong attachments to them are, to a large extent, random. Our values and beliefs are dependent on the happenstance of our birth. If we'd been born in a different country to different parents, we would believe and value very different things.

Our values and beliefs are built in childhood through our lived experience and a process called conditioning. We're all conditioned to see the world in a certain way depending on where and how we grew up. These values and beliefs underpin our sense of 'right', 'wrong', 'good', 'bad', what's 'acceptable' and what's 'unacceptable'. Such rules are passed down to us, largely unconsciously, from our parents, siblings, care givers and the environment and society we live in. We're taught what events or sensations to give 'signal importance' to, i.e., what matters and what we should ignore. Which is why many of our values and beliefs are arbitrary and some are just unhelpful. All of them are dictated by the fluke of our birth.

The conditioning of our minds in this way starts even before we're born and certainly long before we can speak. There are two types of conditioned learning. The first is single trial conditioning which is learning that occurs instantly after only one event. For example, a child doesn't have to touch a hot stove more than once to learn not to touch the hot stove. When an experience is painful, either physically or emotionally, we tend to learn that lesson with only a single exposure to the event or situation.

The other type of conditioning, which is what determines most of our values and beliefs, is less intense. This is called multiple trial learning. As the name would suggest it occurs over time. This multiple trial conditioning is driven by repetition. When we're told something often enough, eventually we believe it to be true – even if it's not true.

In a now famous experiment called *Pygmalion in the Classroom,* Harvard social psychologist Dr Robert Rosenthal demonstrated just how influential teachers are at conditioning their children, and inadvertently determining the outcome based on what they personally expect to happen.

At the start of the academic year, Rosenthal tested 18 classes of primary school children using nonverbal intelligence tests. Twenty percent of the children were identified as being "intellectual bloomers" and their teachers were told to expect significant intellectual gains from those children in the coming year.

Eight months later all the children were re-tested, and the intellectual bloomers had indeed increased in IQ points over the rest of the group. None of the teachers were surprised until they were told that the intellectual bloomers had been chosen randomly. The test was a rouse.

The teachers, expecting the intellectual boomers to do well, almost certainly changed their behaviour toward those children in a positive way and changed their behaviour toward the rest in a negative way. If little Amir was an intellectual bloomer, the teacher would instinctively give him more attention. If he was stuck or confused the teacher would help – after all he was a bloomer, so the extra effort was worth it. Meanwhile, the opposite was also true. Suzie was not in the bloomer group so when she asked a question and needed help, she was prioritised after the bloomers and sometimes there just wasn't enough time to get to Suzie. The teacher expectation and belief became a self-fulfilling prophecy. The teacher's altered behaviour amounted to multiple-trial conditioning toward the children in their class. This conditioning either increases the child's self-belief or not and that determined their success.

Conditioning doesn't just determine what we believe about the physical world, it also determines what 'facts' we come to believe about ourselves, regardless of whether they are true or not. And this applies to everyone around children, not just teachers. If parents constantly tell their child that they're clumsy or useless at maths, the child will eventually believe they are clumsy or useless at maths, whether it's true or not. As a result, that child's self-confidence can be permanently impaired. The same can be said about encouraging children to do well.

But the danger is that if the encouragement is over cooked and we tell a child, with minimal ability, that, "you're a star", this can set an expectation, which if not reached, can create crushing disappointment or toxic perfectionism.[11]

Too many people have extremely low opinions of themselves simply because of repeated 'stories' they were told as children that they accepted as true. Despite understanding this, parents' and teachers' assumptions around a child's potential still stifles many children and staff today.

Any type of change, be that individual or system change, requires us to deliberately step out of the ingrained conditioning we've inherited to design a new context and create a self-authored narrative that supports that change.

Survival Not Sophistication

Part of the reason conditioning is so powerful is because it taps into some of the most fundamental circuitry deep within our brain, and this circuitry is designed for survival not sophistication. A conditioned response is often blunt and can lead to the creation of a whole bunch of faulty beliefs and ideas that can influence us well into adulthood.

If you have an unexplained aversion to prawns, even though they don't make you ill, it's probably a conditioned response coded into your brain when you were a child. If you take an instant dislike to someone and consider the person you just met unworthy of your time, the chances are that something about them triggered your amygdala and alerted you to danger. Perhaps this new person unconsciously reminds you of a neighbour that shouted at you when you were three years old, an experience you may not even remember. This faulty reactivity drives our unconscious bias and often underpins what we believe to be true.

The powerfulness of a belief is down to the degree of threat we perceive and the intensity of the emotion that thought is wrapped in, by our amygdala. The amygdala works by constantly comparing our current reality with all previous experience from the day we're born (hence the reminder of the neighbour). Every new incident, event or situation is unconsciously compared to all the historical data we possess to try to predict if there's any danger. In every moment of our lives, our brain compares all the live sensory data to what it expects, drawn from our amygdala's vast rolodex of names and events, to see if there are any correlations that could spell trouble. And if the amygdala finds a match, it triggers a biological response. This response can make us nervous, irritated or even excited.

When we react to someone we've just met, our reaction may be legitimate, or it may be due to some old historical resemblance to a long-forgotten experience which has nothing to do with the present moment. When we meet educational stakeholders to try to find solutions to the problems we face, our amygdala is working out if we have met someone similar so we can arrive at a quick conclusion about whether we like this person or not or can work with them constructively to find solutions.

We falsely assume that our reaction to this new person is due to something happening live in the moment. We're normally unaware that our reaction may simply be driven by some long-forgotten faulty association that has triggered an outdated and irrelevant alarm. Since we rarely realise our alarm is historical, we mistakenly blame something in the here and now for something that happened in our past, none of which has anything to do with what's right in front of us.

As adults we like to believe that we're rational, but science tells us we are not. What we sense and perceive in every moment isn't sent to our neocortex (the smart part of our brain, where logic and executive function sits). It's first sent to our amygdala then onto the thalamus to be translated into the language of the brain, and only after some processing is it sent to the executive suite that is our neocortex for problem-solving.

Neuroscientist Joseph LeDoux from the Centre for Neural Science at New York University has written beautifully about the neural 'emergency exit' connecting the thalamus to the amygdala. He described how a portion of the original message goes directly to the amygdala, across a single synapse – bypassing the thinking brain altogether and initiating action before the rational brain even knows what's going on. This allows for a faster response when our survival may be threatened – say by a prawn sandwich! And all this happens in a fraction of a second, below conscious awareness. We're basically conditioned to react to potential danger, and this overrules logical processing. This can explain why some children refuse to attend school, or why some very able students struggle to learn, or why many teachers are resistant to change. It's basic psychological safety.

Most of our conditioning occurs before we're even aware that it's happening, and certainly before our brain is fully developed or can differentiate fact from fiction.

Precision decision-making is the domain of the frontal cortex, but the frontal cortex doesn't finish developing fully until our early twenties – after *leaving* university! When we're making all these early connections through the process of conditioning, we don't have the cognitive equipment or capacity to assess the information or experiences we are encountering with any degree of discernment.

By the time we reach adulthood, we've been taught to believe thousands of 'facts', which are often no more than the limited and partial views of our parents, passed to them by the limited and partial views of *their* parents. And these beliefs are embedded in our minds without our permission. And these views aren't subject to any internal critical evaluation. Once embedded, these views take root and can influence our behaviour. They can also change who we believe ourselves to be. And they often determine who we form relationships with, for the rest of our life, unless we wake up to what's happened.

Fortunately, many of these beliefs don't do too much damage, and many of them help us navigate the world faster and more effectively. But that still leaves plenty of beliefs that are nothing more than opinion and bias, which are often unhelpful.

This 'parental brainwashing' has happened to us and to everyone we meet. The specifics of other people's parental brainwashing might mean they have different beliefs and values to us, but they're just as attached to their brainwashed beliefs as we are to ours.

Many of the tensions that occur in our personal relationships, based on these unconscious differences, can be obstacles to aligning a team around what the problems and the solutions in education need to be. We can see such obstacles clearly in racial, economic or disability bias that exists in all societies.

Since this conditioning or brainwashing happened when we were six years old, or earlier, it takes some work to uncover and rectify them. If we're to create an inclusive educational system, we need to lean into our bias and question the way we think and question what parts of what we believe are helpful, and what parts are counterproductive for us today. And we need to do this work with compassion for ourselves and our parents because none of this was deliberate or malicious.

We Don't Appreciate How Values Impact Relationships

In the introduction we looked at how the education system has evolved and how that evolution tracks our own evolution as a species across various value systems. Where we are individually on the values spiral also has a huge impact on our ability to form functional and constructive relationships to solve the issues we face – including education.

Appreciating our own and other peoples' value systems can completely change what we can accomplish inside those relationships. And such a map gives us a way to bridge the gap between different values and see the advantages and disadvantages of all value systems.

Most people don't appreciate that they have different beliefs from others or if they do, they don't know how to interrogate those beliefs for accuracy or learn to put them aside to find consensus. And the same is true for values. When we don't understand value systems, everything becomes a fight. It's too easy to take everything personally which further inflames our biases, belief and value systems. It's not surprising then that progress is often slow and difficult. A repeating pattern in schools, for example, is the 'difficult' parent with a high-needs child. Whilst we may expect a process to be followed for an educational health care plan, the parent is likely operating from a survival value system, overwhelmed by the demands on them and inflamed by their belief that something needs to happen right now!

When we appreciate the primary motivational system at play in such parents and also in any school, which may also be in the same space after a very poor Ofsted report, then the problems that emerge are entirely predictable. And it's not just parents and schools that are evolving through these different value systems, all the individual stakeholders and stakeholder groups are evolving through the value spiral too. This knowledge can also help us to reconcile our differences, reduce conflict and improve the quality of communication. The other person is not being difficult or obtuse, it's just that they see the world through a different values lens and they prioritise different outcomes as a result. That lens is neither better nor worse than our own lens, it's just different.

Think of their lens like colour coded glasses (see Figure 5.6). Those focused on survival have Beige-coloured spectacles on. The world looks a certain way as a result. Each level has a different pair of glasses, where the colour brings different phenomena into focus relating to safety (Purple), status (Red), stability (Blue), success (Orange), social (Green), system (Yellow) and society (Turquoise). As such each values level sees the world quite differently.

When we can recognise those differences, we don't feel so divided or separate from others. What seemed like a chasm, becomes more of a gap to be bridged. Ideally, we become curious about our differences, and the things that divided us become the things that now interests us. When we understand the shared values of various stakeholders and how that stakeholder reality may legitimately vary from our own it can be a source of fascination and exploration rather than a reason to reject or hate.[12]

The differences between us and others, that so often lead to a breakdown in the relationships, are too frequently misdiagnosed as a 'personality clash' or 'attitude problem'.

The differences in values and beliefs between us and others is usually seen negatively, where one side will refer to the other side in a derogatory way. Now we understand that beliefs probably need to be interrogated for accuracy, and we recognise the nuance of value systems we can appreciate that the conflict has very little to do with personality or attitude. Rather it is to do with the different value systems we use to interpret the world. If we can recognise that both our different points of view have merit and are arising from our different value systems, then we're much better placed to find a way to reconcile our differences and find genuine solutions.

If we are to solve the multiple challenges in the education system, then a recognition of value systems can help. We need to move away from a world that defines everything as either/or. Such binary simplification reduces the beautiful nuance of humanity to harsh dichotomous division. We must move to a both/and view of the world and let go of the either/or mindset.

Great teams, great schools and great organisations need everyone, including Beige value systems. Without a survival focus, we won't be here to make the world a better place. Every level from Purple onwards offers significant benefits. Everyone has a role to play that allows the group to tap into the collective strength while mitigating the weaknesses. These insights allow us to appreciate that many of the stumbling blocks in educational reform could be avoided when we effectively blend people who have different values. To be effective we need all the value systems contributing to the solutions so that the solution works for everyone, regardless of the value system they are operating from.

Obviously, the more sophisticated the individual, the more options they have in facilitating the collective to a wiser answer. In other words, the further up the spiral an individual is operating from, the more sophisticated and nuanced their input is likely to be.

If our individual 'I' or collective 'WE' development gets arrested at 15-years-old, we may look like an adult on the outside, but we're still immature on the inside. Such developmental delay results in a belief that we're right and others, who do not hold the same beliefs and values, are wrong. We become wedded to our unique perspective with unshakable certainty. Understanding how to overcome such binary right/wrong thinking combined with the lack of awareness and sensitivity to the views of others is crucial if we want to work effectively with others to solve the crisis in education and evolve the system.

Notes

1 Aiken M (2016) The cyber effect: a pioneering cyberpsychologist explains how human behavior changes online, Spiegel and Grau New York.
2 Maté G (2019) When the body says no: the cost of hidden stress, Edbury, London.
3 Sahtouris E (2016) The secret to human coexisting, YouTube.
4 Collen A (2016) 10% Human: how your body's microbes hold the key to health and happiness, William Collins, London.
5 No Author (2018) Victims of cyberbullying at greater risk of self-harm and suicidal behaviours, Department of Psychiatry, Oxford University.

6 Waldinger R (2015) What makes a good life? Life lessons from the longest study on happiness, TED Talk.
7 Ornish D (1998) Love & survival: the scientific basis for the healing power of intimacy. HarperCollins, New York.
8 Harris P (2015) What children learn from questioning, Educational Leadership, 73(1), 24–29.
9 Kaplan S (2019) Mansplaining: new solutions to a tiresome old problem, The Conversation.
10 Watkins A, Wilber K (2015) Wicked & wise: how to solve the world's toughest problems, Urbane, Kent.
11 Messinger H (2019) Dis-like: how social media feeds into perfectionism, Penn Medicine News.
12 Wilber K (2017) The religion of tomorrow: a vision for the future of the great traditions, Shambhala, Boulder.

Collective Development in Practice

Most people with a desire to change the system in which they're working, education or otherwise, understandably look at the system first and think about what needs to be different. They almost never look inwards and wonder about what they might need to change about themselves and how they lead or work with others. And yet research on leadership development clearly shows that most mature individuals are better equipped to handle the complexity that systemic change requires and are more likely to possess the skills needed to deliver such change.[1]

So, rather than expect or wait passively for some system changes, the journey to educational transformation can start with the development of those responsible for leading the educational system. This is because the inner 'I' change ripples outwards, positively impacting our ability to collaborate effectively with others. And more effective collaboration significantly increases the chances that we can find and implement the solutions that are required to create a better educational system.

Without this 'I' and 'WE' development, we are perpetually stuck, and very little real progress is made. It's worth stepping back into that reality for a moment to remind us just how predictable this dysfunction is.

Think back to the last team experience you had. It really doesn't matter what the team was brought together to solve, or what problem or issue was being discussed, the experience is almost always the same. Initially certain team members align. This alignment may be around the fact that they know each other outside the team, and they see each other as natural allies. Or they instinctively begin to align around their value systems. We can see this happening in real time as an issue is discussed in the group.

Someone who's operating from the Red value system, for example, will become vocal and authoritative, pointing out that the time for discussion is over and the solution is obvious, everyone just needs to get on board and make it happen. Other people in the group who operate from the same value system will nod enthusiastically.

Those from the Blue value system may start to resist because they believe the group hasn't followed its own process and given everyone an opportunity to speak. Other Blue colleagues murmur their agreement, while the Red people dismiss this as unnecessary.

Those operating from the Orange level may start to see the battle lines being drawn and advocate for taking a pragmatic approach and suggest we shouldn't insist on everyone speaking if they don't want to or don't have something to say.

Those operating from the Green level may seem to side with those from the Blue level, but not on a point of process simply in a desire to be inclusive and fair.

Each level is adamant that their approach to the group dynamics and managing the emerging tension is right. And every level is equally adamant that the others from a different values level are wrong, although most will never explicitly say this out loud. Instead, every level tries to push through their solution from their level. Those at Red may become more authoritative, passionate or humorous to win the argument. Those at Blue will try to align people on a point of principle. Those at Orange will use logic, pragmatism and persuasion. Those at Green will use all their interpersonal skills to get their own way.

No one in the room is aware that these values-based dynamics are the root cause of the tension, and they are impacting communication and the ability of the group to align. No one in the room has spotted that each person is adopting a 1st or 3rd person perspective. The Red level tends to favour the 1st person, passion stance. The Blue level tends to switch to 3rd person principles with a little 1st person animation on the importance of principles and the need for robust process. The Orange level will vacillate between both 1st person and 3rd person perspectives to see which one works. They may cherry pick the data that are most compelling and passionately advocate it. They may even claim they are offering the room a shared 2nd person perspective when what they are often doing is passing off their 1st or 3rd person view as shared when it isn't. Such 'sleight of mouth' is common in those operating from the Orange level. The Green level is more focused on soothing and smoothing the tension, supporting everyone's view and advocating that the primary goal is to move forward together rather than get stuck on the specifics of the answer. Their attempts to get consensus may appear too meek or wish-washy for others.

The values misalignments in the group create factions. Each sub-faction may start to plot and scheme in sidebar meetings. Few people are really listening to each other anymore. Instead they're seeking to find ways to get other factions on their side.

Overall communication is poor. Often the group can't even agree on the nature of the problem, never mind how to solve it. There's little or no trust. No shared, agreed position. Usually, the loudest or largest faction wins. But because there is no real agreement, any decisions made still won't get actioned because the passive aggressive battles move to outside the room, and resistance is set up in a wider stakeholder group.

If we accept that the 'I' and 'WE' development of educational leaders is central to a transformation of the system, it's vital to define what level of individual and collective development everyone is currently operating from. It's also essential that those leading the change understand the level of development of the other stakeholders in the system. If one stakeholder has no idea what level of maturity they are operating from or what value system they operate from, and don't have that information for those around them, we'll be relegated to the same old disagreements and differences of opinion that have polluted the discussions and halted progress so far.

We've already explored the benefits of leaders gaining access to more energy, moving up one or two levels in their values and ego maturity lines of development and the gains that can be made around emotional and social intelligence (ESQ). The last three levels of ESQ are of particular relevance in the 'WE' space as they speak to our capacity for empathy, social impact awareness and social intelligence. Feel free to revisit these levels and practice the MAP skill to foster this capability.

Developing your interpersonal capability, as described earlier, enables each individual leader to better manage the inevitable tensions that arise when trying to drive systemic change. Leaders who have levelled up in this way can also reconcile differences in the 'WE' space more quickly. The benefits of 'I' development are therefore reflected in the 'WE' development of leadership teams.

Values Revisited

When each of the team members have also started to do even a little 'I' development and appreciate what values level they operate from under different situations, their insights can be used collectively to improve results.

The real game changer that values identification offers is the resolution of interpersonal tensions in the 'WE' space. When a team charged with solving an issue or making improvements all understand their Complete Values Profile (CVP), they don't just gain an appreciation for their own value system but more importantly, they appreciate how to more effectively work with other people in the team who don't see the world the way they do.

Having a way of understanding the difference between our motivations allows us to better appreciate the upsides and downsides of each value system so we can reconcile our differences, reduce conflict and improve the quality of our communication. This always improve relationships. We've seen, time and again, that the insights gained from the CVP help to dissolve contentious issues so that discussions and negotiations become much more constructive. One head teacher laughed when they read the results and said, "I finally understand why that member of staff irritates the life out of me despite being so lovely with the children! Now I understand why, and I need to shift my lens and how we interact!"

When we can see that all our different points of view have validity and are arising from our different value systems not some personal grudge, stupidity or incompetence, then we're much better placed to shift our position and find a way to reconcile our differences. We learn to see the superpower of each value system as a collective tool to be used toward team success.

When we understand that people have very different motivations, it's also much easier to engage them by using the language of their value system to describe the problem and the proposed solutions. Using the language preferred by the stakeholder in front of you can massively speed up decision making, drive much better answers that include the diversity of views of all available stakeholders. Managing stakeholders in this way saves a lot of time and strengthens relationship bonds.

For example, Matt used to take this approach with Ofsted inspectors. As you can imagine, there is a range of inspectors and it would be impossible for them to remove all their bias. Most inspectors, at least in the first stage, are viewing the school through a Blue stability lens. Initially they may be evaluating and 'inspecting' whether the school is compliant with legal and regulatory process. If the teachers listen carefully, the inspector will provide clues to what they value personally, albeit unconsciously, through the language they use in conversation. Matt would listen for words, phrases and questions that implied they valued status (Red), stability (Blue), success (Orange) or social values (Green). He would then position or reframe the information, results or evidence the inspector was looking for to ensure it matched the value system the inspector was operating from.

A skilled team leader or facilitator can effectively communicate with different people in the group based on their value system. This is not manipulation. It's more about skilfully meeting people where they are and it comes from a greater appreciation of what's driving the team, what messaging is going to land and what it will take to create consensus so the teachers and the inspectors can move forward together. The irony is that most leadership teams know there's often a communication issue; what they need help with is a way to discuss that problem that builds consensus not division. When they've had even a little coaching to better understand the baggage they bring to discussions, based on their values level, maturity or outdated conditioning, they can begin to create new pathways. And when everyone does that, genuine team development becomes possible.

It's also important to recognise that what level of values we operate from varies depending on the context. Thus, what motivates us when we discuss the strategy for the school may be slightly more nuanced than what motivates us when we're discussing managing the staff, or the classroom. We need to adjust our language not just for the stakeholder in front of us but for the situation too.

Fortunately, the values profile has several subscales that can guide us because they reveal how a person's value system varies depending on the tasks they're engaged in. When a head teacher is focused on strategy, for example, they may operate from the Yellow values level indicating an innovative approach. That same leader may then shift into a more Blue stance when discussing how to implement the strategy, seeking to follow process and to ensure the school has the right procedures in place to execute the strategy. The leader may show up differently when discussing staffing issues and become more autocratic and directive, from the Red value system.

Understanding which value system we tend to operate from in different circumstances can create a clear platform for how we can get the best out of ourselves and each other. Matt recalls how leveraging this knowledge had a very positive impact when working with a charity-based school trust.

The trust had a member of staff who was operating from the Red values level. The rest of the team found this difficult and had somewhat dismissed his contribution. His management of others felt too directive for the culture and maturity of the organisation. Yet when the team understood the benefit of all the different value systems, the CEO agreed to set up a new challenge to take advantage of the Red energy, namely fundraising. This brought in £250,000 in the first year. The Red fundraiser also established a network across local businesses that the other leaders wouldn't have imagined possible. He had the impact that he wanted and really enjoyed doing it. In the area of fundraising, he had the power to execute the strategy independently of the team and make it happen. This fit perfectly with his results-driven values-based motivation.

Understanding value systems becomes particularly fascinating when we look at an entire work group or executive team to see where most of the members operate from. This reveals the strengths of the team and the way that the team will fall into conflict. For example, if there is a cluster of stakeholders in the team or group operating from the Red value system, then if this is identified and 'called out', those Red individuals may be able to avoid monopolising meetings and continually overriding the input of other team members.

It's also fascinating to see that our professional values don't always align with our personal values outside of work. We worked with a CEO of a multi-academy trust that had very Green personal values, caring a huge amount about everyone in her life. However, at work she was very Red. She managed their school turn around with the motto 'slash and burn'. This sounded somewhat brutal, but at that point in the school's evolution, this was exactly what was required. This was quite a flex for the CEO and she had to manage the personal tension she felt because she was operating outside of her personal comfort zone, deploying values that were needed but that were not the values that she personally operated from outside of work. Fortunately, she understood that the best way to take care of the school was to be very clear and direct for a short period of time while she turned the school around.

Once the turnaround stabilised the school, she set up a three-year development programme for herself and the team to transform the culture and embrace a more caring Green approach, which aligned more with who she really was. This trust now has one of the best reputations of any large multi-academy trust in the UK. The leader is now far more fulfilled in her work because she's allowed to be herself and care about others, whilst still holding them to account. Her personal journey has even resulted in her developing beyond her Green values into a more Yellow approach. She's become far more innovative. This has resulted in massive and rapid improvement across the schools she is responsible for. Her staff repeatedly say 'I feel valued because I feel invested in', and this is reflected in how engaged the staff are. You can read the full case study of this developmental journey in chapter 13.

Knowing the tensions created by different value systems in different contexts is truly transformational. It also helps to recruit the right people to balance the values dynamics (as long as they are conscious of the underlying variable) in any team to achieve outcomes faster and help the system to develop. For example, those operating from Yellow and Turquoise are particularly useful in strategy meetings because they can appreciate multiple perspectives and may come up with 'out of the box' innovations. Every team needs someone who can do this. But Yellow and Turquoise values play less of a driving role when it comes to implementation of the strategy. Every team needs someone who is operating from a Green value system. They are often skilled at including everyone and ensuring the relationships improve over time. Orange values are needed for adaptability and pragmatism. Blue values often contribute to critical time discipline, build key processes and ensure the team complies with the necessary procedures. Someone in the team who brings the Red energy can be key to ensure pace and change momentum is maintained to get stuff done. A leader operating from the Purple value system will ensure a much stronger sense of identity and belonging exists in the school.

So high performing teams need the healthy version of each value systems to be most effective. Everyone has a role to play, which when understood, allows the group to tap into the collective strength while mitigating the collective weaknesses. Understanding all this allows us to appreciate that many of the stumbling blocks we face in finding solutions to anything can be avoided when we effectively blend stakeholders into effective teams that offer different value-based perspectives we may not have.

Team Development

The task of developing teams is made slightly easier by the greater self-awareness that follows individual leadership development. More mature leaders are better at bringing everyone in their stakeholder group along on the same developmental journey they have been on. Make no mistake, development in the 'WE' domain is the 'final frontier' and is much more complicated than coaching and developing individual leaders.

The ability to create constructive, productive relationships that enables the team to develop and collectively solve problems requires careful diligent work by coaches who have knowledge of adult development and can do a lot more than just take a team through an 'inset' off-site experience, an away day or teach the teachers a few skills.

Collective Development in Practice 149

Unfortunately, most team coaches are unaware of the nine levels of team development. Many operate with the much more simplistic model which refers to the 'forming, norming, storming and performing' levels of team development. This latter model, developed by psychologist researcher Bruce Tuckman in the mid-1960s,[2] may have been sufficient then, but it's much less useful in today's more complicated world. Having worked with leadership teams all over the world for 25 years, we've been able to define nine levels of team development. The forming, norming and storming levels Tuckman describes are, in our view, all variations of a Level 2 team of Battling Experts (Figure 8.1). The performing level Tuckman describes is what happens when a team reaches level 3 – Dependant Experts. Tuckman's model says nothing about how a team becomes high performing or any of the six levels that exist beyond the performing, Level 3. Coaches who work with this model are therefore unlikely to be able to unlock their higher levels of development, not least because their model simply doesn't include them.

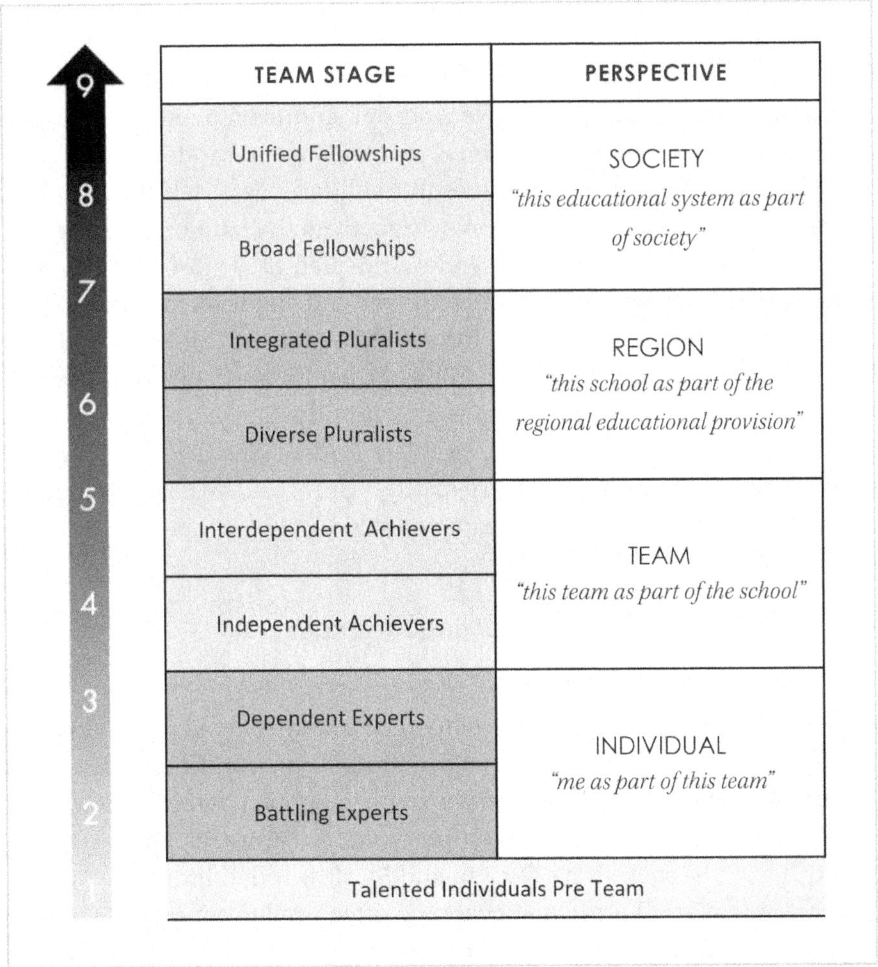

TEAM STAGE	PERSPECTIVE
Unified Fellowships	SOCIETY
Broad Fellowships	*"this educational system as part of society"*
Integrated Pluralists	REGION
Diverse Pluralists	*"this school as part of the regional educational provision"*
Interdependent Achievers	TEAM
Independent Achievers	*"this team as part of the school"*
Dependent Experts	INDIVIDUAL
Battling Experts	*"me as part of this team"*
Talented Individuals Pre Team	

Figure 8.1 The Nine Stages of Team Development

A Level 1 Pre-Team – Talented Individuals

As a team develops through each new level of sophistication, energy increases, speed increases and new capabilities are unlocked. Until a team has a common goal, it's effectively a Level 1 'Pre-Team'. At this point it's a collection of talented individuals. With a shared goal, a team starts forming.

A Level 2 Team – Battling Experts

At Level 2, individuals realise they're paid to deliver results. Team members largely operate from their silo. They see themselves as an individual within the team. They 'report in' to the leadership team meetings, narrate the performance in their own department and jockey for position in the norming and storming phase of development.

Each team member is an individual expert. They battle for authority and try to establish a pecking order within the team. The battle is occasionally explicit but rarely toxic. Polite mistrust is much more common. Subtle briefing or counter briefing occurs, and passive aggression through a careful lack of support is typical.

At Level 2, tensions can become weaponised, and team members can blame or throw each other under the bus. Failure is pointed out and is often used by individuals to deflect attention from themselves in a subtle game of self-protection.

An immature Level 2 team leader may exacerbate the fight or, even worse, play individuals against each other in a widely misplaced idea of internal competitiveness or to create dependency on themselves and condense power in their own hands. Level 2 teams are crying out for strong leadership, and until this occurs, working in Level 2 teams is usually tolerable, rarely enjoyable and always sub-optimal. Even when a strong leader appears, individual team members may switch the focus of their battling to undermine their leader. This may be done through perpetual debate or demands for 'more clarity'. Or there may be a subtle refusal to commit to the journey or allow the leader to lead.

A Level 3 Performing Team – Dependent Experts

Most teams, left to their own devices, can make it to Level 3. At Level 3 teams can drive results, but they're far from developed or consistently high performing. Performance is still very dependent on the team leader. At Level 3 most team members still focus on the delivery in their department, rather than helping the whole team to succeed. This is largely borne of self-preservation. If my department is delivering results, I can't be sacked. It's Darwin and Maslow rolled into one.

The tension that's still present at Level 3 is often used to consolidate an individual's personal authority or defend their department. If failure occurs, it's seen as a performance management issue (Figure 8.2).

Collective Development in Practice 151

	APPROACH TO CONFLICT	APPROACH TO FAILURE
3. Dependent Experts	People use conflict to consolidate authority	See it as performance management issue
2. Battling Experts	Conflict is weaponised	Failure is used to undermine others

Figure 8.2 Immature Level 2–3 Teams

If Level 3 team members start to think about the idea of a team, they may start to subjugate their own desires for the sake of the team. This is what enables a Level 3 team to start performing. But performance at Level 3 is still fragile. On bad days, when the leader is absent, the team often drops back to a subtle battle for control and Level 2. The more enlightened Level 3 leaders will try and flush out and resolve tension, inadvertently making the team more reliant on them.

Sometimes the leadership is provided by a crisis rather than an individual. Many teams describe how they perform better in crisis mode. What keeps many teams stuck at Level 2 or 3 is a failure to fully commit to each other or their joint future together. The team may have articulated a vision for the school, but it doesn't really feel alive or owned by the team, usually because it's either imposed by the leader or defined by someone outside the team. Within the team the focus remains operational delivery in your own department.

If a team ever makes it past Level 3, it normally takes 5–10 years to reach Level 4. However, if the team's coach understands what it takes for teams to develop, then it's possible to deliver accelerated growth and unlock 1–2 new levels in just 18 months.

A Level 4 High Performing Team – Independent Achievers

Helping a team to break out of Level 3 and unlock Level 4 is, perhaps, the biggest game changer for any team. Most leaders have experienced Level 3, and many have become convinced that Level 3 is the ultimate level.

If you're not sure if you've ever been in a Level 4 team, then the chances are you haven't. Level 4 teams feel different. If you look forward to getting together with 'my team' (the highest-level grouping that you can participate in), then you may be in a Level 4 team. The meeting with your Level 4 colleagues should be one of the highlights of your month. It's energising and stretching. This is where you get together with the people who are the most interesting to you. They are there for you and you are there for them.

In contrast, if you think the team meetings are getting in the way of you doing your job, then you are almost certainly in a Level 3 team or below. The fact that so few people have ever experienced Level 4, or beyond, is a testimony to how difficult it is to develop high performing teams. It also reveals how little time or effort organisations invest in team development and how few coaches understand what's required to unlock team maturity. The team's coach must have personally experienced Level 4 or beyond, otherwise they are unlikely to be able to help others to develop to this level.

Level 4 requires a fundamental shift in thinking of the team leader and the team members, which takes time to develop and consolidate. Central to unlocking Level 4 is team members fully committing to each other. One of the manifestations of that commitment is the desire to lean into and work through differences of opinion.

Level 3 teams either 'agree to disagree' or abdicate the tension resolution to the team leader. Level 4 teams understand there's real value in the disagreement and so develop the social and emotional intelligence skills needed to process tensions in a much healthier fashion. Level 4 team members actively encourage each other to share their point of view. They work hard on developing a 'speak up' culture, building trust and psychological safety. They particularly encourage the quieter voices in the team and seek to mine the views of the more reflective team members, rather than letting the noisier team members dominate.

With all this interpersonal work, the team starts to realise that there are many perspectives that must be integrated to deliver smarter, more insightful answers. Better answers become the focus of a Level 4 team. Team members proactively start working across silos in pairs and small groups. Better collaboration is discussed to drive much greater interactivity. There's a desire to set a new standard in team functioning. When team members experience Level 4 team capability, they start to glimpse the power that is yet to be unlocked. This enables them to more fully commit to the process of team development. A Level 4 leader, as part of their encouragement of the team's maturation, starts to talk less and facilitate more.

A Level 5 Best-in-Class Team – Interdependent Achievers

The step up from a Level 4 to a Level 5 team is smaller than the transformation from a Level 3 to 4 team. However, a lot of new capabilities that started to emerge at Level 4 really blossom at Level 5. Level 5 team members work across functionally as a default. They collaboratively swarm to solve the challenges the team faces either within or outside the school or trust. Team members see themselves as school leaders not just departmental heads. The team's shared purpose binds them. All objectives are team objectives, even if the issue mainly impacts one person.

Team members seek out each other's views, spontaneously, because they value each other's opinions. There's a drive to create more interdependency because there's a realisation that this delivers better results. The defensiveness of Level 3 has gone completely. People are encouraged to voice disagreements and ask genuine open-ended questions rather than questions that they already know the answer to or questions that are designed to make themselves look good.

A Level 5 leader prefers to facilitate clarity rather than give answers because they realise this creates greater levels of performance sustainability. A Level 5 team is much better at differentiating the content of a debate from the process of the debate.

Having directly experienced the power of collaboration and interdependent working the team actively seeks to build stronger bonds between different levels of the organisation to ensure there is appropriate leadership at all levels. The team is much faster at processing tensions and aligning outputs, identifying common ground rather than pushing a single point of view. Disagreement is seen positively, as a way to improve team dynamics. Decisions are nearly always made by collectives.

A Level 6 World Class Team – Diverse Pluralists

Very few teams make it to Level 6. If they do, and the team stays together, they're on the verge of becoming world class. A Level 6 team can inspire a new generation of school leaders and establish a better way of leading the educational sector in which they operate. Often a team is broken up just as they are on the verge of reaching Level 6. This is because their contribution, at Level 5, was so significant and the performance impact so great that the leaders are either recruited to fix other schools or the leaders themselves, having developed so much, want to move on to help the system more widely.

If a team, that's reached Level 6, stays together, they can build on all that they've achieved, and step change their capability again. The work to become a high performing team at Level 4 and a best-in-class team at Level 5 comes of age as the team lays the foundations for becoming world class at Level 6 and Level 7. The main change, in moving from a team of Achievers to Pluralists, is the breadth of focus that a Level 6 team can bring. This includes everything that a Level 5 team delivers but transcends it. The core of the shift is from operational optimisation to relationship leverage. Team dynamics are significantly stronger, tensions are resolved at speed and performance is less about high energy and more about flow.

The greater interpersonal capability means that diversity, in all its forms, can be used as an advantage. The focus also moves from performance issues within the school to facilitating wider systemic change in education by working with external stakeholders. Team meetings also shift focus from leading the school to impacting the educational sector. Delegation to and the development of others becomes a major area of interest and how to unlock the untapped potential in everyone.

A Level 7 World Class Team – Integrated Pluralists

Moving from a Level 6 to a Level 7 team is really about consolidating the shift that occurs when the team steps into pluralism. A Level 7 team is genuinely world class, partly because the speed with which team members can learn from each other and convert knowledge into development. Level 7 teams swarm and network quickly. They flow and serve each other and draw in relevant stakeholders as required. Given their much broader focus, Level 7 teams anticipate how the world around them is evolving. They are already thinking about how to plan for an AI-accelerated Web3 devolved future.

Level 7 teams transcend the 'working with diversity', central to Level 6 teams, to integrating the data, views and insights that a diverse group of stakeholders generate. It's integration not aggregation that unlocks the wisdom of the crowd. Innovation in an accelerating world is also critically dependent on the ability to integrate different views and create game-changing answers.

A Level 8 World Leading Team – Broad Fellowships

If Level 7 teams are extremely rare, then there are probably only a few Levels 8 and 9 education leadership teams in the world. It may be difficult to conceive of a level of ability beyond world class. That level is world leading. World leading teams are those that could teach world class teams how to completely change the paradigm. At Levels 8 and 9, the leadership team is less of a team and more of a fellowship.

Level 8 fellowships are capable of everything that all earlier levels of team development are capable of, and can access any of the abilities of earlier levels if required. However, they function very differently. The primary difference for Level 8 fellowships is that they see their role as being less about leading the school, or Educational Trust, or educational sector, and more about impacting society at large. If the team can change the way society sees an issue, then it's an easier task to set up an educational system to mine the benefits of such a transformation. At Level 8, all team members could themselves be highly effective leaders of world class educational teams at Levels 6–7.

A Level 9 World Leading Team – Unified Fellowships

Even when operating at a world-leading Level 8, there's still room for improvement. The team can move from a broad fellowship at Level 8 to a unified fellowship at Level

9. At this fellowship level, everything that a team is capable of operates at a higher level of grace and fluidity. This level is so rare that most will never experience it, or even see it during their lifetime. Even if they do, they may not be able to perceive the difference between this Level and how a Level 5 team operates. This is partly because you would have to be inside a fellowship to experience that difference.

At Level 9 there is a quality of selflessness and service that may be difficult to fathom for most people. This service may manifest in a multitude of ways that look familiar but are profoundly different. For example, there may be robust challenge of each other but even this is in service of achieving a much more nuanced, compassionate and wise view of the world. There's a level of energy and clarity that is exceptional and persistent. Living in such fellowships is like having a spiritual meal.

You can find a detailed explanation of the nine levels of team development in Alan's book *Coherence: The Science of Exceptional Leadership and Performance (2nd Edition)*. Although it's useful to understand the characteristics of each level, what is more important for successful change is to appreciate some of the conditions that, if present, increase the likelihood of genuine team engagement. Understanding these conditions also help you know where your team is currently operating from so you can see how to develop your team further.

The conditions are:

- **Interdependency:** it can help to make one person's success dependent on another team member's input, thereby creating interdependency across functions.

- **Common Purpose:** teams are united by a common objective. This can be broken down into the team's vision or dream, their purpose, their ambition and their strategy (more on that shortly). If a team has made the effort to build a shared version of any one of these, it can serve as a unifying force. If there is alignment across all of these differentiated concepts, team coherence is likely to be significantly higher, and such things can be defined at every level of an organisation.

- **Authority:** every team needs a degree of autonomy and the ability to determine its own destiny within the limits of authority given to it. A team that is clear around what delegated authority it has and what it can change is able to cohere around such authority.

- **Team Size:** with increased size comes increased complexity. The optimal size of a team really depends on a number of factors, such as the team's purpose and the range of capabilities required in delivering its purpose. Many organisations think six is the magic number, but we have seen dysfunctional teams of four people and highly effective teams of 18 people.

- **Commitment to Development:** most people have a justifiable scepticism about 'team away-days'. However, a shared commitment to improving the team's effectiveness and enhancing the team spirit, dynamics and interpersonal relationships can itself be a powerful cohering force. This has to be a sincere commitment, not lip service or 'box ticking'.

- **Leadership:** a leader's commitment to developing a team is the single biggest determinant of that team's success. The leader's sponsorship can be supported or enhanced by other team members, but if the leader is not behind the 'Team Development Journey', the team will never really develop.

- **One Boat:** one of the most vital aspects of team success is the idea that we are 'all in this together', one team, one boat. The 'stroke' in the stern of the boat sets the rhythm and is the equivalent of the CEO, Head Teacher or team leader who is responsible for direction and injecting pace. But everyone in the boat has their role and that role is no more significant than any other. Everyone must play their part and if someone tries to 'be a hero', they will usually slow the team down. Organisational status or hierarchy is irrelevant; what matters is the team result, not anyone's individual expertise. Often leaders who are keen to exercise their own power or authority are the primary reason why the team does not develop beyond the third stage of team development.

It is also worth noting that passively leaving teams to develop themselves or holding team events that are not integrated into a people development strategy may provide short-term improvements but are more likely to keep teams stuck below Level 3. Such an unstructured approach to development is one of the main reasons why schools that want to change fail to do so. If a team gets stuck, this is a major barrier for enhancing the context for learning. Successful transformation requires a much more sophisticated understanding of the levels of team development and how to navigate the levels to unlock the true potential teams offer. High-performing teams are often the difference between success and failure in many schools, and this is vital as we search for solutions in education.

If you're interested to understand what level your team is operating from right now, you can do this using the Team Development Index (TDI). The TDI asks every member of the team a series of questions, and the answers are aggregated to give the team a score across six factors:

1. **Activism:** Laser focus on priorities, taking responsibility for outcomes, delivering what you promise and constantly measuring and improving.

2. **Strategic Power:** Ability to create a powerful school vision and strategy that is compelling and exciting, distinctive, unique, achievable and sustainable.

3. **Entropy:** Ease with which the team can handle conflict and process differences of opinion.

4. **Coherence:** Ease with which the team can find common ground and truly align on a position using flexible decision-making processes.

5. **Relationship Quality:** Sense in the team of psychological safety, strong personal connections and the willingness to support and develop each other.

6. **Personal Engagement:** Strength of personal commitment to the team and alignment of individuals' purpose with the team purpose.

These six factors can be mapped onto the four-quadrant leadership model (Figure 8.3).

Some leadership teams are high on some factors, and some are low. In the early stages of development, battling experts (Level 2) and dependent experts (Level 3), there's a tendency to overestimate capability across these six factors.

Generally speaking, Strategic Power, Personal Engagement and Relationship Quality tend to increase as the team develops. Relationship Quality is often the strongest indicator of the real level of a team's development. The level of Entropy and Coherence varies at different levels, as does Activism. It's also no accident that these six factors that drive a team's development align nicely with the five well-known dysfunctions of teams identified by Patrick Lencioni[3] (Figure 8.4).

In Lencioni's model, he places 'Absence of Trust' at the base of his pyramid. He isn't just talking about interpersonal trust; he suggests the quality of the team relationship is demonstrated when team members are comfortable with showing vulnerability and weaknesses to each other. Without trust, team members are reluctant to be open, honest and transparent. In our six factor approach Lencioni's trust

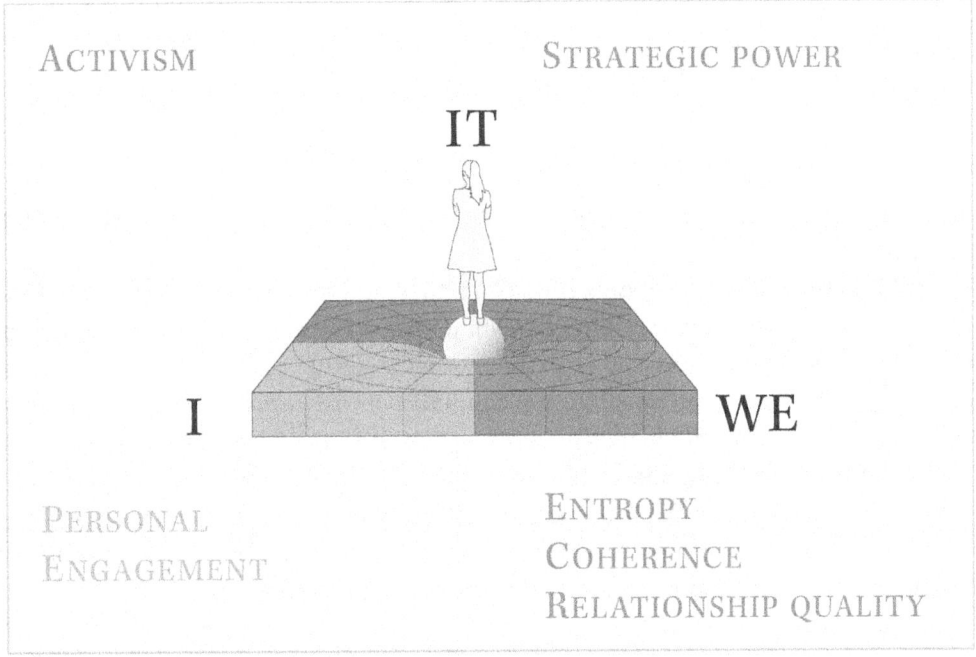

Figure 8.3 TDI Results Mapped to Leadership Model

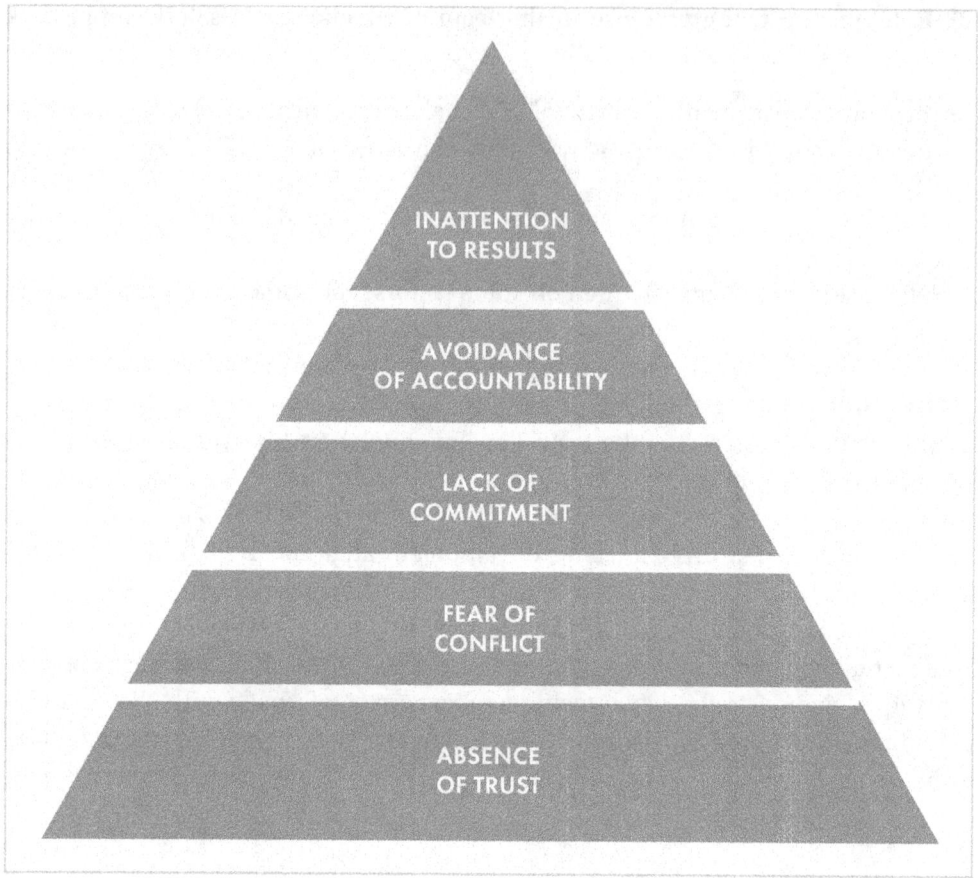

Figure 8.4 Lencioni's Five Dysfunctions of Teams

quality would be picked up by a low Relationship Quality score and a low Entropy score because when there's a lack of trust, team members often engage in conflict avoidance.

Lencioni then talks of fear of conflict. Healthy conflict is essential for productive discussions and decision-making. In a team with low Entropy and low Relationship Quality scores, important issues may be ignored, leading to suboptimal outcomes or a lack of commitment to decisions. Commitment requires active participation and buy-in from all team members. Lencioni's third factor is a lack of commitment.

Immature teams often talk about 'conflict and commit'. But in our experience, this is often idealistic. Immature teams rarely conflict in a healthy way. There may be a team principle of commitment, but in practice their conflict usually produces resistance, or silent opposition outside of the team meeting. Low Entropy scores highlight this fear of conflict.

In our six factors we specifically assess personal commitment. Without commitment there can be no accountability, Lencioni's fourth factor. We assess accountability in our Activism factor, which is more about accountability in action. When there is low Activism team members hesitate to hold each other accountable for their actions and performance. Inattention to results is Lencioni's fifth factor. Insufficient attention to results is picked up by low Activism scores in our model. Our model calls out two critical qualities of a team's development that Lencioni doesn't address: Strategic Power and Coherence. At a stretch one could argue that Lencioni's avoidance of accountability is related to Strategic Power, but in the way he describes it, his factor is more operational than strategic. Either way our TDI model, detailed in the case study in the next chapter, addresses the five dysfunctions of a team and adds a little more precision. We've mapped Lencioni's five dysfunctions of a team on our Leadership Model (Figure 8.5).

As the team matures through the nine levels of development, how the leader and the team show up differs significantly with each new level. Figure 8.6 offers some guidance on what those roles look like at each level.

Most teams in the early stages of their development show up inconsistently and performance varies, often dependent on the topic being discussed. Many Level 3 teams perform at a higher level when in crisis mode. This is because they unite behind a common goal and take a less siloed view. But when the

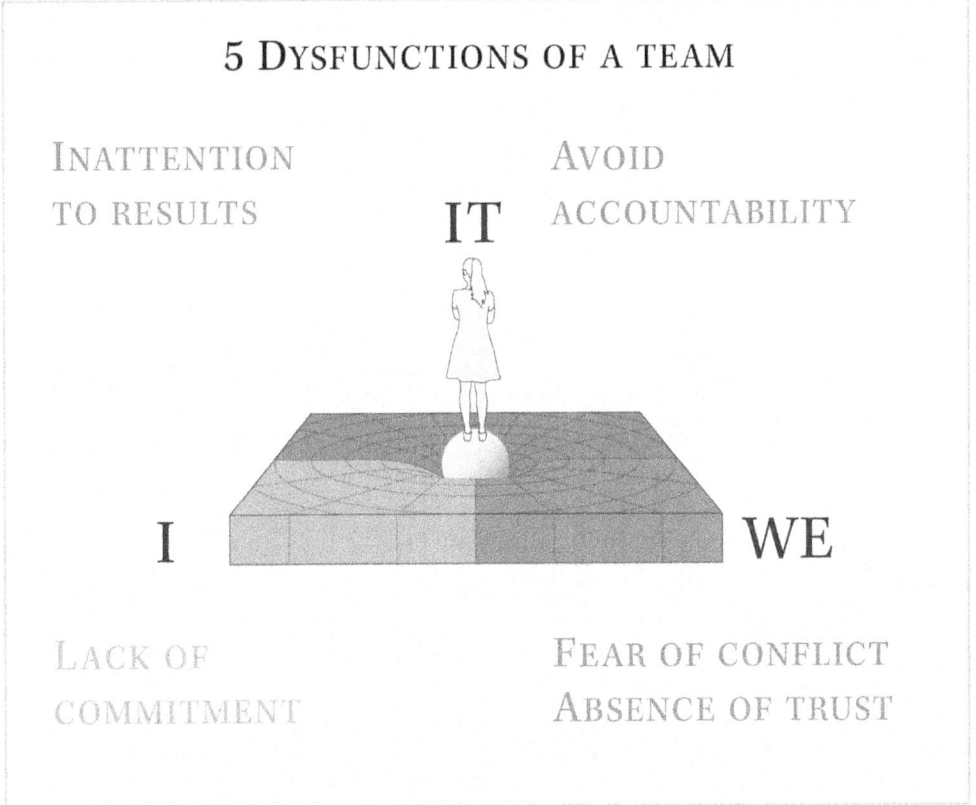

Figure 8.5 Lencioni's 5 Dysfunctions Mapped to the Leadership Model

TEAM STAGE	TEAM LEADERS WAY OF OPERATING	TEAM MEMBER WAY OF OPERATING
9. Unified Fellowships	Leadership is very fluid, disseminated, highly flexible and inspires social change	Team members participate in fluid leadership approach. Everyone moves effortlessly between details and bigger picture, silos and seniority levels.
8. Broad Fellowships	The team acts as the leader, with differentiated roles. Leader is externally facing mission-focus overseeing evolution of individuals, team & system in service of the bigger picture.	Everyone is in service of each other and the bigger mission. Lots of disruptive ideas are flushed to change the whole industry and society.
7. Integrated Pluralists	Leader much more externally focused. Encourages team to make relationships a strategic advantage. Cultivates much more integrative and industry thinking.	Team member work much more fluidly to integrate multiple perspectives and create organisation-wide strategies regardless of role or seniority.
6. Diverse Pluralists	Leader facilitates relationship-based performance improvements by encouraging multiple perspectives, developing diversity and inclusion and silo dissolution.	Look to leverage differences of opinion as a source of competitive advantage. Flush out silent voices and more open to input from other levels.
5. Interdependent Achievers	Works directly to build broader and stronger links across whole team and across multiple levels within the organisation.	Default to working collaboratively, without leader present to solve business problems. High-performance approach where everything can be improved.
4. Independent Achievers	Encourages the development of a team perspective. Wants team members to go beyond their silo and work in twos and threes to deliver results.	Team members actively work to solve business rather than silo issues. Much more proactive problem solving.
3. Dependent Experts	Sets direction, adjudicates conflict and makes final decisions, often run team as hub and spoke. Encourages individual rather than collective responsibility.	Team members report into team meetings, debate with each other and defer to leader. Ineffective delegation is common.
2. Battling Experts	Leader tends to be autocratic & driven. They encourage individuals to express their views and thrash out answers with their option for veto or over-rule.	Team members focus on promoting, protecting and defending their own silo. May gaslight each other. Don't see other's areas as their concern.
1. Pre Team		

Figure 8.6 Level Descriptions by Team and Leader

crisis passes, teams need to commit to and be much more open to change. This change needs to be at the individual and collective level. There has to be a fundamental shift away from the mindset of the 'expert' and much greater curiosity and preparedness to experiment. The greatest challenge for all teams is to invest sufficient time in their own development and allow a developmental coach to guide them. The Expert stance is 'I know'. This makes them resistant to input. But to develop as a team, they need to let go of their own need to be an expert, experiment with different ways of seeing and doing so they can become more of an Achiever, and then ultimately transform the way they see relationships to become Pluralists.

Network Analysis

To facilitate rapid evolution through the stages of team development and to arrive at highly functioning teams and executive fellowships, it can also be helpful to understand the existing networks within an organisation. In our work, we help senior leaders to define the current connectivity within an organisation using our Complete Network Analysis diagnostic.[4] This assessment enables us to precisely define who is connected to whom and why. And we can identify how strong those connections are.

One of the interesting paradoxes we see in business and inside the education system is that while we may have more ways to 'communicate' with each other than ever before, communication is increasingly shallow, superficial or transactional, and as such we often feel less connected. We have the tools for greater connectivity, but meaningful connection is still rare.

It's now clear that top-down traditional 'rollouts' of new educational initiatives from the most senior levels to the far reaches of the system are not effective. We encourage organisations to communicate and engage with their people through 'viral' mechanisms, rippling ideas through the existing organisational networks and forums. A nudge, a wave of excitement and an engaging dialogue with staff are much more effective than most traditional 'internal comms' processes.

Understanding the existing internal networks can facilitate high-speed ripples within the system because if you know who's connected to whom, then you can identify how to spread an operational, cultural or strategic message rapidly by engaging the most influential people in those networks.

Network analysis is based on complicated social networking theory, but we use a much simpler approach that illuminates some very powerful data in just a few minutes. We ask nine simple questions to define three critical networks:

- ***Operational Network:*** Name the people you typically get work-related information from. Name the people you regularly collaborate with. Name the people whom you go to in order to get things done or achieve faster progress.

- **Cultural Network:** Name the people you feel energised by. Name the people you feel you can be open and honest with. Name the people you turn to for support when things are tough.

- **Leadership Network:** Name the people who stretch your thinking. Name the people to whom you turn for leadership and guidance. Name the people who actively support your development at this organisation.

With these questions and some big data analytics, we can flush out a lot of critical information about the structure, leadership, talent pool and performance of your organisation. For example, Matt worked with one of the UK's largest multi-academy trust's leadership teams (including the heads) where the Network Analysis data significantly changed the focus of the leadership team members. One individual's innovation ability was strong, but their peers didn't turn to them for that. Instead, they turned to this individual for information and direction, not stretch thinking. The Trust's best strategic thinker's time was being consumed communicating small bites of information and giving direction. This was draining their energy.

Within the Trust, operational tasks were communicated well, but the cultural communication channel was absent. This meant they lacked the relationship bonds to disseminate more subtle people messages. As a result of the Network Analysis insights, the leadership team significantly changed the way its communication channels worked and the accountability of each leadership team member to disseminate the right messages. They distributed the responsibility for communication more widely and ensured their best strategic thinker was able to 'land' their brilliant ideas rather than being consumed by tactical tasks.

One of the other transformative insights that the Network Analysis revealed was the impact of the team moving one of their leaders sideways in a political reshuffle. This particular leader had very strong cultural connectivity and the change caused significant unrest and a sudden drop-off in performance of a department. Turns out, the person who was moved sideways was culturally key to that department as well as the wider community and it caused many other people in the department to become uneasy and lose trust in the leadership team's judgment. The leadership team realised they needed to reverse their decision for the benefit of the wider system.

The Network Analysis is also brilliant at identifying hidden talents within the system. We've seen repeatedly that the leadership team only sees about 50% of their talent pool. At least half of the rising stars or individuals who should be included in succession thinking are missed. The Network Analysis can literally rank, in a quantifiable way, how much influence one individual has compared to another, and how this varies operationally, culturally and strategically. It reveals how the school or Trust really functions, rather than how the leadership team thinks it should, or could function. The insights generated can be incredibly useful for rolling out initiatives, evolving culture and driving improved performance and succession planning.

Big Picture Thinking

Once educational leaders have got a stronger sense of the maturity of their leadership team from the TDI, the diversity of motivations within the team from the values profile, and how their system really works from the Network Analysis data, they are in a much better place to understand how to improve things and how to gel the team. The next step is to sort out the team's big picture thinking. Specifically, they need to forensically define their answers to the following questions:

a) **Vision:** This answers the question 'WHERE?'. Where is the school or Trust going? A good vision describes a picture of the future, the desired destination. The leadership team must define "a world where . . . what is happening in education?". The Vision is not necessarily a fully achievable state, it describes the direction of travel.

b) **Purpose:** This answers the question 'WHY?'. It's often an emotional (heart) statement that can drive engagement and unlock discretionary effort. It can help define why a teacher works in one school over another. It's the boiled down essence of the school or Trust brand and value proposition. Defining purpose can help to differentiate the school or Trust in the eyes of key stakeholders.

c) **Ambition:** This answers the question 'WHEN?' It a more rational (head) statement about the size, scale and reach of the school when it achieves its ambition. The ambition can be defined in terms of results, student numbers, geographic reach of the school or Trust, student or staff engagement or any other metrics the leadership align on.

d) **Strategy:** This answers the question 'WHAT?' What are the specific things that the school needs to do to grow, achieve its ambition and get close to its vision and purpose. This is often what differentiates the school from its competitors.

e) **Governance:** This answers the question 'WHO and HOW?' Governance defines how the school operates and who makes the decisions. It requires the leadership team to define a series of detailed and robust mechanisms and processes around 'who decides who decides'. Governance drives much greater organisational efficiency, improves the quality of decision making, identifies and enforces precise accountabilities, and delivers greater strategic and operational alignment.

The school's leadership team is responsible for governance. The school's Board of Governors is responsible for overseeing the leadership team's governance and making sure all the other pieces of the big picture thinking, including strategy, are in place, are correct and are delivering improvements in performance of the school. It's not the Board of Governors role to decide the school strategy.

Most leadership teams don't make the distinction between vision, purpose and ambition. Many have done some thinking around strategy, but sadly most of what's included in the 'strategy document' isn't actually strategy. It's usually a series of pressing operational priorities to improve performance. Real governance, is either completely ignored or mistakenly perceived as compliance and operational oversight, both necessary but not governance.

It's common to see insipid vision statements full of meaningless platitudes like 'achievable together' or 'be the best'. Such cliches aren't even vision statements, they're uninspiring ambition statements. The confusion between vision and ambition is most often made by leadership teams at the Achiever level of development.

When teams invest time and energy working on their vision, purpose, ambition or strategy and that work generates hackneyed cliches, it's not surprising that they conclude that their investment was a waste of time. Virtually all teams we encounter have had this experience. Cynicism or at the very least scepticism is the justifiable norm. But if this work is done very well it can drive a significant positive uplift in momentum, align a wider set of stakeholders and give people something to believe in. This can be vital when the wider educational environment is tough, and the school is bombarded with demands and pressure from many quarters.

Even when the leadership team has done some very high-quality big picture thinking, aligning staff around the vision, purpose and strategy can still be very difficult. The most common mistake is for the leadership team to impose its thinking on the school in a top-down, autocratic desire to drive change. Those outside the leadership team, who must action the big picture thinking, are rarely asked for their input. And even if they are, it's often a superficial exercise designed to convince people that the change has not been imposed on them from 'on-high'. It's much more effective to engage those responsible for executing the vision, purpose and strategy in their creation, than to conduct an internal communication roadshow. We've seen some organisations spend thousands of hours talking to staff to explain their strategy with minimal effect. It's much more effective to present staff with the questions, that vision, ambition, purpose and strategy aim to solve, flush out their views and then integrate those views into the final answer. This helps people feel engaged in the process and fosters a sense of ownership in the answer, making executing the answer much easier. This approach taps into their intrinsic motivation and increases engagement (more on this in chapter 10).

Defining the school's big picture thinking in this way, with the widest set of stakeholders, will differentiate the school from most of the other schools in the area. Each building block of vision, purpose, ambition, strategy and governance creates an edge, and together they can create 'clear blue water' between your school or Trust and your competitors.[5]

To hone the strategy and identify exactly WHAT will differentiate your school from the competition, it can be extremely useful to consider the six key areas for education:

1. **Context:** Without the context being supportive and positive, it is likely all other key areas will not sustain. Staff will not remain engaged in their own or learners' development, and both will be demotivated.

2. **Opportunities:** What are the opportunities that exist in this school that don't always exist in other schools? What specific opportunities can the school create for stakeholders inside the school and beyond the school?

3. **Pathways:** What are the unique pathways in the school for various stakeholders? What developmental pathways for teachers, support staff or pupils into higher education or work that could be leveraged to create a competitive advantage?

4. **Diversity:** What sort of diversity does the school embrace, and how could this be used to enhance the future of the school?

5. **Personalised Learning:** Are there processes, systems or ways of working unique to the school that give it a competitive edge in driving personalised learning, and how this can drive real development for all stakeholders?

6. **Outreach into the Community:** Are there ways that the school connects and involves the local community that can be turned to its advantage?

When a leadership team gets the big picture thinking right, something magical happens – trust and confidence start to build within the leadership team. This trust and confidence start to trickle out of the team and invigorate others, who start to wonder if this time things are going to be different. When those outside the leadership team are invited to engage in the same big picture thinking process, they can see how what they do impacts that vision, purpose, ambition, strategy and governance. This restores some meaning and fulfilment back into their roles. Before long the trust and confidence are magnified and virtuous cycles are created, transforming the energy in the school.

Getting it right however requires real skill and a map to design it with. When it's done badly, it can be very demotivating, leading to cynicism and hopelessness. Trust is critical for high-quality relationships and meaningful connection. Like listening, it's a profoundly simple concept. Most people have never explored trust as a specific topic, so few understand the component parts of trust or how trust is created or lost.

In our work we often spend a significant amount of time exploring trust with leaders and their teams. We suggest that TRUST can be seen as an acronym for Taking Responsibility for Understanding Someone else's Traits. The central concept within trust is therefore understanding. If we want to increase the levels of trust in our stakeholder groups, we must take responsibility for building that understanding of other people and their understanding of us. We need to understand how other stakeholders think and feel. As we discussed when we combine thinking and feeling, we can create values and beliefs. When we combine values and beliefs, we can create attitudes. When attitudes become consolidated or crystalised, then they become more stable traits and part of our personality. We used the word 'traits' because it works in the acronym and also because it transcends and includes people's values, beliefs and attitudes.

Understanding someone else's traits, attitudes, values and beliefs requires us to spend some quality time with them to build a personal connection. Having discussed this topic with thousands of people over the years and asked them how they build trust or why it breaks, we discovered there were four key elements to the 'Trust Recipe'. These ingredients are the same the world over regardless of culture or geography. Knowing the four ingredients in the recipe can significantly fast-track results and performance. If you want to increase the level of trust in your team you need to focus on one or all of these elements:

1. **Personal Behaviour:** we make judgements all the time about whether we can trust others based on how they behave. For example, we trust more if they give others credit rather than take credit themselves; or if they take responsibility rather than blame others.

2. **Personal Motives:** we make judgements all the time about whether we can trust others based on what we believe their motives are. Do we think they're honest or manipulative? Do we believe they're transparent or secretive?

3. **Delivery & Competence:** it's easier to trust people who have competency and a proven track record. We trust brands that deliver on their promise and do what they say they will do.

4. **Relationship & Connection:** finally, time may be important. Our trust in someone may simply erode because we haven't seen them for a long time. But it's not just a matter of time. It's the quality of the connection when we have shared time. Trust builds when we collaborate effectively, chemistry is good and empathy is explicitly expressed.

The first two ingredients are more in the 'I' domain, the third is more 'IT' and the fourth is more in the 'WE' domain. Each person operates with different weightings of these four elements, and each of these elements may be present in a positive or negative version to create trust dynamics. But once we know this, we have a tool that allows us to trust others more and help others trust us more.

There are so many simple things we can do to improve our relationships and help children to develop their relationships skills. And we need to practice every day because our future and the future of the education system depend on it.

Notes

1. Rooke D, Torbert WR (2005) Seven transformations of leadership, Harvard Business Review.
   Hunter JE, Schmidt FL, Judiesch MK (1990) Individual differences in output variability as a function of job complexity, Journal of Applied Psychology, 75, 28–42. Zenger JJ, Folkman J (2009) The extraordinary leader: turning good managers into great leaders, McGraw Hill, New York.
2. Stein J (n.d.) Using the stages of team development, MIT Human Resources.
3. Lencioni P (2002) The five dysfunctions of a team, John Wiley & Sons, New York.
4. No Author (2023) The org chart is dead. Welcome to the age of networks, https://complete-network-analysis.com/.
5. Kim WC, Mauborgne R (2005) Blue ocean strategy: how to create uncontested market space and make the competition irrelevant, Harvard Business School Press, Boston.

Collective Development in Action

Let's return to our case study of Adam and how the 'WE' skills discussed in the last chapter were applied in his school and the wider Trust. In working with teachers and educators over the last 25 years, we often see a strong desire to develop skills they can use to better support the children they teach. This is usually borne of genuine care and a passion to make their students' lives better. But we almost always have to remind them that the developmental journey starts with them ('I') and then their relationship to the children ('WE'). This is one thing that Adam got right from the start. He didn't immediately try to 'fix' other people or the system, he started by addressing his own shortcomings.

To some of his colleagues, this looked indulgent or like he was slowing progress. But stakeholders soon started to notice that the changes in Adam's approach delivered changes in the school. Adam was literally practicing what he later 'preached' to others. He worked hard to understand his own values and motivations. He likened it to learning a secret language, and with that language he was better able to understand how others perceived him and how he needed to flex the way he showed up to get the best out of others.

Adam even got quite good at guessing what value system other people were operating from in each meeting he had, based on the words each person used, the metaphors they preferred and the energy they brough to the discussion. Adam developed the ability to create rich conversations around values with the three assistant heads in his team – John, Sarah and Angus. They now shared a common framework for understanding each other's motivations and how they could work more effectively as a team in collaborating and connecting with all the other key stakeholders.

One of Adam's first actions, in the 'WE' domain, was to invest in and commit to a team development journey for his leadership team. As part of this, everyone in the team did their own values profiles. This gave each team member some precise data on their own level of development. Each team member was able to build a personal development plan (PDP) that was more precise and powerful than they had ever created before and share this with their teammates. Team members also

	Purple	Red	Blue	Orange	Green	Yellow	Turquoise
John	5	16	22	17	8	18	12
Angus	6	29	16	16	21	8	2
Adam	9	7	18	20	20	15	9
Laura	18	3	20	11	24	12	10
Sarah	5	11	21	10	24	17	10

Figure 9.1 The Team's Overall Values Analysis

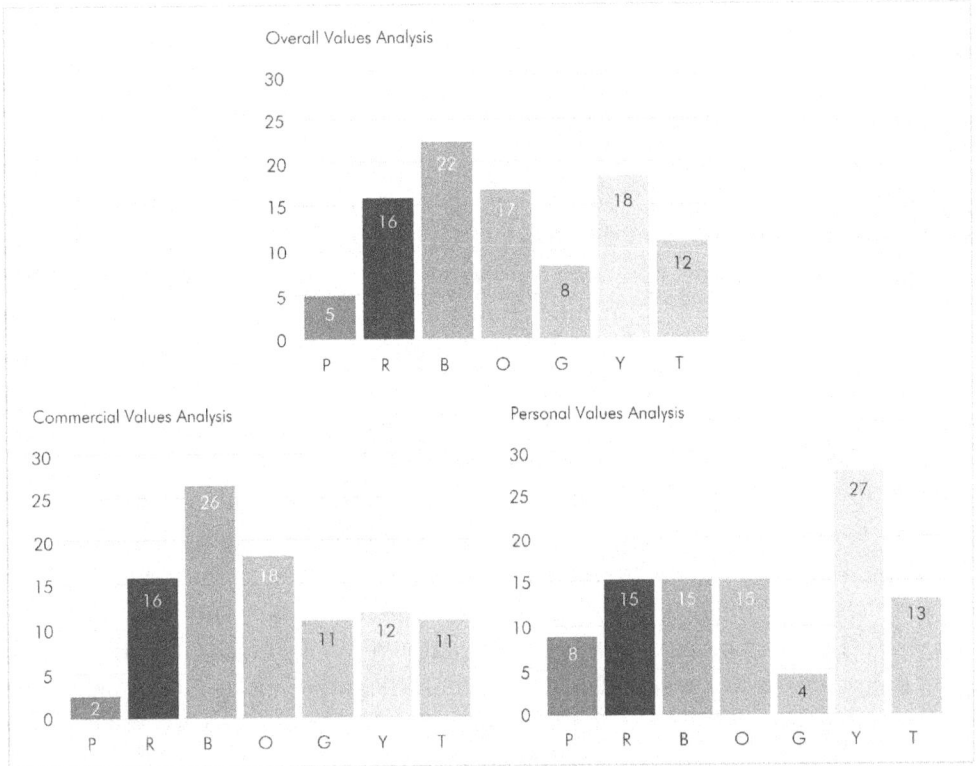

Figure 9.2 John's Values Analysis

openly discussed their own values profiles with each other (Figure 9.1). One of the most insightful conversations the team had, as a result of this data sharing, was to explore why, based on their individual's values profile, certain people were flourishing in certain roles and others were struggling.

They were struggling because the role they were doing wasn't aligned to their value systems. They often felt like their job didn't suit them, and they couldn't bring all of themselves to work. For example, one Assistant Head, John, realised after reviewing his own values data that he had, by his own admission, been going through the motions. He was running a Key Stage but he wasn't fulfilled and he wasn't engaged. So much so that he was thinking of leaving the school.

A deeper dive into John's values profile revealed his personal bent toward innovation (Figure 9.2).

John realised that he had a lot of value to offer the school in terms of his personal innovation but had been showing up with a Blue lens. His Yellow value system showed up very clearly in the personal subscale but less so in his commercial profile. Interestingly John's commercial values sub-scale had a high Blue score, and he found this was often in tension with his Yellow personal driver. John's perception that he had to be process driven restricted showing up in line with his personal values often made it difficult for him to be disruptive when the team was discussing strategy. He perceived his input to be rocking the boat or stepping outside his remit so he didn't.

The team acknowledged John's nervousness, but encouraged him to share his disruptive thinking. He was given the space to do so and was relieved, even if ultimately the team decided to move in a different direction. When the team realised that allowing John to share his innovative ideas was vital to his motivation, they were happy to give him this space. This was reciprocated by allowing other team members, who operated from the Orange value system, to evaluate whether John's ideas would work in practice. Essentially everyone was given the room to 'be themselves', bring their magic and work effectively with the diversity of values everyone brought.

With these team agreements in place and some coaching, John found the courage to put forward many great ideas from his digital marketing and research background. His role has now changed to better align with his values and he has since gone on to create a deliberately developmental coaching model for Early Career Teachers. This helps them transition much more easily into the school culture by understanding themselves better and how their values relate to the school's approach. Twenty members of staff were prompted to take on additional development programmes. As a result of staff growth, the lethargic legacy mindset has been overcome. All this work was pivotal to the leadership team's decision to become a research school (more on that shortly).

John has demonstrated a flair for innovation, and Sarah also uncovered a real passion for research with the help of E-Bank and Complete Values Profile (CVP). The E-Bank was instrumental in allowing team members to better understand what tasks and responsibilities were draining them or energising them. These energy insights led to a reshuffle of the leadership team responsibilities. The team made sure they had 'the right people sitting on the right seat of the bus'. Prior to working on her own development, Sarah had been struggling with a heavy teaching timetable, and she didn't feel as though she had the time or energy to focus on her primary passion and interest – research. She was reluctant to discuss this with Adam because she didn't know how to.

Following some coaching, Sarah was able to articulate her thinking to Adam. Like John, Sarah had also been thinking of leaving the school to pursue her interests, and it hadn't even crossed her mind that she could follow her passion without changing jobs. The work and support from the team helped her turn things around, and instead of leaving the school, she started pioneering research into the impact of how a deliberately developmental approach impacted early career teaching.

The values framework was instrumental in building new layers of trust in the team because each team member understood their own values level and how that differed from their teammates. As a result, they were better able to step into each other's shoes in meetings. With cognitive and emotional empathy, it was much easier to find solutions and align around ideas. This increase in trust and the development of more aligned action has been repeated across many educational leadership groups and is captured by the phrase: 'when we're invested in, we feel valued'. A coaching culture emerged, and specific training around staff's own values has led to shifts in their curriculum framework, pedagogical approaches and behaviour management strategies.

After such success at the leadership team level, the school cascaded these skills and insights to the wider staff to help them understand who they were, what gives them energy and how to better align their values with their roles to create much greater levels of engagement. The common language around 'lines of development' resulted in a professional development system being put into place, alongside the existing performance management system with a coaching network to facilitate people's journeys towards their goals.

The team journey has allowed the leadership team to understand the benefits of development as well as experience them. Each team member felt more engaged and aligned in 'one boat', a metaphor for pulling together towards a common goal. They implemented a staff audit, allowing staff to share their professional backgrounds and experiences inside and outside of education, as well as interests and hobbies. These data were essential for informing the school's strategy. Future plans ceased to be just about the budget and Ofsted. The school strategy started to reflect the uniqueness that everyone brought to their role.

People described how their developmental experience was 'done with' them instead of 'done to' them. As one teacher said: "I don't feel judged by my teammates, I feel supported". The team contract that was created is now present in every meeting as a reminder of what they expect from each other.

In addition to using the E-Bank skill and values profile to develop a much better strategy, that hinged around being deliberately developmental, the team also reviewed what level their team was operating from using the Team Developmental Inventory (TDI) data. Figure 9.3 shows where the team was before they embarked on their 'WE' developmental journey.

Unsurprisingly, given that most of the team members were largely operating from the people-centric Green value system, the TDI data showed that Relationship Quality was the team's highest score compared to the global benchmark (0.0) of all teams who have completed the TDI. The Relationship Quality construct includes a level of psychological safety, strong personal connections, and the willingness to support and develop each other.

The second highest team score was for Strategic Power. This construct includes the team's ability to create a powerfully compelling vision. In contrast, the team scored less well in their ability to convert their vision into action (Activism). Having previously received an Ofsted assessment of 'Outstanding' the team had mistakenly started to rest on its laurels, feeling it was a case of 'job done'. After working with Matt for a short period, we helped the team increase its ambition leading to the development of a compelling strategy, even though Ofsted never mentioned this.

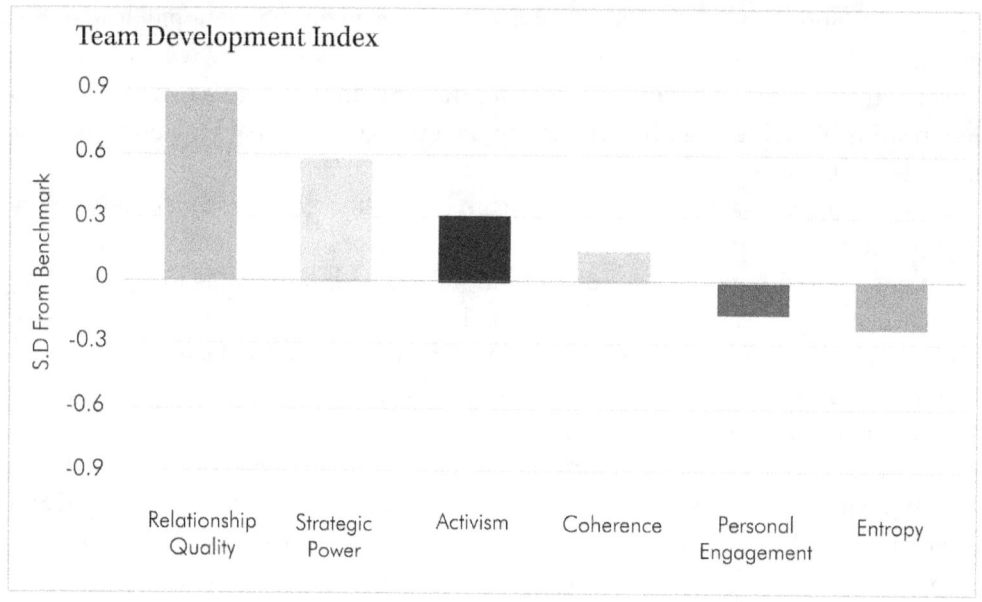

Figure 9.3 TDI Results Before the Developmental Effort

It's worth pointing out that, certainly in England and Wales, the strategy of each school is, at least broadly, already laid out by Ofsted guidelines. Ofsted assesses every school against four areas (although Ofsted offers no guidance on whether it thinks schools should consider these areas for strategic focus or just for incremental operational improvements):

1. Leadership and Management

2. Quality of Education

3. Behaviour and Attitudes

4. Personal Development.

As a result, most schools restrict their operational and strategic conversations to just focusing on these four areas. Adam and his team did exactly that, initially. However, we encouraged them to stretch their thinking and consider their unique selling point (USP) or point of difference and how this might enhance their strategic objectives. This resulted in Adam's team choosing to add research and networking as the fifth areas for strategic focus.

With the team's centre of gravity being around the people-centric Green value system, we felt the team needed help with their ability to align because the TDI data on the Coherence construct were much lower than expected. The Coherence construct refers to the ease in which a team can find common ground and truly align everyone behind a decision, without the need for 'conflict and commit' rules. The team's Green gravity meant that genuine consensus was rare and conflict avoidance was common. People didn't speak for fear of rocking the boat. This tendency for avoidance was borne out by the low Entropy scores as well as the low Personal Engagement scores in the TDI data.

The initial TDI data helped the team admit that they were operating at Level 2 of team development, called 'Dependant Experts'. This helped them set an ambition to reach Level 4 as a team or become 'Independent Achievers'.

To achieve that ambition, we worked with the team to design a meeting schedule for strategy and implementation. Adam invited others to take greater responsibility. He created much clearer succession plans and he realised his ability to design an improved curriculum would have greater impact if it was systematised, scaled and owned by all the staff. To this end, each team member took responsibility for one of the strategic initiatives that aligned with their own values. This created a much greater sense of agency for each individual. That team member became the 'captain' for that initiative. Each captain nominated a 'coach', someone who may have relevant knowledge or experience (some were outside of the school) in that strategic initiative as well as a 'right-hand' and 'left-hand' person to support them in implementation and delivery of their strategic initiative.

A meeting schedule was created to help the captain, coach, left- and right-hand to distribute the accountabilities and create forward momentum. To address the low entropy score, the captain was also asked to seek open challenges from their group as part of the meeting design. Key actions were agreed and taken away from these meetings in the relentless march through agreed milestones to implementation and delivery. The team's own development journey was now a much more conscious affair, driven not by Adam but by the team itself.

The importance of these meetings was further emphasised by all team members signing a meeting contract and creating meeting best practice guidelines. We helped the leaders better understand (often for the first time) the three different phases of a meeting to ensure faster and more effective meetings. Finally, the captain was asked to appoint a meeting 'Chair', which was usually the person in the coach role. The coach was able to create more momentum than would have been possible if the captain had chaired the meeting.

How we helped Adam, and his team, isn't rocket science. The benefits are a result of the quality, skill and precision of the guidance through a carefully thought out and curated series of steps. Part of the challenge is that, in a busy school day, competing priorities mean doing the right thing often gets lost, ignored or forgotten. But with a captain for each strategic objective who had the delegated authority to move things forward, the captains and support team for each strategic objective were invested in the outcome. And the low Coherence and low Entropy started to rise. Milestones are achieved collectively, confidence builds and a virtuous cycle is created. Relationship Quality, which was relatively high initially, increased further, and the delivery team no longer saw the leadership team as the centre of the wheel, but as part of a network of professional

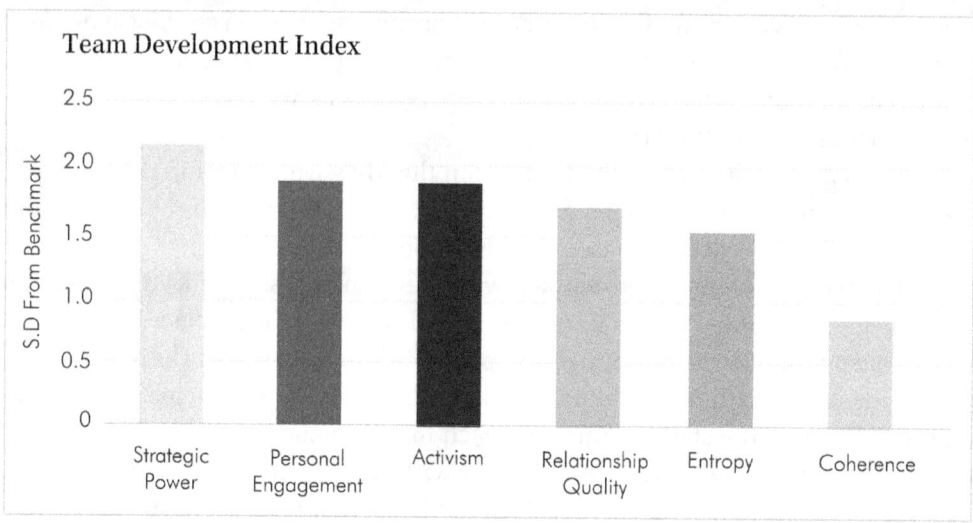

Figure 9.4 TDI Results After the Development Effort (Six Months Later)

practitioners, each accountable for a developmental culture, reinforced by developmental tools and specific coaching.

The leadership team, instead of looking to Adam for all the assurance and direction, characteristic of Dependant Experts, became more independent and collaborative, more in keeping with their ambition to be Level 4 'Independent Achievers'. Their real progress fostered a deeper level of trust and collaboration across the school. And the leadership team went on to create an observation classroom with a digital platform partner to enhance professional practice within the school and disseminate the learning nationally.

All this progress reflects a significant step change in the quality of thinking and a new performance culture. We also saw an upgrade in leadership behaviours. Whilst having some of the highest Standardised Assessment Results (SATs) in the region, the school hasn't had the time to document what they've achieved and are yet to share their learning. The school is in the process of doing this and creating an outreach offer (more on this in chapter 12).

The team's improved collaboration has increased their level of Coherence and instead of pretending to agree and then complaining about the decisions outside the meetings, they've been able to reach genuine alignment much faster. The team has also become more confident in aligning with a much broader set of stakeholders.

What was inspiring was that it didn't take long for all these changes to happen. A 'speak up' culture was established in meetings; more views were shared sparking more debate and dialogue which raised the Entropy still further. Because the team started as a highly Green team, their capacity to share ideas very quickly tipped into the upside of Yellow. They became innovative problem solvers.

Figure 9.4 shows the team dynamics when the team re-tested on the TDI.

What is so game changing about TDI and the development around teams is that it creates a path to purposefully address the problems that keep us stuck in the 'WE' dimension. It gives structure to elevate the quality of communication, it gives us insight on how different people are, and how we can harness those differences towards a better future rather than complain or get stuck on those differences.

 Behaviour and Systems Development in Theory

The start point for many, in an 'IT' addicted world, is to focus on what we can DO to improve results, or what systems we can put in place to change the outcomes. In the classroom a teacher is always considering what they can DO to encourage better behaviour ('IT') from their pupils or how they can teach a little differently to get better results. This isn't wrong, it's just an insufficient answer. One of the reasons so many peoples' attention is on action is that actions are visible. If a pupil misbehaves, it's obvious. If a teacher does something wrong, pupils notice. But getting people to change their behaviour, and 'do the right thing' isn't easy.

The difficulty in changing behaviour is mainly because there are many things that we can't see that determine whether people do or don't do something, as discussed in chapter 5 when we explored the Integrated Performance Model (Figure 5.1). Starting at the bottom of the model, physiology determines what emotions we have. Our emotions are the composite stereotypical patterns of energy that we may be able to feel. Our feelings determine what and how well we think. Our thinking determines what we decide to do, which is the behaviour that others can see. And of course, it is behaviour that determines results.

The fact that behaviour starts with physiology is why the physical and emotion lines of development, in the 'I' quadrant, are so important. Mastery of these lines of development make a huge difference to the results we get. Unfortunately, most of us have never been taught how to regulate our physiology or emotions, so consequently we have very little control over what we think and how we feel. Whether we succeed or fail is unpredictable. Sometimes things go well, sometimes they go badly. We often have no idea why.

What the Integrated Performance Model tells us is that our interior landscape determines our exterior results. The bridge between our inner world and our outer world is paved by motivations and engagement. If we want to design solutions that can change outcomes, we must understand that bridge a little more.

Intrinsic and Extrinsic Motivation Theory

For many years academics believed humans had just two motivational drives, intrinsic and extrinsic. The most basic intrinsic motivation is the biological imperative to survive. This is underpinned by the need to eat, sleep, breathe, drink and breed. Manipulating these variables can have a very powerful effect, but such motivations are not precise, they lack subtlety and nuance. This basic drive isn't that helpful if we want to reinvent the educational system.

For example, threatening a teacher with redundancy may be a powerful motivator, but it's unlikely to elicit the subtle shift in behaviour needed to help them improve their performance in the classroom. Similarly, threatening a pupil with exclusion may put them in survival mode, but it's unlikely to cause them to reflect on how they become a better learner or how they might develop better interpersonal skills. Once the immediate threat has passed, they will revert to their old behaviour patterns. The most we can usually hope for is belligerent compliance or passive aggression.

The second recognised motivational drive is reward and punishment. Reward and punishment are known as extrinsic motivational tools because the impetus to change is coming from external sources. According to these motivational forces, the only way you can get people to change their behaviour is to reward them when they do something positive and punish them when they do something negative. These motivational tools (the carrot and stick; star charts and demerits; chocolate or the naughty step) have been used in society, including the education system for centuries. They emerge from the Red value system as simple control mechanisms. Historically many schools literally used the stick, as part of a corporal punishment strategy. This was very much in keeping with the understanding about motivation – at that time.

The problem is that whilst this approach to motivation is still very much alive and well in the school system, scientific research has now proven this Red reward and punishment approach doesn't work. Worse still, it has several unhelpful side effects.[1] The carrot and stick approach to motivation can:

- Actively reduce motivation
- Reduce creativity
- Impair results
- Actively inhibit good behaviour and foster bad behaviour
- Be addictive
- Be expensive to administer and breeds complacency

In one study with pre-schoolers, psychologists Mark Lepper and David Greene identified a group of children who chose to spend their free play time drawing. They created an experiment to assess what happened to those children when they were rewarded for doing something they were already motivated to do and enjoyed.[2]

The children were divided into three groups – 'Expected reward', 'Unexpected reward' and 'No reward', and after just two weeks the kids from the unexpected or no reward group were as enthusiastic as ever about drawing. Those who had previously received a reward for the activity, however were much less interested in drawing. The rewards had turned something that was enjoyable into a chore.

Princeton psychologist Sam Glucksberg discovered that giving individuals a reward reduced creativity. When faced with a conceptual creative challenge, the group that was incentivised took three and a half minutes *longer* to complete the challenge than the ones that were not rewarded. Harvard Business School professor Teresa Amabile, who is also one of the world's leading authorities on creativity, discovered that creativity drops when people are rewarded for doing something they love or are good at anyway![3]

Plus offering rewards diminishes results. The Federal Reserve Bank in the US commissioned research into the effectiveness of rewards on performance and commissioned four economists from MIT, Carnegie Mellon and the University of Chicago to investigate and report on their findings. They concluded that, "In eight of the nine tasks we examined across three experiments, higher incentives led to worse performance". The London School of Economics also confirmed these findings after analysing 51 studies of corporate reward schemes. They reported that, "We find that financial incentives . . . can result in negative impact on overall performance".

Edward Deci, Professor of Psychology and Gowen Professor in the Social Sciences at the University of Rochester and director of its human motivation program along with two colleagues, went back over 30 years of research assessing 128 experiments on motivation, and they concluded that, "tangible rewards tend to have a substantially negative effect on intrinsic motivation". The long-term damage caused by offering short-term rewards is one of the most robustly proven findings in social science and yet it is constantly ignored.

The impact of a rewards-based education system also ripples across learners and educators – no wonder there's a retention crisis in the system.

And the punishment side of the carrot and stick equation doesn't fare much better, and it certainly doesn't stop bad behaviour. Economists Uri Gneezy and Aldo Rustichini found that punishment can actively encourage bad behaviour. They studied a childcare facility to see whether imposing a fine on parents who collected their children late reduced this behaviour. When children are not collected in time, then a member of staff obviously has to stay with the child until someone collects them. The first four weeks of the study was to observe behaviour and calculate how many parents were late to collect their children. Prior to the fifth week, all the parents were told about the imposition of a fine to tackle late pick-ups and yet the result was twice as many parents collected their children late!

It's impossible to know exactly why this happened but the assumption is that prior to the fine, parents had a social and moral responsibility to collect their kids on time. They presumably liked the people who cared for their children and didn't want to put them out or upset them. But the fine provided them with a way to buy off their guilt. They could now legitimately be late, because after all, they were now paying to not pick up their children. The moral dilemma was removed which allowed them to quantify the inconvenience and erase their guilt.

The same outcome was seen in a study of blood donors. Instead of increasing the numbers of people who gave blood, the offer of payment reduced participation. For most people, the desire to give blood is an act of selflessness, connection or altruism, and the offer of payment somehow sullied that experience.

And finally attempting to motivate people through rewards is expensive and addictive. Russian economist Anton Suvorov concluded from his studies that once rewards become expected and normal, the desires, effort or activity plateaus. This means the reward provider must constantly increase the reward to illicit the same behaviour. Brain scanning studies have even established that anticipated rewards cause a surge of dopamine to a particular part of the brain, and rather alarmingly it is exactly the same surge of dopamine to exactly the same part of the brain that is experienced by people with addiction! This is what most social media platforms tap into.

Once people get used to being rewarded, they become addicted to being rewarded and they will constantly have to increase the reward to get the same results. Addicts are looking for the 'next hit'. This can completely erode any sense of fulfilment, which is exactly what happens in 'doom scrolling' on social media platform. Social scientists Philip Brickman and Donald T. Campbell suggested that as someone is rewarded, their expectations and desires rise in tandem which results in no permanent gain in happiness or fulfilment.[4] Many children and adults today are totally addicted to their phones as a result of the need to get their next dopamine hit in the false hope that this may make them feel better.

The evidence is overwhelming; you can't reward or scare people into changing their behaviour.

Extrinsic motivational tricks may work short term, but they are unsustainable. If people are only doing what you want them to do because they're scared of the consequences of non-compliance or they've been promised a juicy reward, then as soon as the reward has been delivered or the danger has passed, they will revert to their comfortable behavioural type.

The distinction of intrinsic and extrinsic is, of course, slightly arbitrary because the 'extrinsic' punishment we may be avoiding is 'guilt', which is clearly an internal state. Similarly, the 'extrinsic' reward may be satisfaction, which is also an internal state. In addition, some external motivations like the promise of using a car for passing an academic test could trigger internal motivations such as a sense of freedom. This is why it's key to understand someone's value systems which can be internally or externally triggered.

It's also worth noting that the reason much of society is still operating with a very blunt Red motivational system is because reward and punishment *are* sometimes effective. It's the word 'sometimes' that creates the addiction. But it inhibits development, it inhibits real progress, it inhibits fulfilment and it impairs health and performance.

Motivations, extrinsic and intrinsic, can also be linked to the nature of the task. Behavioural scientists often divide tasks into 'algorithmic' and 'heuristic'. Algorithmic tasks are routine tasks that follow a set path to an ideal conclusion. Humanity during the Industrial Revolution built machines to take many algorithmic tasks off us, to reduce the drudgery of repetition. If you want to motivate people to do some algorithmic tasks, which are often tedious and boring, then reward and punishment *will* work. We've seen many algorithmic tasks performed by lawyers, doctors, accountants, pilots and even teachers taken over by AI. The future work of humanity is clearly not in algorithmic work. Machines and computers can do it faster, more safely and more accurately than any of us.

But heuristic tasks are very different. They are tasks where the outcome can be reached in several different ways, where the individual needs to experiment and be creative to come up with something new. According to McKinsey & Co, algorithmic task-based jobs will account for only 30% of job growth now and into the future. This means that 70% of job growth will come from heuristic work and heuristic work does NOT respond to reward and punishment.[5] Edward Deci and Richard Ryan's research suggest that intrinsic motivation delivers a much greater uplift in performance than extrinsic motivation not just in productivity but also in well-being.[6]

It's time to relegate reward and punishment in education to the history books because it just doesn't change behaviour. We need a much more nuanced view of motivational systems.

Thankfully, behavioural science has discovered and fine-tuned our understanding of a third motivational drive. This far more subtle type of intrinsic motivation relates to the actions and activities we do for their own sake, for the pleasure and satisfaction it provides.

US psychologist Harry F. Harlow first hinted at this instinctive drive in the 1940s after he conducted experiments on rhesus monkeys. The monkeys were given puzzles to solve. And what he found was that the monkeys solved the puzzles without reward or punishment. He reported at the time that, "The behaviour obtained in this investigation poses some interesting questions for motivation theory, since significant learning was attained, and efficient performance maintained without resort to special or extrinsic incentives". Harlow suggested that there must be something missing from the accepted understanding of motivation, but he was ignored.

In 1960, MIT management professor Douglas McGregor wrote a book called *The Human Side of Enterprise*. He too challenged the idea that we are only driven by the need to survive and reward and punishment. McGregor believed business was missing a major opportunity because of false assumptions about human nature. He argued that command and control style management actively stifled motivation. Again, command and control are still very much alive in the education system.

Abraham Maslow, one of Harlow's former students, also questioned the standard view of motivation and he introduced the world to Maslow's Hierarchy of Needs and later developed humanistic psychology in the 1950s.

Self-Determination Theory

But it wasn't until the mid-80s that this third drive made it into the mainstream. Deci and Ryan proposed self-determination theory (SDT) in which they defined three critical elements for intrinsic motivation to work. These elements were the need for:

- Autonomy
- Competence
- Relatedness

Autonomy

For us to be intrinsically motivated, we have to experience the first element which is some measure of autonomy. If we want to change the education system and get all the stakeholders on board and motivated to buy-into that change, then the stakeholders must enjoy a sense of autonomy.

It was Dr Ellen Langer and her colleague Judith Rodin who alerted the world to the importance of autonomy through a now famous study in a nursing home. The purpose of the experiment was to make residents more mindful of their day-to-day activities and help them engage with life more fully.

In one group, the elderly participants were encouraged to find ways to make more decisions for themselves such as when to see visitors and when to watch TV. In addition, each participant was asked to choose a house plant which they would look after and be responsible for.

In the second group, the residents didn't have any autonomy over their choices and although they were given a houseplant, they did not choose it for themselves and they were told the nurses would look after it.

A year and a half later the residents were re-tested against the same battery of tests they took before the experiment began. The first group was found to be more cheerful, active and alert. They were also healthier! Less than half as many residents from the first group died over the term of the experiment compared to the group who could not exert any autonomy over their day-to-day lives.

In short, we need to feel some measure of control over our situation in order to feel motivated and engaged. On this basis alone, it is easy to see why so many children feel demotivated at school. Children need a teacher that promotes their autonomy not a controlling teacher.

Competency

The second element crucial to self-determination is competency. It was the late Hungarian psychologist Mihaly Csikszentmihalyi who helped us appreciate the role of competency in motivation. Csikszentmihalyi is probably best known for his work around high performance and his discovery of 'flow'. Flow is often characterised by a complete absorption in the task where the individual loses all track of time.

Csikszentmihalyi called these moments 'autotelic experiences' from the Greek *auto* meaning self and *telos* meaning goal or purpose. He suggested that when we are 'in a flow state', the reward is the task itself. It enables us to experience a level of competence and progress toward mastery.

Csikszentmihalyi even conducted a series of experiments to demonstrate just how critical a feeling of competence is to well-being. Having identified areas where individuals experienced flow and a sense of competence, he asked people to remove 'flow' from their daily lives. The results were almost immediate. People became sluggish, started complaining about headaches and had difficulty concentrating. Csikszentmihalyi noted that, "After just two days of flow deprivation ... the general deterioration in mood was so advanced that prolonging the experiment would have been unadvisable."

In other words, without an opportunity to demonstrate competence in anything, even something trivial, we begin to exhibit symptoms that are remarkably similar to serious psychological disorder such as depression. Parents and teachers have a crucial role to play in boosting a child's sense of competence.

Building someone's sense of competence is critical for the current education system but is absolutely vital as we transition to a new system. There is always going to be a stage of incompetency in any change process. Our loss of motivation that results from periods of temporary incompetence make it very easy to give up on the initiative and fall back to old behaviours.

Relatedness

The third element of Deci and Ryan's self-determination theory is relatedness. People need each other, as we discussed in the 'WE' chapters. When we're connected to people we like, respect or care about we are intrinsically motivated.

Think how important relationship bonds are for students when they transition from one school to the next. We organise visits so children, about to start pre-school, can visit their future primary school and be shown around, to ensure the transition goes smoothly. But this rarely happens when children move from primary to secondary school. There are rarely any insights offered about the change to relatedness and motivation that can happen during these transitions. When a child is happy and content in a primary school, but their friends move to a different school, they can be rocked by the experience because they lose their relatedness network. These transitions can also impact their sense of belonging and dent their sense of identity.

When people can express autonomy, competence and relatedness, their level of intrinsic motivation is high and they're more likely to be creative, enthusiastic, productive and vitally engaged (Figure 10.1).

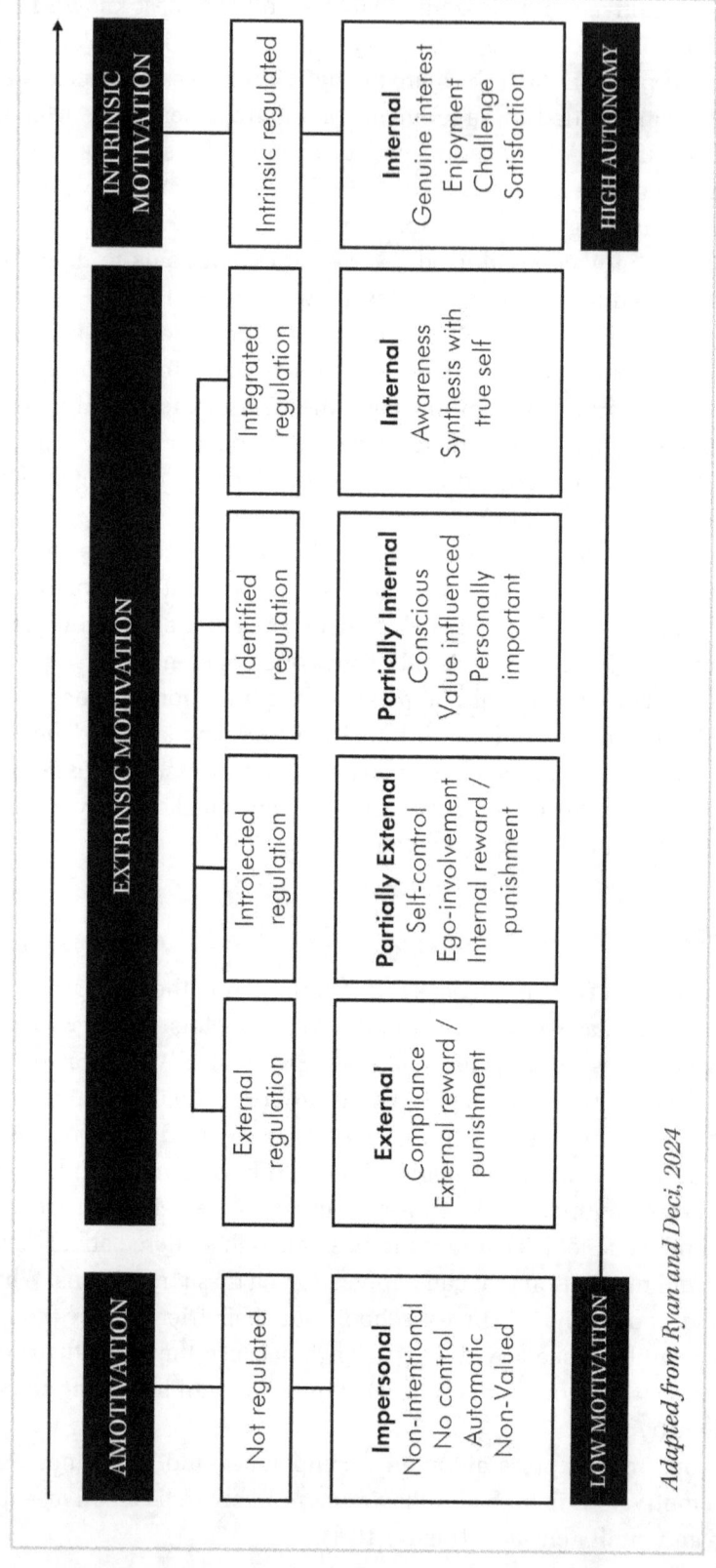

Figure 10.1 Potency of Self Determination Theory

When these needs are inhibited their intrinsic motivation plummets. Our current education system is designed around power, rigidity and individual success. Aggressive competition and the need to demonstrate competence can reduce relatedness. Little wonder then that the current school system isn't full of intrinsically motivated children, and why so many are disengaging.

This more nuanced view is also provided by our understanding of values, as we've discussed throughout this book. The more nuanced approach of evolving value systems allows for individual and collective diversity, the shifting patterns of motivation in different situations, and even the change in our own motivations at different moments in time. An understanding of evolving value systems also provides a very powerful framework to enable us to align different stakeholders and flex how that alignment works as people's values mature. Such understanding is very different to the bluntness of punishment and reward.

When building a better system, we must understand human motivation and ensure the elements of self-determination are present, at all levels, across all stakeholder groups. We must also understand how motivations link to engagement levels.

Engagement Theory

In addition to embracing a more sophisticated understanding of motivation, we need a more mature understanding of engagement. Many people use the terms interchangeably but they're not the same thing. Motivation is the inner drive or ignition for behaviour, whereas engagement is the consequence of motivation. Motivation is personal, engagement infers a relationship to a person, group or task. As such, engagement is often the visible consequence of an invisible motivation.

In the classroom, engagement can be seen in how well pupils learn and develop. Most organisations measure employee engagement because it's known to be highly correlated with performance and productivity. It can also determine a colleague's attitudes and response to change.

Engagement has four parts to it, all of them visible:

1. **Cognitive Engagement:** This sounds like an internal thing, but we mean the visible behaviours that flow from the mental effort that someone puts in when they're cognitively engaged. For example, someone may be cognitively curious, leading them to hunt for an answer to a problem. They search the internet, read a magazine or book, maybe phone a friend. We can observe their seeking behaviour because of their cognitive engagement. Cognitive engagement infers some depth of processing, maybe some strategic thinking, or at the very least the application of cognitive resources to comprehend and master material. Cognitive engagement often drives the development of competence.

2. **Emotional Engagement:** This also sounds like an internal thing. But emotional engagement can be seen in the degree of intensity with which someone

engages with a person or a thing. It manifests in a pupil's or teacher's emotional reactions in the classroom, their level of interest or their expressions of enjoyment. It's often driven by the personal relevance to the content or subject in focus.

3. **Agentic Engagement:** This type of engagement is the trickiest to understand. It relates to free will and our sense of control. If we feel we have sovereignty over ourselves, this is called agency. We can make our own choices. With agentic engagement we choose what we want to pay attention to and connect with. We can take control of our environments. This is strongly related to our sense of autonomy and proactivity.

4. **Behavioural Engagement:** This is the simple observable behaviours and actions we take when we are an active participant in an activity like learning. They are driven by our attitude, values and beliefs.

The agentic part of the puzzle was brought to light by American psychologist Johnmarshall Reeve who pointed out that if individuals didn't feel any sense of control of the outcome, they would naturally disengage, and conversely if they did feel a sense of control, engagement would increase (Figure 10.2). This is vital for learning and development. If pupils feel that learning is being done to them rather than something they choose and are involved in, then we can expect the levels of pupil engagement to be very low. Likewise, if teachers feel put upon by the school inspectors, the school governors or their colleagues then engagement scores will be low.

Sharing preferences, asking questions and communicating their likes, needs and desires to the teacher are all ways students engage in agentic participation. Beyond verbally participating in the classroom, engagement may also show up through one-to-one discussions, student feedback and collaboration. All of which increase connectivity between students and teachers. The same is true for interactions between leaders and staff.

The lack of agentic control over their learning experience was almost certainly one of the key reasons why, in 2022/23, the Office for National Statistics published data showing 22.3% of pupils were thought to be "persistently absent" from school.[7] The Department for Education suggested that this is equivalent to missing 10% or more of possible school sessions or around 19 days per academic year.

Motivation and engagement are particularly challenging in the digital age. The battle for attention often comes down to where the stakeholder feels the most autonomy. At home for example, a young person may have far greater autonomy and agency than they do at school. If their psychological needs are not being met, they will be more motivated to stay home than go to school, particularly when their digital reality is designed to sustain attention. At home they can play video games or scroll social media feeds, where they appear to have almost complete autonomy. Add in some extremely addictive algorithms, delivering dopamine hits every

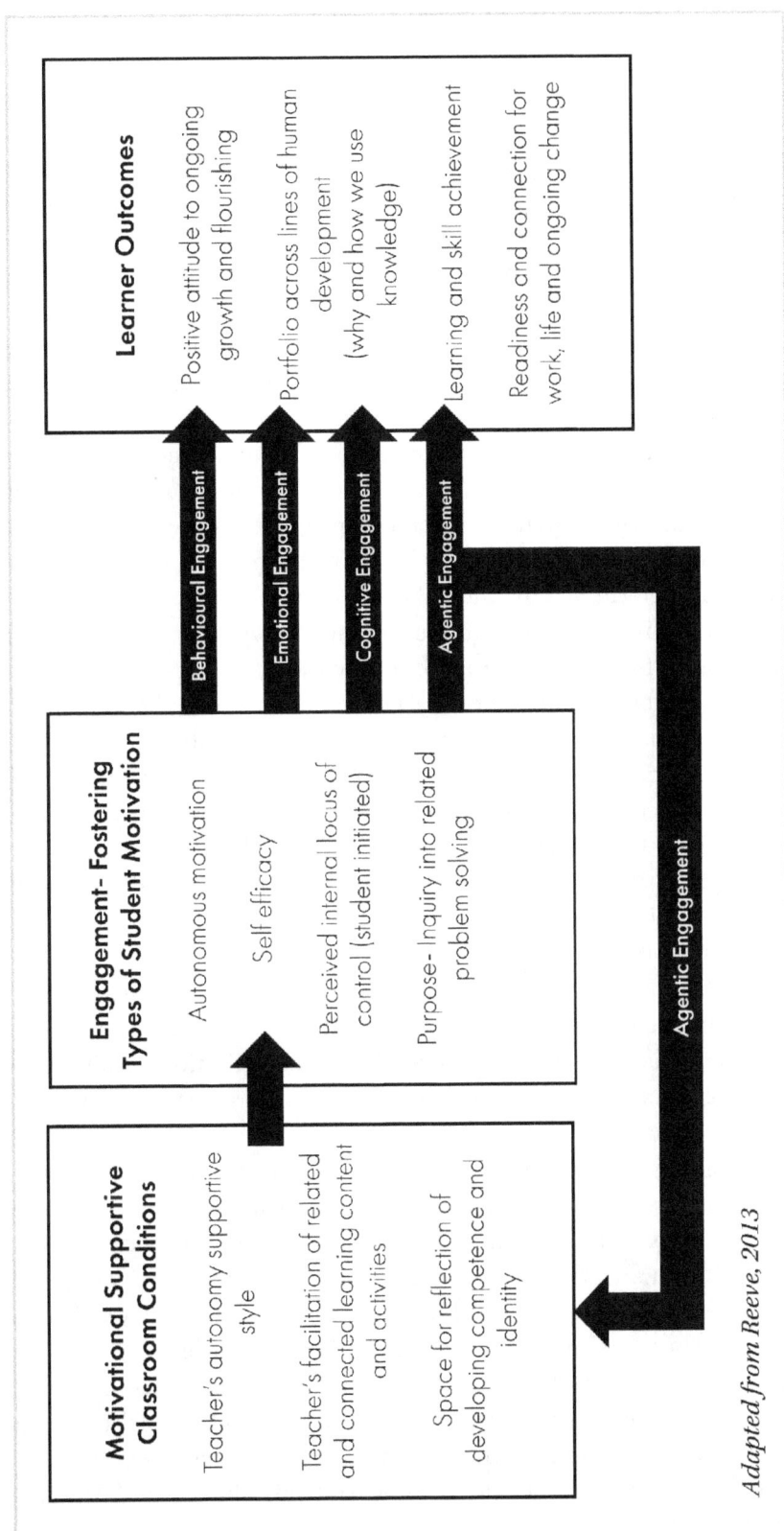

Figure 10.2 Motivation and Engagement in the Classroom for Lifelong Learning Outcomes

couple of minutes and the result is a far more emotionally compelling world than the one they experience at school – the perfect cocktail for school absence.

Of course, it's not all bad. When online gaming, children are often using their initiative to solve problems and they've learnt to adapt so their character or avatar can flourish. They often play with other users all over the world, so they may be exposed to some cross-cultural diversity. They may be part of a gaming community which requires them to participate in diplomatic community building.

But 'in real life' (IRL) their school or home environment may be far less motivating. Children may struggle to generalise any skills they have acquired online into the real world. Not least because real-life demands and relationships are far more complicated. There are few cheat-sheets, and you can't 'Control-Alt-Delete' your way out of your homework or reboot your maths lesson.

The challenge for schools is how do they make the experience engaging enough to keep pupils turning up and help them to build meaningful real-world connections. Fining parents when their kids don't turn up doesn't work. Providing the learners with more agency is also a key part in the process towards becoming self-regulated, self-determined learners.

It's also worth noting that one of the unintended consequences of spending a significant amount of time in a virtual online world is that it distorts children's expectations. Many children, fuelled by energy drinks, may be able to power through several levels of a game, find the treasure and finish a game. In the real world there are no confetti guns going off when they arrive in the classroom. There's no fanfare when they answer a question correctly or solve a problem. There's just the next task. And of course, when those children leave school and enter the workplace, there are no confetti guns there either. Finding or creating something valuable IRL may take years of work but the online world does not foster patience or resilience.

We've heard from employers everywhere that many new recruits believe they should get a fabulously well-paid job while not doing too much, and then be rewarded with significant salary uplifts even if their contribution hasn't improved.

The widening discrepancy between the virtual world and the real world isn't helped by a flurry of social media 'Influencers' pretending they have a dream lifestyle and are making tons of money with little effort. Many influencers fuel the toxic perfectionism we discussed chapter 7, or fear of missing out (FOMO). They create a fantasy built around immediate gratification because YOLO (you only live once). Influencers will constantly push their own artificial world at every turn in case you missed it (ICYMI), designed to up their 'likes' from faceless 'followers'. There are legitimate concerns about the absence of responsibility, particularly from the tech giants that create these platforms, because they drive a superficial comparison culture with fake 'highlight reels' that create a pressure to measure up to an unrealistic standard.[8] The outcome is a widespread quest for social validation rather than truth. And this shift is undermining the very fabric of society.

The education system is in the front-line battle for the minds of the future. If we don't reinvent education and help children to develop the skills they need to flourish in the real world, not in some corporate 'metaverse' designed to line the pockets of the few, we can expect the problems of today to become much worse in the next few years. The good news is that when we understand motivation, engagement and our own development, we can reinvent the system and change the outcome.

Systems Theory

Change in the 'IT' dimension relates to individual behavioural change and also how we go about changing systems. There is little doubt that the education system needs to be reinvented. But this type of change is hard, and it requires us to understand much more about systems theory.

Systems theory is a broad and interdisciplinary framework for understanding, analysing and managing complexity. It originated in the mid-20th century and has since been applied across various fields, including biology, engineering, sociology, psychology, ecology and business management. Education reform is also in urgent need of systemic thinking.

In chapter 2 we looked at examples of educational reform that were working, or at least represented a marked improvement on the mainstream offer. The irony is that we often know how to fix a lot of the issues we face. The problem is we often limit those solutions to pockets of improvement because we rarely think about the system as a whole. People who want to change the system focus on small scale change, be that in their classroom or their school. Whilst understandable, and in most cases commendable, systemic change requires a far greater appreciation for the complexity of the whole system. Tweaking the specifics in a classroom or school is no longer enough. What's required is a much more comprehensive, systematic upgrade across the entire education system itself. And system theory provides a framework for that urgent work.

At its core, systems theory views systems as entities composed of interrelated and interdependent parts that work together to enable common goals or functions to be achieved. These component parts can be physical or abstract, and they may interact with each other and with their environment. There is a tendency in the education system and many other systems to focus on the parts of the system rather than the whole system, whereas systems theory emphasises the relationships, interactions and dynamics within systems rather than focusing solely on individual parts. As such it gives us a valuable framework for reinventing the education system in several ways:

- **Complete Approach:** The education system is complex. There are multiple stakeholders, including students, teachers, administrators, parents, policymakers and the broader community. To reinvent the system, we must understand the system in all its breadth and depth. That means we must consider the interactions and relationships among all the various people and parts of the systems operating at every level of the system rather than focusing on individual elements. By adopting a complete approach, policymakers and educators can address the interconnected challenges facing education more effectively.

- **Interdisciplinary Collaboration:** As we understand the relationship dynamics between all the parts of the system, we must work in a more interdisciplinary way to bridge the gap between the different disciplines and multiple fields of knowledge in the system. We must develop better interdisciplinary collaborative capability and improve our ability to integrate diverse perspectives. This also means specifically and proactively dissolving the silos between subjects and fostering greater collaboration across disciplines. Educators can then create more integrated and meaningful learning experiences for students.

- **Feedback Mechanisms:** A systemic approach requires more thoughtfulness about feedback loops, which are essential for maintaining stability and promoting learning within the education system. Systems theory highlights the importance of both positive and negative feedback mechanisms in driving improvement, adaptation and progress. By establishing effective feedback channels, educators can gather insights from students, parents and other stakeholders to continuously refine and enhance educational practices.

- **Adaptability and Resilience:** Better feedback loops improve a systems' adaptability and more importantly its resilience. This enables a reinvented education system to respond more effectively to changing societal needs, technological advancements and economic shifts. Systems theory also emphasises the importance of self-organisation. This requires a culture of innovation and flexibility. A more innovative mindset means educators can ensure that the education system remains responsive to evolving challenges and opportunities.

- **Equity and Inclusivity:** Systems theory encourages us to be more thoughtful about the distribution of resources, opportunities and outcomes within the education system. This drives greater equity and inclusion, and enables policymakers and educators to more effectively address the systemic barriers and disparities that hinder access to quality education for all students. This may involve restructuring policies, implementing targeted interventions and promoting diversity and inclusion initiatives.

- **Longer-Term Thinking:** Systems theory requires us to take a longer-term perspective and consider the broader implications of educational decisions and interventions on the wider societal system in which that educational system sits. By understanding all the interdependencies of different elements within the education system, policymakers and educators can anticipate potential consequences and design strategies that promote sustainable and equitable outcomes for future generations.

- **Continuous Improvement:** Education systems should embrace a culture of continuous improvement, where stakeholders collaborate to identify challenges, experiment with innovative solutions, and learn from both successes and failures. Systems theory provides a framework for iterative problem-solving and experimentation, allowing educators to adapt practices based on real-time feedback and evidence-based research.

Clearly, systems theory provides a very powerful framework for understanding the complex dynamics of any system which can range from biological to social organisations to ecosystems. By applying systems thinking principles to the education system, researchers, policymakers and practitioners can analyse and intervene effectively, leading to improved decision-making, problem-solving and management strategies. By applying systems thinking principles, education stakeholders can work together to create a more inclusive, resilient and effective education system that meets the needs of diverse learners in the 21st century.

We believe that systems thinking is so important to the future of education that it should also be taught to children as a key school subject. Unless we start to cultivate systemic thinking skills at an early age, the problems in the education system, health care, justice and economic systems will continue to get worse. And this deterioration is largely down to ill-thought out short-term, parochial or partial 'solutions' that make things worse because no one was taking a system-wide view.

We must reinvent the education system to reflect the fact that a system built around knowledge is woefully out of date. Children don't need to rote learn facts and figures and prove their memory skills in an exam. Assuming they have access to a device, they already have immediate 24/7 access to the internet where they can find any piece of knowledge or information they need via their mobile phone. There's little point assessing written essays or reports when teachers already know that ChatGPT has probably done most of the work. While children need some basic level of knowledge on reading, writing and mathematics, what's more urgently needed is a complete paradigm shift to a deliberately developmental education system that prioritises and has at its core a focus on:

1. Critical thinking and root cause analysis

2. Systems theory and systemic problem-solving

3. Creativity

4. Emotional and social intelligence

5. Collaborative capability.

When we reinvent the educational system around these central organising principles, then teachers become more like coaches or educational guides. They can shepherd a child's learning and development. Subjects become much more integrated and focused on interdisciplinary topics that children find interesting and relevant, using frameworks rather than pre-loaded content. Such a reinvention is better placed to equip the next generation with the capabilities they need to flourish in tomorrow's world.

In fact, the shift to a more interdisciplinary educational model is already happening in tertiary education and universities. The Singularity University,[9] founded in 2008 by Peter Diamandis and Ray Kurzweil, builds its programmes around an interdisciplinary focus. Other dedicated institutions have emerged with a similar ethos such as the Ubiquity University,[10] The California Institute of Integral Studies[11] and more recently the London Interdisciplinary School.[12] But an interdisciplinary systems focus isn't just confined to these specialist universities. The mainstream has woken up to this urgent need. Most major academic institutions are developing their credentials in this area. For example:

1. Stanford University offers an Interdisciplinary Graduate Fellowship (SIGF).[13]

2. MIT in its Schwarzman College of Computing aims to integrate computing across all disciplines.[14]

3. Cambridge University has a Centre for the Study of Existential Risk (CSER), which brings together experts from various fields to address global risks.[15]

4. University of California has the Berkeley Interdisciplinary Graduate Fellows Program (BIG), which supports Ph.D. students pursuing interdisciplinary research. It also has interdisciplinary research centres focusing on areas such as energy, health and the environment.[16]

5. University of Tokyo has set up the Interfaculty Initiative in Information Studies and the Integrated Research System for Sustainability Science (IR3S).[17]

6. Zurich School of Technology has established the Zurich Future Cities Laboratory, which explores sustainable urban development through interdisciplinary research.[18]

7. University of Amsterdam fosters interdisciplinary research and education through programmes like the Amsterdam Institute for Social Science Research (AISSR) and the Amsterdam Centre for Law & Economics (ACLE).[19]

This new operating principle centred on development and an interdisciplinary, systems focus is necessitated by the accelerating pace of change over the last 20 years. And if we take an even broader view of societal evolution, the case for reinvention of the education system becomes even more compelling.

This first great leap forward in the sophistication of society happened in about 1760. As discussed in chapter 1, the first industrial revolution saw the emergence of mechanisation, particularly in the textile industry, which literally became 'steam-driven'. With the invention of the steam engine, the power loom and the spinning jenny, society moved from farm to factory, from a craft-based economy to a manufacturing economy.

This first revolution lasted about 100 years and was followed by the second industrial revolution, which started in about 1850 and ran for another 100 years. It was powered by the widespread adoption of electricity. We saw the development of the telegraph and telephone, the expansion of railroads connecting towns and cities, and advances in steel production. Central to this second great leap forward was the assembly line and mass production techniques. Such were the benefits to society, especially between and after the world wars, that the efficiencies of the factory were translated into the educational system. We started to teach children in aged-defined batches. They were moved along the assembly line of the education system to deliver citizens ready for factory work. Our current educational system still largely operates on the same system today.[20]

The third industrial revolution started in about 1970 but this one was more digital than industrial. The age of computing had arrived, and this revolution was accelerated by the invention of the internet or Web1. These were the hypertext transfer protocols (http); file transfer protocols (ftp), that emerged with the world wide web (www). There was a new hypertext markup language (html), allowing us to locate and communicate with static web pages using a uniform resource locator (url). We saw the emergence of simple mail transfer protocols (smtp) enabling us to email each other at our unique internet protocol (ip) addresses. The digital acceleration created by the third industrial revolution's Web1 was then amplified by Web2. This created all the software and Apps that run on the new train tracks of the internet. For example, Web2 delivered blogs, Wikis, APIs, social media, cloud computing, e-commerce. The big plot twist in Web2 was the mobile phone. Mobile phones created mass scale distribution of knowledge, democratised access to all this knowledge and connected people in new ways that had been impossible just a decade earlier.

The impact of increased connectivity, driven by the internet, is clearly visible when we consider speed of adoption between the various industrial revolutions. For example, the second industrial revolution's technology, like the telephone, took 50 years to reach 50 million users, electricity 46 years and television 22 years. In contrast technology in the third industrial revolution like the PC took just 14 years to reach 50 million users and the internet just seven years. Connectivity exploded with the emergence of the smart phones which allowed various platforms to flourish. YouTube reached 50 million users in four years, Facebook took three years and Twitter took just two to reach 50 million users.[21] And ChatGPT surpassed 50 million users in its first month of release.[22] Each version is more sophisticated than the last and there is simply no way to put that particular genie back in the bottle. It was ChatGPT that triggered the AI boom we are currently living through (2024).

In this information age it's not surprising that the school systems attempted to double down on learning and the dissemination of knowledge. If we are operating in a knowledge economy, where knowledge is power, the system needs to graduate knowledge workers to feed this knowledge economy.

Of course, the problem with this entire narrative is the speed at which knowledge advances and often becomes obsolete. By 1982, as discussed in chapter 1, knowledge was doubling every 12 to 13 months. And today it's every 12 hours, possibly faster. Even experts can't keep up. Even if an expert knew everything in their field, within a week their knowledge base is reduced to less than one percent of what is known within their own area of expertise. Expertise is dead as a way of creating advantage and certainly as an organising principle of the modern education system.

Clearly, the current education system, based on the 19th century factory system of the second industrial revolution, has now been overtaken by the technology of the third industrial revolution. Knowledge doubling renders that approach pointless, particularly as the third industrial revolution has given way to the fourth industrial revolution. The fourth industrial revolution is a term coined in 2016 at the World Economic Forum as AI and the internet of things (IoT) gripped the imagination.

Since we've already moved beyond a knowledge economy, we believe the case for a new educational operating principle is overwhelming. And, as we suggested earlier, this new principle must be development, not learning. Not least because the massive acceleration we've seen because of Web2 is only going to increase as Web2 is replaced by Web3 technology[23] and Web4 beyond that.

Web3 basically reinvents the rail tracks on which the digital age is built. Its impact will be even greater than the impact of the internet. There are several critical Web3 technologies, which have already emerged, that will make an already outdated educational system seem positively prehistoric. The first is blockchain technology.

Introduced in 2009 by someone under the pseudonym Satoshi Nakamoto, Bitcoin was the first successful implementation of blockchain technology. Since then, numerous blockchain projects and cryptocurrencies have emerged, each with its own features and functionality. One of the most promising is Ethereum (ETH). While both Bitcoin and Ethereum offer the use of digital money without payment providers, third-party intermediaries or banks, Ethereum offers far more flexibility.[23] Although the only thing the Bitcoin blockchain can record is Bitcoin transactions, this lack of functionality makes it very secure – ideal for a new currency. But Ethereum was the world's first *programmable blockchain*. It is a decentralised, open-source blockchain platform that enables the creation and deployment of self-executing smart contracts where the terms of the agreement are written directly into the code. These contracts are then automatically executed when predefined conditions are met or allowed to lapse when those conditions are not met.

The idea of blockchain is already disrupting many systems and organisations around the world, including education. It's disrupting monetary systems with the emergence of crypto currencies. As monetary systems change the way education systems are financed will also need to change. In addition to monetary system disruption, blockchain is also disrupting knowledge and the ability to verify information. In fact, one of the great benefits of blockchain technology is its ability to verify things – clearly an important issue to rectify in a post-truth world.

The world we now live in is unrecognisable to the one we occupied just 30 years ago. The internet changed everything, and it's been an explosive advance ever since. The world our children will grow up in and the one our grandchildren will grow up in is almost impossible to imagine. And yet we are teaching children as though it were still the 20th century! We urgently need behavioural, developmental and systemic change.

Notes

1. Pink DP (2011) Drive: the surprising truth about what motivates us, Canongate, London. Kohn A (1999) Punished by rewards: the trouble with gold stars, incentive plans, a's, praise, and other bribes.
2. Lepper MR, Greene D (2015) The hidden costs of reward: new perspectives on the psychology of human motivation, Psychology Press, London.
3. Pink DP (2011) Drive, Canongate, London.
4. Brickman P, Campbell DT (1971) Hedonic relativism and planning the good society, Academic Press, New York.
5. Johnson BC, Manyika JM, Yee LA (2005) The next revolution in interactions, McKinsey Quarterly Nov 1.
6. Ryan RM, Deci EL (2000) Self-determination theory and the facilitation of intrinsic motivation, social development, and well-being, American Psychologist.
7. No Author (2023) Pupil absence in schools in England, UK Gov.
8. Watkins A, Jones S (2023) Lie-ability: how leaders build and break trust, Routledge, London.
9. https://www.su.org/.
10. https://www.ubiquityuniversity.org/.
11. https://www.ciis.edu/.
12. https://www.lis.ac.uk/.
13. https://vpge.stanford.edu/fellowships-funding/sigf.
14. Reif LR (2018) A step into the future: The MIT Stephen A. Schwarzman College of Computing Letters to the MIT Community.
15. https://www.cser.ac.uk/.
16. https://isf.ugis.berkeley.edu/fellowships-and-scholarships/.
17. https://www.u-tokyo.ac.jp/en/academics/grad_interdisciplinary.html.
18. https://fcl.ethz.ch/.
19. https://aissr.uva.nl/?cb.
20. Robinson K (2010) RSA animate: changing education paradigms, YouTube.
21. Cook GC (2022) Web3: the end of business as usual, Whitefox, London.
22. Cerullo M (2023) ChatGPT is growing faster than TikTok, CBS News.
23. Cook GC (2022) Web3, Whitefox, London.

Behaviour and Systems Development in Practice

Throughout this book we've made the case for putting development not knowledge, at the heart of the education system of the future. To enable this to happen, many of the structures and processes within a school need to change. This starts with restructuring teacher training, moving away from topic-based training to include a much more sophisticated understanding of a child's physical, cognitive, emotional and social development. If teachers are expected to adapt the curriculum to the individual child, they need to know how to assess that child's developmental level, and how to support that child to level up.

Many teachers already understand some of this. For example, as mentioned in chapter 4, when toddlers enter school for the first time, some of them are not yet mature enough to understand the concept of ownership. This is why it's possible to witness a five-year-old 'steal' their classmate's pencil and then flatly deny the 'crime'. They will claim the pencil is 'mine' even when it clearly isn't. This isn't deceitful, it's developmental. Some five-year-olds are only just beginning to develop an understanding of possession and the importance of sharing.

Another example would be that a six-year-old thinks in very literal terms.[1] This is because the nerve tracks in the front part of their brain are not fully myelinated. In contrast, a 12-year-olds brain can operate at much higher speeds because it is fully myelinated. Faster brain speeds enable a 12-year-old to engage in abstract thinking. This means you can teach them algebra. It would be pointless trying to teach most six-year-olds algebra because their brains aren't physically developed enough to cope with letters and numbers in the same equation. A six-year-old could sit in front of a simple algebraic problem all day and still decide the answer is 'my shoe', whereas a 12-year-old could solve the problem in ten seconds. This is a perfect example of how, when you level up, capabilities emerge that enable much greater speed and the ability to handle greater complexity.

Key Stage 1 and 2 SATs would be much more useful if we included an assessment of developmental level rather than simply inferring a level of knowledge transfer from a child's SATs score in reading, writing, maths and science. Falsely assuming children to be less intelligent because they do badly in such tests is unfair, especially then the real issue may be that they just haven't matured yet. Given we age-batch children through school it's common for the August babies, who are usually the youngest in the year, to be at a disadvantage compared to children born later in the year, who may be nearly 12 months older.

Surely the goal of teaching should be to pay attention to the developmental level of the child and then help that child to mature rather than just acquire knowledge. This changes how classrooms are set up. Batching children according to developmental level rather than age would probably be much more compassionate and much less likely to create a stigmatisation of less 'able' children, who are simply less mature. Children at different levels of maturity learn at different speeds. If this was included in the way we set the system up, we might be able to reduce the risk of labelling children as 'slow learners'. Children would learn at a pace that's more suitable for their level of development and more aligned with their needs relevant to this stage.

When teaching the foundations of any subject the curriculum should be adapted to focus on the mastery of the basic rules or principles of that subject before progressing to more complex rules. This is exactly how the human mind develops. But in many schools, there's a drive to 'get through' the curriculum, even if the content doesn't land. Children are often moved on before they've understood the rules of an earlier level. This is the equivalent of building the fourth floor of a high rise before the structural integrity of the third floor has been checked. No structural engineer would advocate such a thing, but that's often what happens in school because the system provides no other choice other than 'catch up'. No wonder then that after 14,000 hours in school from the age of 5 to 16 years that 25% of 15-year-olds have a reading age of 12 or below; 20% a reading age of 11 or below, and 10% a reading age of 9 or below. Such developmental delays are often spotted much earlier. One study showed that 24% of its students enter Year 7 (age 13) with a reading age of only five years old.[2] At age 15 years, 53% of girls have a reading age of 15 and higher, compared to only 47% of boys. By comparison the average reading age of the UK population is 9 years old.[3]

Making sure children don't progress to the next level before they've understood the previous level minimises the risk of a collapse in understanding, leading to a fatal disengagement with the curriculum and learning throughout life as children feel out of their depth. Ensuring learning is consolidated at each level before we attempt to progress is a foundational principle of the Khan Academy, which from its inception in 2008 now has more than 150 million registered users in 190 countries in the world.

Direct instruction is useful to start the education process off and create a solid foundation but as the learner makes sense of the world, the need for scaffolding or direct instruction should diminish. Instead, young people do better when they can self-determine their learning alongside a guide- known as Heutagogy. We are not pitching for this to be a constant, but if the Montessori method facilitates learners making choices at an incredibly young age, we know it is possible for learners to maintain a sense of agency throughout their journey. This more adaptive and fluid learning approach is not just more engaging for the learner, but it is essential in the face of a constant state of flux and 24-hour access to the internet that can tell any learner how to do anything anyway!

Plus, if we maintain this traditionalist direct instruction scaffolding throughout school, the learners are not prepared for life beyond school when there is no scaffolding at all. This is often why we see so many disenchanted young people drop out of university or regress as employees in the workforce. Shifting away from only teaching knowledge around subjects to at least including the teaching of capabilities such as creativity, critical thinking or reflection, collaboration and communication would also be timeless. And these capabilities would be of far greater use in the wider world than knowledge about soil structure or how to ask the way to the swimming pool in French. They would be used daily in a young person's life as they navigate work, relationships, friendships and the normal ups and downs of human existence because they can question 'why' and consider 'how' as part of their decision making.

Of course, if we look at changes to teaching methods, it's already exhausting, largely due to the global education reform movement or GERM, mentioned in chapter 2. Adopted as an educational reform orthodoxy since the 1980s, GERM advocates for at least five globally common features of education policies and reform principles:

- Standardisation of education
- Focus on core subjects
- Search for low-risk ways of reaching learning goals
- Use of corporate management models and
- Test-based accountability policies

These have been increasingly employed to try to improve the quality of education and fix the apparent problems in public education systems. All of which have spawned endless initiatives of how teachers should now teach. Although each one promises to revolutionise results, they are usually short term, PISA driven initiatives that do little beyond increasing teacher turnover. Teachers are leaving the profession in alarming numbers – and with this endless shifting of the educational goalposts, it's little wonder. Humans do not respond well to change or excessive top-down control.

Besides, no behaviour is really being changed, except greater disengagement from students and resignations from teachers. No one is asking or involving the stakeholders in these changes, and the same can be said for all the stakeholders in the education system. GERM for example is often promoted through the interests of international development agencies and private enterprises through their interventions in national education reforms and policy formulation.[4] But was a single teacher or student even asked for their input?

Such poorly thought through attempts at transformation go to the heart of motivation and engagement. As human beings we are always far more interested and invested in change or initiatives that we had a hand in designing and are bigger than us. This is why direct instruction is so futile in the modern world – there is no autonomy, a crucial ingredient in both motivation and engagement. We need a far more open, fluid way to teach that gives more autonomy back to the learners *and* the teachers, so the learners have a say in what they learn and why. The teachers become more like conductors of an orchestra where they play to the strengths of the students in front of them. This will also increase the sense of competence and relatedness, the two other component parts needed for motivation to flourish.

The current education system is limited in the understanding of motivation and engagement across any stakeholder group and that must change. Only when it does, and each stakeholder group is involved and consulted about the change and help to design it will we be able to tap into the far more powerful intrinsic motivation and maintain high engagement levels.

Designing Motivation and Engagement into the Solution

If individuals are aware of their own intrinsic motivations, what they value (and how this matures) and understand that others may have alternative views that we can tap into, then the healthy tension of different views, that fosters innovation, is much more likely to enable these individuals to drive the solutions themselves. Self Determination Theory (SDT) helps us to craft more motivating and engaging solutions for the individual, team or the system. Individuals can then tap into existing competency, and cultivate relatedness and some level of autonomy to help with their role or the task in question. This applies to all stakeholders.

The good news is that a lot of the insights needed to drive better engagement and motivation will already have been flushed out during the 'I' and 'WE' development work. For example, the values profile provides insights on what each person in the team values and how they interact (relatedness) with their teammates. This helps recruit the right people into the role and team at the right time based on their values as described in chapter 9, enhancing the standard talent assessment processes most organisations run.

A talent audit to identify stakeholder interests and passions can also help when distributing accountabilities. Giving people the option to volunteer according to the audit, competencies and value systems provides a sense of autonomy in what they do and how they do those tasks or roles rather than simply being instructed. There is always a balance to be struck between tapping into existing competency and allowing an individual to grow in an area they're interested in but may not yet have developed their abilities.

You may remember in chapter 9, when Adam's leadership team each chose a strategic objective, they wanted to lead; the individual's choice was always based on that person's level of existing competence and what motivated them as identified via the values profile and a talent audit. This activated their sense of autonomy. Each leader nominated a project coach, who was someone with the relevant knowledge or experience in that area, further increasing their sense of competence and relatedness. The appointment of a right-hand and left-hand person to support them in implementation and delivery also increased relatedness. All of this increased the leader or captain's sense of support.

When designing 'IT'/'ITS' solutions, the key aspects to consider are:

- **Sense of Purpose:** As much as possible, all activities must be aligned to each individual's sense of purpose to make that activity meaningful.

- **Connection with Others:** Ensuring greater interdependence and collaboration is necessary for task completion, as well as encouraging some social interactions reduces any sense of isolation and the propensity to feel overwhelmed.

- **Positive Emotions:** Designing tasks that can trigger positive emotions, such as joy, gratitude and a sense of accomplishment is key to maintaining momentum. Positive emotions are key to overall well-being and resilience, especially when workloads are high. Recognising key events with high emotions also support memory as we timeline our learning to make sense of it (why can we not remember much about Covid lockdown?).

- **Motivation and Engagement:** Meaningful activities are often intrinsically motivating and increase engagement and a sense of flow.

Designing education solutions with motivation and engagement in mind has yielded significant benefits. For example, research by Frédéric Guay on the application of SDT in education, showed that solutions with autonomous motivation had more positive consequences for students and predicted better school outcomes. Increasing a sense of competence, autonomy and relatedness also increased parental and teacher fulfilment.[5]

When pupils were more intrinsically motivated to do their work, it enabled teachers to focus on teaching rather than relentlessly trying to get pupils to engage.

Schools as DAOs and DDOs

When looking around the world to see how other complex systems are changing, either within an educational context or outside, two models are worth considering that may help us understand how to design schools for the future. These are

Decentralised Autonomous Organisations (DAOs) and Deliberately Developmental Organisations (DDOs).

DAOs emerged because of Web3 blockchain technology. In a DAO, decision-making processes are encoded into smart contracts and executed autonomously without the need for traditional hierarchical management structures. For DAOs to work well, governance must be decentralised and collective decision-making is required. Pulling this off in practice requires careful facilitation to unlock the inherent wisdom of the crowd.[6]

DAOs lock in and protect the integrity of information within the blockchain. Once the information is inside the blocks and connected to the blockchain, it's impossible to change or contaminate that information. This creates a transparent and tamper-resistant record of ownership, record keeping and cybersecurity. Blockchains deliver much greater levels of 'interoperability', leading to cross-chain communication. Such ideas are leveraged by the specialist universities already mentioned in the last chapter, such as the Singularity University,[7] the Ubiquity University,[8] the Californian Institute for Integral Studies[9] and the newly formed London Interdisciplinary School.[10]

Blockchain driven education is fundamentally different from the red brick or the 'Russel Group' of universities. Knowledge is more tokenised and can use NFTs, and gamification as a central teaching methodology. DAOs and blockchains will contribute significantly to change the face of a reinvented educational system not least because the gaming industry is already worth more than double the film and music industry combined. Blockchains may also decimate the supply of teachers and talent to the educational system.[11]

DAOs have their rules or 'articles of association' and 'shareholder/stakeholder agreements' coded into a smart contract using a platform such as the Ethereum network. There is no management structure, board of trustees, employees or shareholders in the typical sense. Instead, membership is recorded on the blockchain, and members meet via chat apps like Discord and vote to govern decisions. Joining a DAO is signalled by 'financial cooperation' in the form of tokens, via a crypto wallet which provides members with owner's tokens, which correspond to voting rights.[12] The more tokens someone owns, the more voting power in the DAO. Smart contracts determine deliverables between various stakeholders, including teachers, leaders, students and employers who are all incentivised to participate.

In education, this could translate to token rewards for students who excel in their studies, contribute to open-source resources or the evolution of the school itself. NFTs (non-fungible tokens) could be awarded for student's participation in local community initiatives. This could create a more dynamic and engaging learning environment. DAOs could help develop a more decentralised systems for credentialing and certifying students and teachers. Instead of relying solely on traditional institutions, individuals could earn credentials through a distributed network of validators within a DAO. This might help in recognising a broader range of skills and experiences. They could facilitate the creation and maintenance of educational platforms. These platforms could be owned and governed by the community itself. This would deliver a more tailored and responsive learning experience. All participants could have a direct say in the platform's features, content and policies.

Multiple educational DAOs could pool resources and allocate funds based on community decisions. In education, this could mean crowdfunding initiatives for educational projects, scholarships or infrastructure improvements. It could democratise the funding process and direct resources to areas that need them the most.

DAOs also operate a decentralised and transparent governance model. In education, this could mean that decisions about curricula, policies and resource allocation are made collectively by stakeholders, including students, teachers, employers and administrators. Instead of big employers lobbying government for changes to the education system so that young people leave school with skills that are pertinent to that employer, the employers may simply be part of the DAO and seek to encourage participation in the community. This could lead to more inclusive and democratic decision-making processes or specific pathways for students into employment.

One of the greatest disruptions that educational DAOs could deliver could be a transnational collaboration, without the need for a centralised authority such as government. DAO schools and trusts could collaborate globally on research projects, shared educational resources and cross-cultural learning experiences. Students and educators from different parts of the world could collaborate seamlessly.

Another disruptive Web3 technology has impacted student identity by changing something called 'self-sovereign identity' (SSI). This is where users have much greater control over their own identity without having to rely on centralised authorities. We're already seeing this impact from those who own the data that computer systems or organisations have on us. We're moving to a world where personalised data are owned (and possibly traded) by the individual rather than by centralised authorities. In Web2 the mantra was 'if the service is free, you are the product', in Web3 and beyond the mantra is 'play-to-earn' or 'play-to-learn'.[13]

This data ownership is key to the verification of a teacher and a student's qualifications, their test results and frankly any demographic or personal data that are relevant to their future employment.

Perhaps the most well-known Web3 disruption is generative AI (GenAI) and the use of large language models (LLMs) and natural language processing (NLP), which enhance the human-computer interface. Of these, Open AI's release of Chat GPT4 has already transformed education. An increasing number of students are using it to do their homework or as an online tutor. And an increasing number of teachers are using it to mark homework. And it's already significantly disrupting a student's employability with many organisations now refusing to employ juniors unless they can add more value than ChatGPT – and many can't!

Beyond basic subject comprehension, which students will still need, the information that students have acquired in the current system can become outdated or rendered irrelevant by new insights, new understandings or new ways of knowing. And given the knowledge doubling rate, it's impossible for anyone to keep up. Technologies such as ChatGPT make an IQ of 120 on any subject available to any pupil or teacher already. This lessens the need to retain such information in our own minds.

The disruption and speed of change driven by the fourth industrial revolution requires us to change the focus from *what* we know to *how* we know it. From the absorption and interrogation of information to being able to make meaning from that information. This is the only way we can protect ourselves from the speed of change and the evolution of knowledge. This means all schools and educational establishments should become Deliberately Developmental Organisations (DDOs), where stakeholder development is the central operating principle, not knowledge transfer.

A deliberately developmental organisation (DDO) is a concept introduced by Robert Kegan.[14] It is an organisational model that prioritises the growth and development of all the stakeholders as a central part of its mission and operations.

Key characteristics of a DDO include:

- **Continuous Development and Growth:** In a DDO, development rooted in learning is not just an occasional activity, but a constant process integrated into the daily work environment. Stakeholders are encouraged to continuously develop more sophisticated skills, perspectives and capacities.

- **Feedback Culture:** Feedback is not only welcomed but actively sought in a DDO. All stakeholders receive honest and constructive feedback on their performance, allowing them to identify areas for improvement and how to accelerate their development and personal growth even more.

- **Transparency and Vulnerability:** DDOs cultivate an environment where individuals feel safe being vulnerable and sharing their challenges and failures openly, after all this is a sign of a mature individual. This fosters trust and deeper connections among team members and the wider school community.

- **Shared Responsibility for Development:** In a DDO, everyone is responsible for their own development as well as the development of others. Teachers and school leaders play a crucial role in supporting and facilitating the growth of their students and fellow team members.

- **Purpose-Driven Work:** Stakeholders in a DDO are aligned with the school or Trust's mission and values, and they find meaning and fulfilment in their work. This purpose serves as a guiding force that drives individual and collective growth.

- **Experimentation and Innovation:** DDOs encourage experimentation and innovation, recognising that failure is an essential part of the development process. Stakeholders are empowered to take risks and explore new ideas without fear of reprisal.

The goal of a deliberately developmental organisation is to create an environment where personal and professional growth are not only encouraged but integral to the organisation's success. By investing in the development of its students, teachers, leaders, governors and other stakeholders, a DDO aims to create a culture of continuous improvement, adaptability and resilience. The good news is that personal development already exists in the Ofsted handbook, it's just not considered significant. But imagine the impact on leadership, behaviour and the quality of education if we made development central to the future. It would be the catalyst for an incredible transformation.

If we focus on how to interpret information rather than just the knowledge itself, then we can stay ahead of the game. And that means focusing on our children's development. On their ability to interpret what they are experiencing and reading. One of the key signs that we are maturing is that we can generate more sophisticated interpretations of the information in front of us. This is what we should assess, develop and reward in schools. Children should get an 'A', not for their ability to remember facts and regurgitate them under exam conditions. They should get an 'A' for the sophistication of their interpretation of the information presented to them or their ability to interrogate that information to determine its veracity. And how to apply it and then adapt it.

In summary, we must reinvent the education system and put development at its heart. We must cultivate our ability to make better sense of information and become meaning makers not knowledge jockeys. The fourth industrial revolution can help us. Educators everywhere must wake up to this fact if we are to deliver an educational system that prepares our children for the future.

Notes

1 Day J (2006) Children believe everything you say: creating self-esteem with children, Element Books, London.
2 Quigley A (n.d.) READ ALL ABOUT IT: Why reading is key to GCSE success, GL Assessment.
3 Jackman P (2019) The average reading age is . . ., Guerillaworking.com.
4 Sahlberg P (2012) Global educational reform movement is here!, Pasisahlberg.com.
5 Guay F (2022). Applying self-determination theory to education: regulations types, psychological needs, and autonomy supporting behaviors, Canadian Journal of School Psychology, 37(1), 75–92.
6 Watkins A, Stratenus (2016) Crowdocracy: the end of politics, Urbane Publications, London.

7 https://www.su.org/
8 https://www.ubiquityuniversity.org/
9 https://www.ciis.edu/
10 https://www.lis.ac.uk/
11 Cook GC (2022) Web3: the end of business as usual, Whitefox, London.
12 Ibid.
13 Ibid.
14 Kegan R, Lahey LL (2016) An everyone culture: becoming a deliberately developmental organization, Harvard Business Review Press, Boston.

12 Behaviour and Systems Development in Action

When it comes to documenting change across the various dimensions, it becomes next to impossible to tease out what is an 'I' change from a 'WE' or 'IT'/'ITS' change. They are interconnected and interdependent aspects of life. And we can see this clearly when looking at what happened with Adam and his team.

Most of what we will recap on here we mentioned in chapter 9, because of the interconnected and interdependent nature of change. There was a huge uplift in motivation and engagement within the team, not only because they were given tools to understand themselves better and appreciate the differences in the team, but they were then able to use those insights to choose what strategic objectives they wanted to be involved in. They could either volunteer as 'captain' or in a support role as either right-hand or left-hand person or coach, where they perhaps had experience and knowledge to share but didn't want to get involved in delivery. All of which tapped into SDT and their intrinsic need for autonomy, competence and relatedness to feel genuinely motivated.

And of course, this motivation was infectious. Because the leadership team was beginning to kick goals and were excited and enthusiastic about the work they were doing, the school cascaded these skills and insights to the wider staff team. Taking each teacher through the same developmental approach to help them understand who they were, what gives them energy and how to better align their values with their roles created much greater levels of engagement. Everyone in the school understood the concept of 'lines of development', and a professional development system was put into place, alongside the existing performance management system. And a coaching network helped to facilitate people's journeys towards their goals. As a result, a coaching culture emerged and specific training around staff's own values has led to shifts in their curriculum framework, pedagogical approaches, and behaviour management strategies.

The staff audit also allowed staff to share their professional backgrounds and experiences inside and outside of education, as well as interests and hobbies. These data were then used to get the right people working on the right projects, in areas they could deliver value in or brought them joy. Remember John, the deputy head, his past knowledge and experience led to the creation of a coaching model for Early Career Teachers which helped new teachers transition into the school culture. Sarah, another deputy head, started pioneering research into the impact of having a deliberately developmental approach to early career teaching.

Adam's school was already considered 'Outstanding' by Ofsted before the developmental work but the school itself, it's culture and systems were transformed by the collective efforts. Staff turnover reduced even further and there was real energy and passion running through the corridors. The school is in the process of creating an outreach offer where parents and other members of the community can access adult learning, which also includes some subtle development tools such as emotional regulation which can help them to navigate family life.

As Adam unlocked his Yellow values level, he spent more time on strategy. This became one of the strongest assets of the school. The school started to see itself as a research hub and operated as such. This changed Adam's approach to the new build the school was embarking on, and he promoted the development of a digital classroom as a model for developing best practice, nationally thus disseminating their learnings to help others. And finally, he stepped back from teaching maths and now delivers training regionally on the principles behind developmental system design, knowing that his team is in place when he's offsite and that they're more than capable of running the school in his absence.

A SEND Case Study

We've tested virtually every aspect of the interventions shared in this book in schools all over the UK and other parts of the world, over the last 20 years. We've seen the incredible impact even parts of the 'I', 'WE' and 'IT'/'ITS' recipe can have in the primary, secondary and tertiary arms of the education system on children, teachers, parents and virtually all key stakeholders in the system.

In this section we would like to demonstrate the flexibility of this approach by sharing some of Matt's astonishing results using the ideas and tools outlined in this book when he was head teacher at Shaftsbury High School, a SEND school. If mainstream schools are suffering at the hands of an outdated system, then that distress is amplified ten-fold in SEND schools where resources are stretched even further and engagement is notoriously low.

The point here is to emphasise the impact that is possible when you reinvent the system, and that reinvention can occur in any type of school or educational environment even within the existing system. What follows is just one specific example, to clarify how 'IT' changes can be implemented.

When Matt took over, Shaftsbury was running a traditional secondary curriculum model with 175 students from 11–19 years old. Needs ranged from Autistic

Spectrum Disorder (39%) to Moderate Learning Difficulties (41%) and social, emotional, mental health (19%) including students with complex needs. Only a very small number of students achieved an academic outcome that led to either employment or further education without having to take 'catch up' courses.

Students attending this SEND school didn't typically go on to higher academic study, so the purpose of their education was somewhat different to a mainstream school. It's worth pointing out that even in a non-SEND school, there are countless students who will also not go on to higher academic study. The idea that SEND-students are somehow less than those who go onto further education or that SEND-students won't or can't be of value or find meaning in their lives is incredibly discriminatory and simply not true. A definition of ability and potential that is too narrow, in SEND and in mainstream schools is robbing students of access to meaning, resilience and of learning how to flourish in life and within their communities.

As we have said many times through this book, it's incredibly hard to make any change unless you start with the individuals who will be expected to make the change. For Matt that involved his own development, his 'I' dimension, and then work with his team in the 'WE' dimension as discussed in earlier chapters. The key take aways from that developmental work for Matt were:

1. Understanding the raw physiological data his body was providing, but he was not tracking and shifting the whole school timetable to better manage their energy and emotions.

2. Being able to understand his own values lens and why perceptions of his leadership changed for different people. This acknowledgement of difference helped to dissolve resistance and fine-tune roles and responsibilities so all stakeholders could flourish.

3. The ability to listen at a much deeper level and rapidly find the true meaning behind what was being said (or not), whether that was with stakeholders or the voices of his own internal narrative. This transformed his change management and created much greater buy-in across key nodes of his network and far beyond the school gates.

4. The first three insights quickly mapped into how he led and listened, and Matt became more compassionate. Instead of worrying that his new approach was wrong, he simply focused on communicating it more clearly, using other people's values level. It also ensured a digital communication and coaching culture was modelled and the quality of interaction with all stakeholders facilitated a shared experience and nurtured true behaviour shifts.

5. How to manage change, engaging the whole community in setting a developmental purpose, vision and culture for the organisation over a five-year period. The clarity of this plan and the alignment it created meant the significant

changes were finished two years ahead of schedule and the buy-in came organically from the middle of the school.

For Matt, step changing how the leadership team functioned also set the stage for the incredible progress the school subsequently made. Collective clarity in the leadership team on big picture thinking, as outlined in chapter 8, was absolutely crucial.

Having spent some time looking at his own development, Matt, like Adam, encouraged his leadership team to embrace their own development. They had noticed differences in Matt's behaviour, outlook and communication style and this increased their engagement with the idea of becoming a DDO from the start. Sponsorship by the leader is just as vital in schools as it is in business, and without a personal commitment to change little happens. Matt's team felt they had autonomy and choice about how they engaged and what parts of the programme would work for them individually and collectively. This helped step change their own motivation whilst creating a collective energy behind the change cycle.

Nearly all developmental journeys start with clarifying where the team is going. This meant creating a collective vision for the school. Amazingly this was something the school had never done before. Vision describes the future world the team wishes to create. It answers the question 'where' are we going. Vision must not be confused with purpose (why), strategy (what), governance (who and how) or ambition (when we get there how big will we be).

Shaftesbury's leadership team's vision was to create a world where the school was 'carving pathways into employment'. This was logically and emotionally motivating for the staff, given that only 5.7% of adults with learning disabilities and an educational health care plan ever find employment after school in the UK.[1]

In defining what needs to happen to deliver that vision, the team also identified a series of high-level strategic objectives. Specifically, they recognised that they must:

1. build a curriculum and culture framework that fosters intrinsic motivation and the character required to develop,

2. achieve academically and socially in education and beyond it,

3. define real pathways for students where they could flourish in social or employment roles.

These answers were created by the leadership team rather than being handed down from Matt. The team arrived at them through consultation in and out of the school, and created an ongoing learner focus group rather than having those strategic objectives inflicted on them by the school, local government or because of a change in central policy. Top-down approaches rarely work and fly in the face of motivation theory. If those impacted by the vision are not involved or consulted, it simply amplifies the lack of clarity in the system. We have seen so many examples of schools or businesses that have some definition of vision, ambition, purpose, strategy and governance, but if the senior stakeholders haven't been involved in the creation of these answers, then they remain nice words on the annual report or displayed as a strap line on email signatures but nothing changes. Such outputs don't act as a North Star in the organisation.

What often happens in most systems is a handful of people often with good intention, who are interested or want to make a difference cluster around pet projects, scrimp and scrape for funding and design a project or two. Then they try to make them happen and hope the work sticks.

What Matt did at Shaftsbury was the antithesis of that. He took a systematic approach where the leadership team made sure they aligned what people did consciously to the vision, ambition, purpose and top-line strategy that the school community had collectively decided was worth pursuing.

The leadership team also involved their key stakeholders, the children, in designing their collective future together. In any SEND school there is a wide array of disabilities. The students have a 'spikey' ability profile, where each individual is stronger or demonstrates more competence in one area over another. To accommodate and work with individuals with spikey profiles, Matt and his team asked students to identify areas of interest or problems they would like to solve in their local community. The students, working with Matt and his team, identified six projects that excited them:

1. Art and Design
2. Digital Design and Technology
3. Food Technology
4. Life Skills
5. Performing Arts
6. Sports Leaders

Once these areas of interests were identified, the school invited people to come in and be part of the six working groups to put together the content and parameters of each project. Participation was voluntary to ensure that whoever showed up was motivated to be there, not expected to be there. From each group a 'project lead' was nominated. The project leads were teachers who met a year in advance to ensure that each project had a clear timeline and milestones that each student could progress through. The project leaders also needed to identify the learning outcomes within each project and how they related to each core subject. Such an interdisciplinary approach to teaching subjects was a radically different way of teaching, so there were some teachers who were excited about the opportunity, and volunteered to be project leads, and there were teachers who were, frankly, very resistant to the whole process. The weekly peer-to-peer review sessions opened feedback loops to the leadership team and strong trust was built. The structure was slowly removed over the year, and the group took on its own leadership role with clear governance.

Students in Key Stage 3 (age 11–14) then rotated through each of the six projects, twice. This gave them a better sense of what each project involved. Before the students moved into Key Stage 4 (age 14–16), they had to apply to the project of their choice. This approach was deliberately developmental and designed to mimic the application process, they would need to get a job after school or to gain a place in further education. It also provided a space for students to demonstrate they had worth and believed they could add value to the project. Whilst maintaining core subjects in the curriculum including literacy, numeracy, science, PSHE and physical education, the students entering Key Stage 4 were therefore given much more control than they would have previously had over what they studied.

This reinvented process tapped directly into the students need for autonomy and increased their agentic engagement. Competence was amplified through the time each student spent on these projects, which was 400 hours per academic year rather than the meagre 36 hours they would have normally committed to such activity. Thirty-six hours rarely delivers anything approaching mastery or a sense of competence. The 400 hours meant that deeper learning could occur, skill mastery could occur and often a meaningful qualification was achieved, something that had been extremely rare prior to this reinvention. Of the 400 hours, 120 hours were dedicated to the qualification such as a BTech or Arts Award. Since all the projects were interdisciplinary and being taught in groups, they also significantly increased relatedness in pupils, peers and teachers, tapping into all the key motivators of self-determination theory.

The commitment of 400 hours in each project also allowed other subjects to be built into the learning, transforming how the curriculum was delivered each term. Colleagues would peer moderate that their subjects were sufficiently considered and covered, creatively finding ways to weave the 'why' rather than the 'what' into the projects. One of the best examples of this was within the projects themselves. When the final curtain fell on the school production of *Bugsy Malone*, every student from every project stepped onto the stage to take a bow.

Each student in the Performing Arts group had directed their own scene, the Art and Design project group created the set, and the Digital Design and Technology group worked on the props, sound and lighting. The Food Technology group provided the catering, the Life Skills group sold it to attendees, and the Sports Leaders group played the more athletic roles. Everyone on stage embraced each other at the end of the show and in so doing, modelled to every stakeholder and the audience that they could work together to achieve a fantastic outcome. It was a significant event that step changed the expectations of everyone who witnessed it. Imagine the impact on the lines of development for each individual that was part of that event? Although different for each individual, there was little doubt this approach created ripples of change that elevated each individuals' lines of development but also across the capacity of the organisation as a whole.

The focus on skill mastery also allowed time for reflection and helped build and strengthen their sense of identity in a space they felt they belonged to. Each student was able to see their own progress and appreciate the nature of failure and how to get better over time. Each teacher encouraged the project group to reflect on what had been achieved each week and figure out what they wanted to achieve in the following week. This developed goal setting skills as they were held to account against their self-authored goals. Self-esteem increased as milestones were achieved and celebrated alongside the mistakes it took to get there. When things didn't go well, students were encouraged to develop their ability to find resources, foster resilience and try again, with new insights on board. Staff created an impact process where progress was measured, those results were provided as feedback and the outcomes to that process were then recognised through peer-to-peer and community events. These events act as showcases to encourage ever rising standards to facilitate double loop learning to occur – vital in creating change (Figure 12.1).

Each term, the project was based on a local, global or community-based problem the children felt connected to, thus creating an emotional connection to the learning that created meaning. This approach also gave learners the opportunity to add value, one of the most effective strategies in creating identity and a sense of belonging.

The projects created virtuous feedback loops where the autonomy to choose increased their motivation and the desire to engage in the various projects. They were dealing with real world issues and received real world feedback that challenged internal and external assumptions. Engagement increased learning, which increased competence, which amplified motivation as progress was recognised. As the group worked together more closely, the bonds in the group strengthened, increasing engagement and relatedness even more.

In one instance two students who fought every single day both opted to join the Preforming Arts group, and the project leader was understandably nervous. Early in the project the group went on a theatre trip and these two students never fought again. Because they were able to bond over a shared interest and experience, the irritations that had niggled them previously simply fell away. The assumptions they had both made that they didn't have anything in common based on how they looked became redundant. A similar approach was used to address the stigma around disability, with adult artists with their own mobility needs from the Camden Art's Centre partnering with the Performing Arts project to evidence that their passion was possible to take forward. The external connections shifted expectations and provided a bridge into those networks, with one learner sharing his mental health poem to 20,000 people at WE Day at Wembley Stadium and went on to perform in the West End.

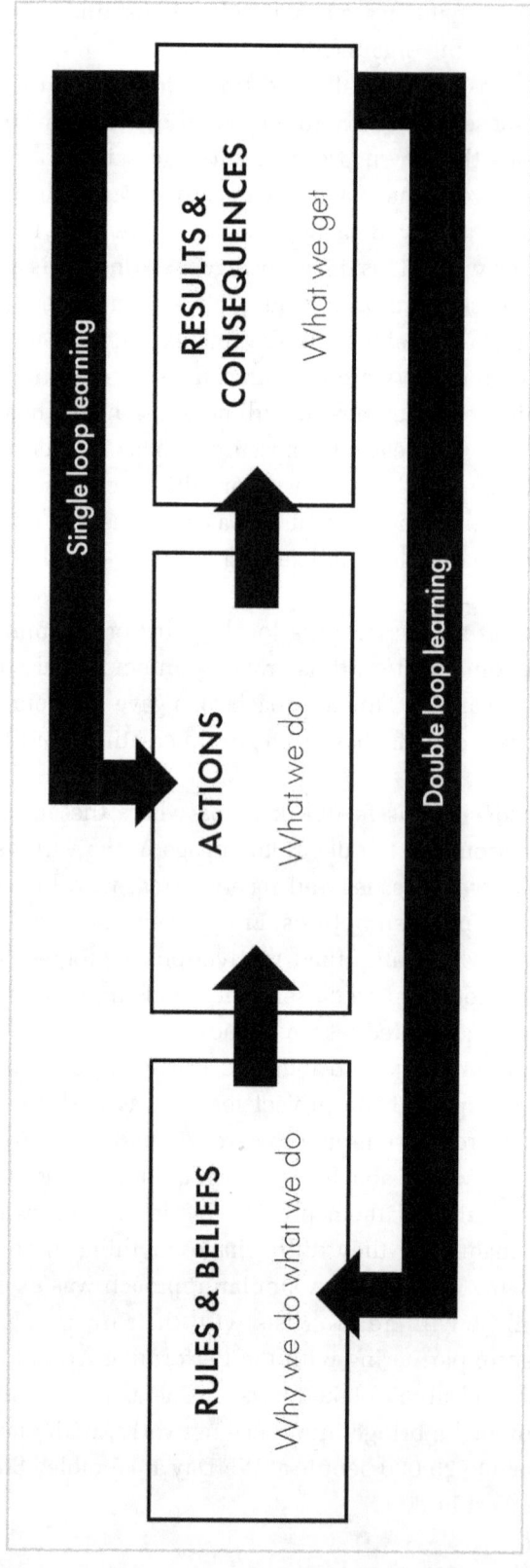

Figure 12.1 Double Loop Learning

Each project was built around the '3i's' of Ofsted's curriculum guidance: intent, implementation and impact. This helped ensure Ofsted was onboard with Matt's plan and enabled them to assess the outcomes and results of the school. The whole project focus built on each child's educational health care (EHC) targets and embraced the 6Cs of 21st century living[2] (collaboration, creativity, communication, critical thinking, character and citizenship). Developing these six functional skills enabled students to better access the curriculum and adhere to the Gatsby benchmarks around high-quality career guidance to support students into relevant employment.[3]

The reinvention of the entire curriculum hinged around well-being, core subjects and the six projects (this number was based on the scale of the school). At the start of every day, students began with a well-being session where they developed the ability to regulate their emotional state and ensure they were ready to learn. This benefited both the students and teachers. It was led by the teaching assistants who had revealed a passion for yoga, meditation and martial arts, as part of the talent audit and practitioner development meetings. Everyone in the room contributed to creating an environment for energised and constructive learning.

After the initial well-being session, Matt and his team deliberately scheduled project work every morning because the students really wanted to do this. Starting with project work reduced student absenteeism still further. The core subjects, such as maths and English, were scheduled in the afternoon and was aligned to the morning project work, increasing its relevance. Better project and core subject alignment boosted enthusiasm for the core subjects too. Students, often for the first time began to believe in themselves and the notion of going on to further education became a real possibility. They also understood that if they were to make that possibility a reality, they needed some of those core subjects such as maths and English, and this recognition dramatically increased their attention and engagement with the work.

Instead of being told that English and maths were important, they were able to appreciate for themselves why they were important in relation to what they were trying to achieve – get a job or get into a further education role using what they covered in their project. Despite being an extrinsic motivator, the learners were able to value the influence of the qualification rather than seeing it as either unachievable or some form of compliance issue.

As one student said, "I think core subjects improved because we know at the beginning of the year, they presented what exactly we're going to be doing, for this year, what qualification we're working towards, what it would allow us to do, and before that it was just a bunch of English work just thrown at us."

Such positive feedback loops became an important part of the project learning as significant events provide a time stamp in their memory and allowed the students to make sense of the learning sequence. Everything in the projects became much more meaningful to the students because it was in context. They were recognising their own patterns of limiting beliefs and purposefully making new self-authored beliefs about what they were truly capable of.

The sessions were also shortened slightly so they were less of a slog for students and core subjects were broken up by more active subjects like PE or IT to better manage energy. Finally, continuous measurement allowed Matt and his team to assess impact against the vision of 'carving pathways to employment'.

Collectively the programme of activity outlined above allowed Shaftsbury High School students to make significant steps toward gaining employment. This deliberately developmental approach resulted in 80% of students going on to subject specific courses at college, as opposed to just 5% prior to the reinvention of the curriculum. In addition, four students achieved internships – the first in the school's history.[4]

Academically, the first year of results showed approximately double the quantity and quality of qualifications achieved. And the incidents of negative behaviour fell by an astonishing 83%. Shaftsbury was ranked 'Outstanding' by Ofsted a year after the new teaching framework had been in place, and it's now leading on the strategic vision for SEND schools within the borough, with networks reaching out far beyond its borders, including an eight-school collaboration that looks to develop innovative teaching, learning and leadership.

The students and teachers loved it. Even the most initially reticent teachers were able to see and feel the difference in the school, the results and the culture. Staff absence dropped by a whopping 47%.

Teachers' leadings different projects had daily planning sessions, and where two projects were working on the same core subjects that day, the project groups would merge and exchange ideas. This helped to build relationships across the classes and projects to create a more collaborative professionalism between teachers, a fact that also positively impacted the culture.

The teachers involved in the projects were very keen to keep the reinvention going with one adding, "I would now not only keep the model; I would expand its principles beyond the six projects and into all areas of the curriculum". Another agreed: "The projects enable students to find pathways for future learning and employment and find an area of study that they enjoy." Another teacher noted, "'Students are now recognising the skills they've learned have applications, which can form an essential part of their own long-term learning pathway, beyond school and into adult life."

Parents were also very pleased with the results, with one parent noting, "Despite the challenges in getting up and running, it's been the most successful year at the school. This past year has seen my child blossom. They now show a real interest in school, they are forming real friendships and learning to love working for the first time. The project lead has been amazing and very proactive in making the work stimulating and then show casing it."

When a school becomes deliberately developmental in its approach, it's not just the children who benefit but the teachers, leaders, employers and the wider community too. Every developmental effort in the education system has a disproportionate ripple effect that has the impact to not just change education but change the world.

Notes

1 No Author (2023) Written evidence from DFN Project SEARCH (YDP0043). https://committees.parliament.uk/writtenevidence/125064/pdf/
2 Kristoffy J (2018) 21st century skills: the 6 C's, Right Track.
3 No Author (2023) Careers guidance and access for education and training providers, Statutory guidance for schools and guidance for further education colleges and sixth form colleges, Department of Education UK Government.
4 Silver M (2021) Motivation, engagement and outcomes in curriculum development in a specialist SEND School in England, Support for Learning, 36: 133–146. Silver M (n.d.) An exploratory study of the impact of a meaningful, mastery project based learning curriculum structure based on self-determination theory and agentic engagement on motivation, engagement and outcomes in a SEND secondary school in England.

13 TKAT Case Study

Our final case study is the Kemnal Academies Trust (TKAT), one of the largest multi-academy trusts in the UK with 45 primary and secondary academies. TKAT decided that improvements couldn't wait for government intervention or some other external miracle, and worked with us to embark on a reinvention of their multi-academy trust using a programme of development as outlined in this book.

The Catalyst for Change

In total, TKAT has 22,000 children and 3,350 staff in its 'family'.

TKAT Deputy CEO Liz Harrison demonstrated her desire for change when she started researching leadership development solutions in September 2019. Liz recognised that improvements would be essential, and this view was confirmed by the results of an external multi-academy trust review in January 2020.

- "The feedback from teachers and staff in the schools aligned with the leadership team's recognition that we weren't getting things right in terms of communications and impact. We realised the culture had to change."

- "Our culture was one of top-down command and control. The impact of that was that people and schools were working in silos. We wanted more collaborations, more interconnectivity and less distance between the TKAT board and headteachers and staff."

- "Every school and every leader had something powerful to contribute that supports holistic outcomes for children. We needed to share this to garner everyone's strengths and skills and create a community."

The Development Journey

This developmental programme combined diagnostic assessments, team development and individual coaching. Initially, the eight members of TKAT's senior leadership team (SLT) was the focus, but over time the work was extended to include the wider leadership team of 15 people.

In addition to assessing the leaders using the diagnostics outlined earlier in this book and the team development index (see below), our coaches started working one-to-one with four key individuals: Karen Roberts (CEO), Liz Harrison (deputy CEO) and two senior education directors.

Assessment

TKAT's journey started by assessing the level of team sophistication using their Team Development Index (TDI) with the SLT in addition to the Complete Values Profile (CVP) for the wider leadership team. The results were striking.

Team Development Index

In June 2020, the TKAT SLT was below benchmark on four of the six dimensions of the Team Development Index (see Figure 13.1).

Furthermore, three of the areas the SLT scored low on Relationship Quality, Strategic Power and Coherence. Fundamentally, the SLT was a group of motivated individuals, but it wasn't operating as an effective team. Everyone was working hard, and they were busy 'doing' things but they weren't all pulling in the same direction. They were expending significant energy but not getting the results they deserved.

The TDI was then repeated in September 2021 and the improvements were dramatic. The left of each pair of bars is the score from June 2020, while the right of each pair of bars is the result in September 2021 after the developmental intervention.

The team is now in the top 10% of all teams surveyed for all six dimensions and in the top 3% for Coherence and Strategic Power.

Figure 13.2 gives some examples of the huge improvement in percentage agreement in the responses to the survey questions.

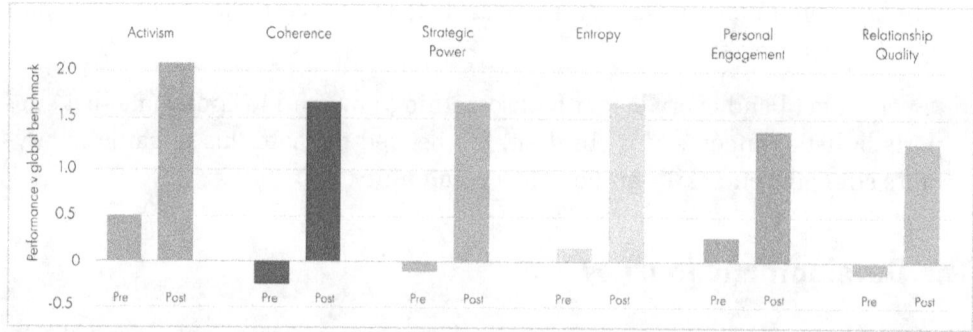

Figure 13.1 TKAT TDI Results

SURVEY QUESTION	JUNE 2020	SEPT 2021
We can resolve disagreements between team members without the team leader having to adjudicate	29%	60%
The team leader imposes the final decision on the team	93%	27%
We have a vision that will be a game changer for our industry	43%	93%
The vision of this team is inspirational to people in my area	64%	100%
The strategies in our separate areas come together with clarity at the team level	57%	93%

Figure 13.2 Response Change to Survey Questions

From the initial team assessment data, it was clear that the team was focused on the short-term 'IT' dimension of the Leadership Model (see Figure 13.3). It was a breakthrough for the leadership team to understand that they needed to invest time on the longer-term 'IT' as well as the 'WE' and the 'I' dimensions of leadership.

Complete Values Profiles

Next the team did their Complete Values Profiles (CVP) to precisely define which of the eight value systems they were operating from (see Figure 13.4). The CVP defines what every leader considers important (what they value) and therefore what they are likely to focus on to unlock a new level of performance. The data from the initial values assessment revealed why the SLT was failing to fulfil its potential.

The aggregated results of the TKAT SLT's values before the developmental intervention are shown in Figure 13.5. As Liz Harrison noted: "As a team we were incredibly 'Red', particularly in relation to man management."

The Red (power) value system can be passionate and entertaining. People operating at this level can bring a clarity that can be immensely useful in a crisis. However, like every level, the Red value system can also have a negative impact. People operating from a less healthy Red perspective can become overly directive, egotistic and struggle to see the bigger picture. There was certainly significant unhealthy Red motivation at TKAT. The desire for collaboration was very low and there was no common purpose.

School Performance

- Deliver Ofsted desired outcomes
- Develop educational offer and services
- Build holistic metric tracking
- Control operational risks
- Run staff performance management
- Increase school revenue streams

System Leadership

- Clarify vision
- Set ambition
- Uncover purpose
- Identify strategic building blocks
- Establish effective governance & innovate system

IT

I   WE

Personal Performance

- Improve quality of thinking
- Develop boundless energy
- Increase resilience and wellbeing
- Understand human development to ready pupils and staff for learning
- Understand behaviours

People Leadership

- Drive culture transformation
- Develop community values
- Build sustainable leadership teams
- Create intrinsic drive
- Build collaborative networks, (including outside of education)
- Increase stakeholder engagement

Figure 13.3 The Leadership Model

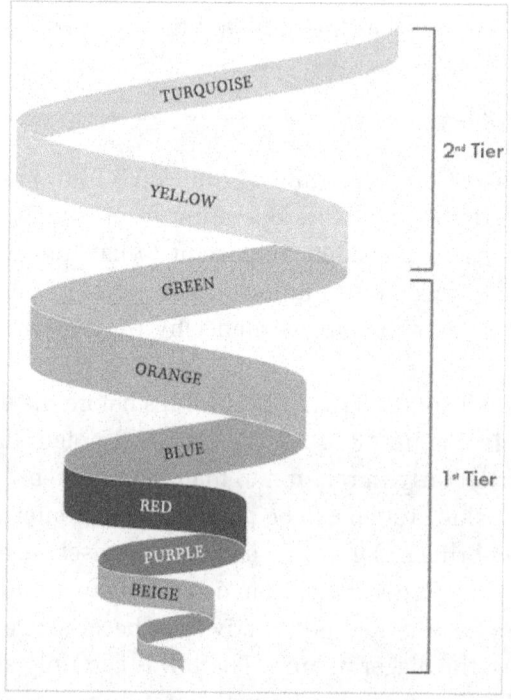

Figure 13.4 The Values Spiral

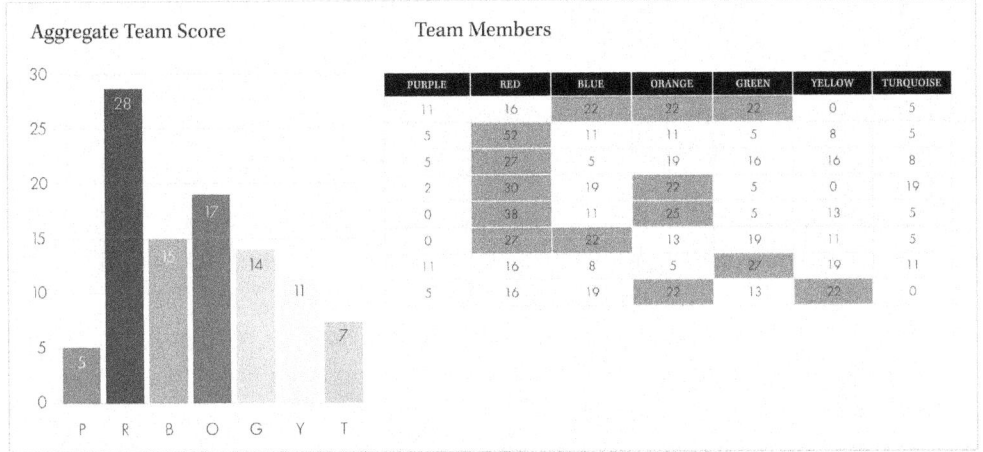

Figure 13.5 CVP People Management Results June 2020

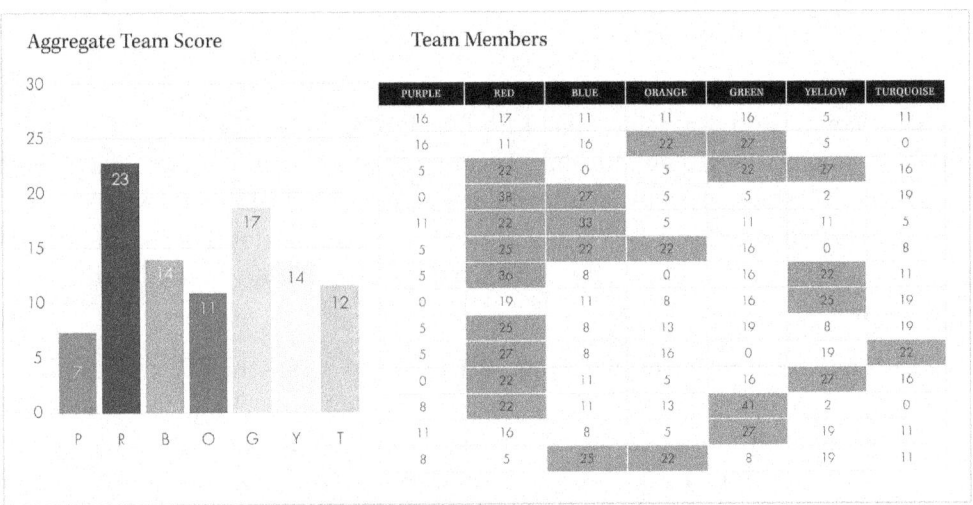

Figure 13.6 CVP People Management Results September 2021

Figure 13.6 shows the result of significant development over the 15 months of the intervention. This change reflects how the team reinvented itself and now brings more innovation, creativity and disruptive ideas to the table, as reflected by the significant increase in the Yellow and Turquoise value system. The SLT is focusing more on the longer-term systemic changes needed (increased Turquoise), with a strong value around caring (slightly increased Green values).

The excessive directiveness of the Red value system and the overemphasis on results of the Orange value system also reduced, but not so much as to undermine the importance of academic achievement. Access to Red and Orange values remains important, but the growth in the higher levels of the spiral is transforming how the team works together to deliver much better and more balanced outcomes for the Trust.

Developmental Intervention

As well as using the results of the assessments to focus the coaching and team development interventions, the SLP were also involved in eight days of team development which included the following modules:

1. **Context set with the 4D framework:** The team was introduced to the 4D leadership framework (see Figure 13.3). This was essential to broaden the team's perspective beyond their focus on short-term tasks, targets, goals and metrics ('IT' dimension). The team now works together collaboratively, spends more time on longer-term strategic thinking and on continuously developing themselves and their teams.

2. **Understanding individual and team values:** We assessed the team's values in detail which helped to build a common language around motivation, culture and cultural transformation. It also clarified how the team could operate more effectively and leverage their collective strengths.

3. **Creating more entropy:** Once a common language and a leadership model had been created, there was an urgent need to focus on helping people get all the ideas and challenges on the table. This included helping the team to achieve a level of radical candour that allowed tensions to be raised and resolved much faster and more effectively. Radical candour is not brutal honesty but rather saying what you think, while also caring for the person you are in conversation with.[1]

4. **Building new ways of working:** We actively strengthened the relationship bonds between individual team members by teaching the team how to listen much more deeply to develop much better understanding of each other, while welcoming diverse views and opinions and managing conflict constructively.

5. **Moving to a distributed leadership style:** The team moved to a less directive, more inspiring and empowering leadership style. This brought new clarity and precision to what the team and the leaders needed to improve outcomes. The team have been surprised by how quickly they've seen people step up.

6. **Understanding and adapting the organisation's culture:** The team assessed the current culture by looking at the customs, rituals, symbols, myths, metaphors and stories that are prevalent in the organisation. This was very insightful and helped the team realise that the culture further down the organisation still reflected the old way of working. The team agreed actions to role model and drive the cultural shift.

For the TKAT programme participants, the coaching and team development has been transformative.

Key Benefits Delivered

The key change from the developmental work outlined in this book has been a move from a centrally led, directive style of leadership to a distributed leadership approach. This has led to a culture of much greater empowerment and inclusion, more creativity and systemic thinking, with strong care and support for everyone. The TKAT leadership team coined the acronym ICE to Inspire, Care and Empower. The level of trust, collaboration and comfort with different views has increased dramatically.

The changes at TKAT led to several new strategic initiatives. These are already showing good results.

Specifically:

- TKAT's created a 'Champion for Every Child' initiative with 7,000 children having a named, consistent adult champion. The result was a big improvement in attendance rates and a 13% increase in age-standardised reading scores for the primary children involved.

- A Phonics initiative, rolled out across 28 schools, lead to 88% of children passing their phonics test compared to 77% in 2019, surpassing the national average of 82%.

Since their developmental work started, all schools have held or improved their Ofsted grading. While this can't be solely attributed to the developmental interventions, there's a strong belief that the programme has been a major contributing factor as all Leadership and Management is considered good or above. All TKAT headteachers surveyed said they appreciate the culture change and especially the way they are now able to work with the senior leaders. This has been reflected in 100% of heads staying in post or promoted to more senior roles.

TKAT CEO's Transformational Journey

As the TKAT CEO, Dr Karen Roberts is a significant role model for leaders at TKAT. Her behaviour has a significant impact on the culture of the organisation. She credits much of her recent leadership transformation to the relationship with this developmental work and her coach, Dave.

While the details of Karen's one-to-one coaching sessions are confidential, Karen was happy to openly share how it has helped her so that others can see its value.

"From the outset, Dave has been fantastic. He met with me before the group sessions to tell me what everyone had been saying and to explain the results of my values profile."

"It was raw and brutal for me to listen to – the feedback from my team and my profile showed me to be a dragon. If someone was disloyal, my reactions would be fierce and reactive. I would be quick to make decisions or force people to make decisions and didn't allow enough reflection time. It was very reactionary. If I included people in my deliberations, it would be a limited amount of people, not a wider stakeholder group."

"I had the misconception that the right thing to do was to make quick decisions and move fast. Sometimes it is, but more often than not, it's not the best way."

"Dave and I agreed we should share the insights from my assessments with the rest of the SLT and work with it. Naturally, I was reluctant, but I knew it was an essential part of my leadership journey and my transformation."

"The first meeting with the team was really difficult. However, having Dave as my coach as part of the programme has been invaluable."

"My leadership journey has been phenomenal. I was caught in a legacy, leadership style, which wasn't really me and wasn't making me happy in my job. Not only that, but I also wasn't getting any results in terms of moving the organisation on."

"Exploring my whole leadership style, linked with who I am, has been transformational for me. I would use that word 'transformational'. There's still a bit of Red in me – I'm driven and focused, but it doesn't manifest in a 'bad' Red anymore. I'm allowed to enjoy people."

"I don't have all the answers, but we now work as a team to find the answers together. I've been able to develop so much that it's permeating to different levels of the organisation as well – beyond me."

"The most important thing for me is allowing myself to be me – giving people time and really valuing them as people and professionals. What I thought was most effective in terms of leadership quite clearly wasn't."

"Part of this whole process for me has been understanding that if you're a leader, you need to open up and be more transparent, to have closer relationships. Before, I didn't know myself or my team well enough."

"I didn't know what I didn't know. I just didn't know all this was out there. Now I listen to other education colleagues – CEOs – and I think they haven't got close to what this developmental work has brought to us."

As Deputy CEO Liz Harrison explained, for some members of the TKAT SLT the insights into their individual and collective values profiles had a dramatic effect:

"The work around our own values profiles was hugely illuminating for everyone. For some, it was life changing. There were some dramatic changes and some less obvious, but everyone's changed. It has transformed working lives dramatically."

Coaching for the Senior Leadership Team (SLT)

While the results of the assessments clearly sparked the necessary change in TKAT's SLT, it has been the personal coaching and the team development activities (as outlined above) that have cemented the transformation.

David Linsell describes himself as a "minister without portfolio" at TKAT. He leads on curriculum and is currently responsible for governance in the academies, but he takes on whatever projects the SLT and Liz Harrison requires. He had observed the changes the work was generating, but considered himself a little outside it, as he explained: "I was watching its impact on other people and thinking it was having a brilliant impact, particularly in terms of the discussions and insights it brought. But, I was on the outside and I thought I was already there in terms of my development."

Two one-to-one coaching sessions with Matt changed David's view. "Matt challenged my view of self and my world perception. When I judge somebody, I thought it was an objective judgment. I knew we had perceptions, but one of the most powerful things to have come through from my interactions with Matt is that when you make a judgment, you're actually projecting yourself onto that other person. You're judging their reaction against how you would have reacted. I'm now much more aware of this trait in myself, which is helping me control it, but I'm also aware of it in other people too".

Leadership Development for Headteachers

Following the initial assessments, team development and coaching work with TKAT's SLT, the programme expanded to include headteachers within TKAT.

Jo McKeown was one of the first headteachers to participate in the leadership development programme which was specifically designed for headteachers and other senior leaders across TKAT, but she admits she was a little reluctant initially.

"At the time I was clear I didn't want a TKAT-funded coach. I felt there was a network of colleagues that I could pick up the phone to if I felt I needed help, but I wanted any other conversation to be outside of TKAT. I worried that it wouldn't be completely confidential. The other reason I was hesitant was that I didn't really understand what coaching was – nobody had really explained what it was. I confused it with mentoring. I probably thought I'd done it. I didn't know what I was missing".

Jo also acknowledges that it can be hard to find the time for coaching. "In the first years of headship you don't come up for breath. Any thought of coaching just felt selfish – I wasn't putting the school first. Now my understanding is very different."

"What I've learned is that the coaching sessions are hard. You must be present and willing. But what they have given me has been transformative. They have given me the practical tools to rein myself back in when I feel that imposter syndrome rearing its head and causing me to doubt myself. Now I can re-write that narrative in my head. The coaching with Matt has been really practical in many ways – things like visualisation techniques – but it goes much deeper than that. It's had a huge impact".

"I'm now actively building in much more reflection time for myself. I'm much more aware of my core purpose, vision and values in everything I do. That's impacted how I lead meetings, how I plan, how I work with other leaders in the school. Not a day goes by when I don't think about what I'm doing and how it's connected to my values and my work".

David Moss is another headteacher who's benefitted from the leadership development programme. While he snapped up the offer for some development, he admits to some trepidation. "I had experienced other leadership coaching before, and it hadn't worked for me. I'd enjoyed previous coaching but had reverted to old habits straight afterwards".

David's developmental coaching experience was very different right from the start. "I had a real revelation in that initial session – that our physiology is linked to our behaviours. The iceberg model [Integrated Performance Model] was transformative for me. To the extent that at that point I made the decision that I would never again behave in the way I had before".

This model, as discussed in chapter 5 and 10 explains how our physiology is ultimately linked to our behaviours through our emotions and feelings.

David explained how this insight changed his thinking: "I could be quite reactive, and I let things bother me and get to me. Until that point it hadn't occurred to me that I didn't need to let it bother me. That I could be in control of my feelings".

For David, out of all the coaching sessions, the 'iceberg' session was the most impactful. "It really kept me engaged with the programme. Despite the challenges we've all faced in the last few years, I've managed to hold fast to those principles: in particular the practical things I've learned like the breathing techniques to manage my responses to situations".

"The next stage for me is to spread that training to the rest of my leadership team. I can see one or two others behaving in the way I was, and I know they would benefit from this developmental approach".

This is the first leadership work David has done that's had a meaningful impact. "It's been a revelation to me and I can start to see how various things have impacted my performance. Since then, I've become more effective and more efficient in what I do. It's also helped me achieve greater clarity around my decision making."

"I've been in teaching for more than 20 years and I thought I couldn't help the way I was. Now I know differently. I've done Myers Briggs in the past – it's interesting but it seems to reinforce who you are. With this developmental approach, you can develop and evolve – your behaviour is not fixed".

The Transformative Impact

The impact of undertaking this developmental work has also been transformative at the very top of TKAT. Liz Harrison explained how the quality of the coaching has helped the SLT, including CEO Karen Roberts, understand how they could evolve through the spiral and become more sophisticated. "We saw the change in our day-to-day work almost immediately. The biggest change has been in our CEO. It's been absolutely phenomenal".

It's a change that CEO Karen Roberts is the first to acknowledge. Karen further explained: "Now I don't get angry anymore. It's literally done wonders for my blood pressure – I've had issues for a long time, and it's now the lowest I've ever had".

According to Liz, the change in the CEO has enabled the SLT to work in a way that suits them much more: "We've been happier and more productive at work as we've moved away from the Red value system that dominated us as a team. We've realised that it's not always about speed. Distributed leadership has become more important. There has been greater trust and more examples of co-creation".

"All of that has led to people being confident in their roles. They are now able to put forward ideas, to make decisions and they have been unlocked from a particular way of working into a new way that is far more collegiate and collaborative".

"Headteachers are also telling us that they feel far more valued. They see the executive team more often and they feel closer to them. We have joint working parties involving the executive and the headteachers are being given real power on those – they're not just talking shops, the headteachers have a genuine role".

"The executive has been really up front about the journeys we've been on and the headteachers have recognised that and are supportive of it".

TKAT is moving away from a very traditional, hierarchical organisation and a leadership style which was directive with all decisions made centrally, to a much more distributed leadership style in which people are inspired by TKAT's purpose and vision.

People are included, involved and empowered to make decisions. They are supported by being part of a deliberately developmental organisation that cares and provides very practical support.

Already, TKAT have witnessed:

- Directors taking the lead on key aspects of TKAT's strategy

- Head teachers much more involved in determining the way forward for TKAT and in key decisions

- Much more focus on long-term, sustainable improvements rather than quick fixes to turn around under performing schools

- A high level of trust, inclusion and listening in senior leadership team which was not there before.

Future Plans

The developmental work outlined in this book has been transformative for senior leaders at TKAT, right from the start and the first moments of the development work. Leaders describe 'lightbulb' moments when they realise, for the first time, just what they need to achieve and are able to develop far better working relationships.

Senior leaders are already allocating more time for reflection and strategic thinking which is impacting the quality of the decisions they're making and that is having a positive knock-on impact in schools too.

TKAT is confident that the huge impact of the work will continue to cascade throughout the organisation and ultimately impact the young people in their schools, as Liz Harrison explains: "We are hoping that the staff will have a better work-life balance, will be more creative in their thinking and that ultimately TKAT will become the employer of choice and we'll attract great people because of our culture".

"When we have happy, productive and creative leaders, we inspire better teachers, which impacts on better outcomes for children".

"We can't underestimate how significant the change created by Complete has been and, we expect, will continue to be".

TKAT has begun to author its own journey and therefore their own narrative for their community to buy into. This is creating a context for leaders to thrive in and frameworks to take back to their schools and implement it. Each leader, team and school will be at their own stage on the journey, but having a clearly defined purpose that is context led, is beginning to show up in their leaders' retention (100% in 2022/23) and learners' performance on a number of levels across each key stage. Innovation on how to meet the diverse needs of their learners is emerging with a digital re-engagement school and a one-to-one support system for those with pupil premium funding.

Note

1 Scott K (2017) Radical candor: how to get what you want by saying what you mean, Macmillan, New York.

Conclusion

It's thought to take around two years for a new minister in charge of a government department to become familiar enough with the subject and challenges to even start to be effective. The Conservatives were in power from 2010 to 2024 and in that time there were 10 Secretaries of State for Education. One, Michelle Donelan, became the shortest-serving cabinet member in British history, when she resigned from the post just 35 hours after being appointed. Kit Malthouse lasted all of seven weeks. The insidious nature of populism in politics has meant that often posts are filled based on perceived loyalty to the then leader and rarely on experience or capability. But we see this reality regardless of which political party is in power.

The idea that somehow, somewhere, the government is going to come to the rescue and fix the broken elements of the education system is clearly a fantasy. No one is coming. No single stakeholder group is going to ride in on white stallion and save the day.

The late Sir Ken Robinson laid this out in his Death Valley TED Talk:

"There's a wonderful quote from Benjamin Franklin. *'There are three sorts of people in the world: Those who are immovable, people who don't get it, or don't want to do anything about it; there are people who are movable, people who see the need for change and are prepared to listen to it; and there are people who move, people who make things happen.'* And if we can encourage more people, that will be a movement. And if the movement is strong enough, that's, in the best sense of the word, a revolution. And that's what we need."

In other words, it's up to us.

And that's exciting because if we commit to the developmental journey across all stakeholder groups, we empower ourselves to not only reinvent the education system but foster the diverse skills and capabilities we need to help us to solve the many issues we face.

We've described how the reinvention of education requires us to develop change capability and rapidly move through the steps of the Change Wheel (chapter 3) to achieve an educational revolution. A revolution is required because the strain on the system is too great, and time is running out.

Right now, teachers and leaders are leaving the profession in their droves, crippled by the futility of the system and dwindling resources. Far too many children are being left behind, either dropping out of school altogether or treading water until they can leave. But without high-quality education, their life is made immeasurably harder, forced to work for minimum wage or on zero hours contracts whilst facing the biggest employment threat of all time (AI). We must provide a meaningful pathway that changes the narrative of the education system, that highlights the incredible commitment of our educators. The learners within the system must again see the value in their journey through the system whilst they are in it, as well as with hindsight.

For this we require the energy, maturity and sophistication of thinking to take the majority of the system around this revolution and reinvention of the system. If designed well, around developmental frameworks, the momentum can drive a more considered second revolution towards levels of innovation, integration and augmentation required to constantly evolve the system and solve and re-solve the wicked problems created by humans going through a dysfunctional educational system.

We need a movement of deliberately developmental organisations (DDOs), schools and Trusts that bring diverse views to a shared framework that allows them to see the value their resistance holds. We need to take the initiative, like those leaders at TKAT to turn our own corner of the system around and create something that is fit for purpose. Something that empowers all the stakeholders in the system from the pupils to the teachers and beyond to fulfil their potential. We need a network to drive and unite these courageous leaders and parts of the system so we can experience a transformation of the entire system, borough by borough, county by county, nation by nation.

High-quality education is central to a good life. It offers hope and opportunity for all. At least it should. In his book, *The Coming Jobs War*, author and CEO of Gallup, Jim Clifton, writes, "What the whole world wants is a good job. Humans used to desire love, money, food, shelter, safety, peace, and freedom more than anything else. The last 30 years have changed us. Now people want to have a good job, and they want their children to have a good job. This changes everything for world leaders. Everything they do, from waging war to building societies, will need to be carried out within the new context of the need for a good job."[1]

Drawing from deep advanced analysis from Gallup's US and World Polls, macroeconomic data on job creation and trends in world economics are clear – what people want in their lives is meaningful work.

The Global Well-Being Index is the result of six years of Gallup research, including two million interviews in the US and 133,000 interviews across 135 countries. It is the largest global study into well-being ever undertaken. What they found is that regardless of where we live, our well-being comes down to five elements:

1. **Purpose:** liking what we do each day and being motivated to achieve our goals.

2. **Social:** having supportive relationships and love in our lives.

3. **Financial:** managing our economic life to reduce stress and increase security.

4. **Community:** liking where we live, feeling safe and having pride in our community.

5. **Physical:** having good health and enough energy to get things done daily.

Education, in one form or another, is central to each of these outcomes. In analysing the results of the index, Gallup classifies responses as "thriving" (well-being that is strong and consistent), "struggling" (well-being that is moderate or inconsistent) or "suffering" (well-being that is low and inconsistent).[2] Without a solid educational base, too many children are entering the world to suffer and struggle instead of thrive. Each of these elements requires a better understanding of ourselves and others. This calls for a reinvented education system. One that is built around development not knowledge transfer.

As the creator of the first school in England, St Augustine one said, "the words printed here are concepts. You must go through the experiences". We hope that this book has inspired you to know that there is a solution and there is a way to go through the experiences and make sense of them so these frameworks can be shared in making education better for everyone. We hope you are inspired to become deliberately developmental in your own life and create deliberately developmental organisations around you.

As Carl Ward, Chair of the Foundation of Education Development (FED), reminds us, "Whatever evolutionary stage is coming next, it's vital it's co-created by those with a stake in it". For education, that is each and every one of us.

Notes

1 Clifton J (2011) Coming jobs war, Gallup Press.
2 Standish M, Witters D (2014) Country well-being varies greatly worldwide, Gallup.

Index

Page numbers in italic indicate a figure and page numbers in bold indicate a table on the corresponding page

abstract thinking 72
academic outcomes 7, 24, 53, 81, 86, 87, 109, 225, 232
academisation 15
accountabilities 158–159, 162–163, 175, 202
acetylcholine 93
Achievers 115–116, 124, 151–153, 161, 164, 175–176
"action logic" 68, 112
active listening 131
activism 130, 156–158, 173
adaptability 148, 192, 207
adrenaline 92–93, 120
adult development 62, 68, 74, 129, 148; journey 74; levels of 67–68; society and law on 74; theory 112; transpersonal swamp 73–74; *See also* child development, stages of
adult maturity 74, 112, 113
agentic engagement 188, 214
aggressive behaviour 97–98
AISSR *See* Amsterdam Institute for Social Science Research
algorithmic tasks and motivations 183
all quadrants all levels model *36,* 60
alternative schooling methods 16
Amabile, Teresa 181
ambition 155, 163–165, 173, 175–176, 212–213

Amsterdam Institute for Social Science Research 194
amygdala 138
anabolic hormones 94
anaesthetics 73–74
anger 98–99, 115
anti-social behaviour 72, 86
anxiety 26, 70, 82, 100, 112, 127, 129
apartheid, in teaching 18
appreciation: and gratitude 100; importance of 103; way to increase levels of 104
apprentice style teaching 23
AQAL model *See* all quadrants all levels model
arts-integrated learning 50
assembly line and mass production techniques 195
assessments 15, 28, 31–32, 40, 42, 48, 52, 53, 79, 81, 111, 113, 115, 161, 173, 199, 221–223, 226, 228–229
association learning 29
'Attachment Theory' 127
attendance exemptions 10–11
attention 60, 63, 81, 87–88, 101–102, 105, 127, 131, 137, 150, 179, 188, 200, 217
attitudes 27, 75, 134, 166, 174, 187, 188
Augustine, St 6, 18, 235
authority 11–12, 16, 31–32, 72, 79–80, 112, 119, 150, 155–156, 175, 181, 205

autonomy 15, 53, 81, 155, 184–185, 188, 202–203, 209, 212, 214–215
"autotelic experiences" 185
awareness 43, 59, 61, 63, 65, 68–70, 72, 75, 82, 88, 90, 97, 104, 111, 133, 135; conscious 106, 138; emotional 91, 97, 100; evolution of 68

Baker Act *See* Education Reform Act of 1988
Balfour Act *See* Education Act of 1902
Battle Hymn of the Tiger Mother (Chua) 33
battle of wills 72
behaviour 31, 36, 68, 70–71, 73, 82, 86, 92, 98, 104, 111, 137, 139, 174, 179–183, 187, 201, 203, 205, 211, 213, 215, 217, 227, 230; behavioural engagement 188; development 179; difficulty in changing 179; factors driving *85,* 86–87; management strategies 173, 209; and physiology 179
beliefs 104, 132–141, 166, 188; composition of 135; and values 132, 139
Bell, Andrew 8
big picture thinking 163–166; key areas for 165–166; questions answered by 163–164
Binet, Alfred 12–13
Binet-Simon Intelligence Scale 12–13
bitcoin blockchain 196
Black Death 6
blockchain driven education 204–206
blockchain technology 196–197, 204
blue value system 109, 144
Board of Education 12
Bowlby, John 127
brain 26–27, 29, 72, 91, 101–102, 137–139, 182, 199
Breathe Rhythmically Evenly And Through the Heart Every day skill *See* BREATHE skill
BREATHE skill 91, 120–122
breathing 88, 91, 120–121
British Schools 10
broadcasting 75, 105, 129–132; obsession with 129–130; and thinking 131

bullying 32, 93, 129
burnout and disillusionment 30–32
business performance principles 15
Butler Act of 1944 13

Campbell, Donald T. 182
Campbell, Joseph 63, 65
cancel cultures 103
Career-related Programme 52
caring 51–52, 147, 225–226
Carnegie, Andrew 8
Carney, Mark 15
carrot and stick approach, to motivation 180–181
CAS *See* Creativity, Activity, Service
catabolic hormones 94
Centre for the Study of Existential Risk 194
'chalk and talk' 130
change: approach to 63; capability 77; challenges of 62–63, 65–66; cycle of 63–65; navigating 65; path followed by 65; perceived as risk 63; road map for 63; wheel 63–64, *64,* 233
ChatGPT 26, 43, 76, 193, 195, 205–206
child-centred learning 49
child development, stages of 67–68; cognitive capabilities 72; 'conceptual self' 69; 'concrete self' 71; consciousness 71; emotional self 69; fifth level of 71–72; first level of 68–69; fourth level of 71; morality and ethics 70; physical sensations 68–69; pre-conscious level 68; second level of 69; self-awareness 72; self-identity 69; third level of 69–70; transpersonal self 72–73; transpersonal turbulence 72–74; *See also* adult development
child mortality 127
Chua, Amy 33
Class sizes 30
class teachers 51
Clifton, Jim 234
CMP *See* Complete Maturity Profile
coaching 124, 148, 172, 176, 226, 228–230; culture 173, 209–210, 211; network 173, 209; and team development 226

cognition 47, 82, 87
cognitive development 46, 80
cognitive empathy 104–105
cognitive engagement 187
cognitive line 87
cognitive sophistication 79–80, 87
coherence, in classroom 91
collaboration 15, 45, 49, 68, 80, 112, 129, 143, 153, 176, 188, 192, 201, 203, 217, 221, 223, 227
collaborative learning 54
collective change 63
collective development: big picture thinking 163–166; case study of 169–177; network analysis 161–162; team development 148–161; values and 145–148; values-based dynamics and 143–144
colour-coded values levels 2, *4*
commitment 53, 124, 152, 155, 157–158, 212, 214, 234
communication 80, 129, 131–132, 144–145, 161–162, 201, 217, 221; broadcasting 129–131; interruption 131; listening 130–132; perspective taking 132–133; quality of 140, 177; reception 130–131; superficial 131–132; transmission 131
community involvement 51
compassionate empathy 105
competency 166, 184–185, 202
Complete App 90, 95, 120, 122
Complete Maturity Profile 115
Complete Values Profile 111, 123, 145, 172, 222–223
compulsory assessments 15
computing age 195
conditioned learning 136–139
conditioned reflex 59
conditioned response 137
conditioning 136–137, 139
conflict 7, 94, 140–141, 145, 147, 156, 158
connectivity 195
consciousness 68, 71, 82, 87
constructivism 46–47
continual assessment 28, 40

continuous learning 46
Cook-Greuter, Susanne 68, 112
cooperation 128
corporal punishment 11
cortisol 94
CP *See* Career-related Programme
creative thinking 48
creativity 17, 48–49, 51–52, 54, 80, 124, 180–181, 193, 201, 217, 225, 227
Creativity, Activity, Service 52
'Creativity Crisis' 31
critical thinking 17, 26, 45, 47, 49–50, 52, 80, 193, 201, 217
cryptocurrencies 196–197
CSER *See* Centre for the Study of Existential Risk
Csikszentmihalyi, Mihaly 65, 184–185
'Cult of the Expert' 24, 25
cultural network 162
culture 25, 51, 61, 63, 81, 121, 124, 132, 134–135, 147, 166, 192, 210–211, 218, 221, 226–227; changes 5, 227; of continuous improvement 193; speak up 152, 176; war 5
Curran, Thomas 26–27, 42
curriculum 10, 12, 14–15, 19, 24, 29, 45, 48–50, 54, 119, 199–200, 212, 214, 217–218, 228; for child-centred learning 49; developmentally appropriate 50; IB program 52; Steiner education 50; teachers 24–25
CVP *See* Complete Values Profile
cyberbullying and self-harm, association between 129

DAOs *See* Decentralised Autonomous Organisations
Darwin, Charles 150
DDOs *See* Deliberately Developmental Organisations
Decentralised Autonomous Organisations 203–206
Deci, Edward 181, 183
dehydroepiandrosterone 94
Deliberately Developmental Organisations 124, 203–204, 206–207, 212, 231, 234–235

democracy, in education 45
Department for Education (DfE) 188;
  on school building collapse risk 31;
  workforce survey 30
development: basic levels of 74;
  developmental intervention 222–223,
  226–227; developmental journey 65,
  71–72, 74, 76, 87, 119, 148, 169, 173,
  233; importance of 75; and knowledge
  acquisition 76; levels and learning 76;
  lines for personal capability 77–78,
  78; moral 68; personal 27, 106, 174;
  physical 24, 71, 78, 81; social 47,
  199; *See also* adult development;
  emotional development; inner lines
  of development; personal capability
  development; team development;
  vertical development
development level: age as blunt proxy for
  134; assessment 199; characterisation of
  134; and learning 76
Dewey, John 16, 45–46, 45–46, 59
DHEA *See* dehydroepiandrosterone
Diamandis, Peter 194
differentiation process, in education 43–44,
  49, 54, 60
digital age, motivation and engagement
  challenges in 188–190
discovery learning 47
'disease of meaning' 73
disillusionment 29
disruptive behaviour 32, 93
diversity 109, 112, 134, 136, 146, 153, 163,
  165, 172; inner 134; outer 134
Donelan, Michelle 233
double loop learning *216*

E-Bank skills 90, 121–122, 172–173
economy 7, 15, 18, 33–34, 109; educational
  system impact on 33–34; and education
  system 15
EDI frame: evolution meta-steps using 59–60
education: factors preventing
  transformation of 87; importance of
  1; Latin roots of 6; purpose of 23; and
  status, link between 8

Education Act of 1902 12
Education (Schools) Act of 1992 15
educational DAOs 203–206
educational exclusion 18
educational health care 140, 212, 217
educational innovations 55
educational leaders 60
educational philosophy 8–9
educational reform 54, 191, 201
educational stalemate 15
educational standard 10
educational system 1–2, 5, 10, 11–12,
  15–18, 21, 23, 27, 29–30, 34, 37, 43–44,
  48, 53–55, 59–60, 62–63, 65, 68, 75–77,
  80–81, 82, 87, 97, 107, 111, 112, 115,
  128–129, 132, 139, 143, 154, 161, 166,
  180, 183–184, 191–195, 199, 202, 204,
  205, 210, 233–234; challenges 2, 5;
  change capability 2; concept of 75;
  failures of 2, 17; new way of looking at 2;
  reinventing 1–2; 'Seven Great Waves' of
  change in 2–3, *3*
educational thinking 14, 16–17
education policies and reform principles 54
Education Reform Act of 1988 15, 24
educators 8, 30, 46–49, 55, 68, 80, 101, 169,
  181, 192, 205, 234
ego maturity 80–81; Achiever narrative
  115–116; assessment 115–116; definition
  111, 115; developing 115; importance
  of 111–112, 115; levels of 112, *113, 114*,
  115; model 115–116; Torbert and
  Cook-Greuter's work on 112
EHC *See* educational health care
elementary education 10
Elementary Education Act 10
elitism and disparity, in education 7
emergence phase of evolution 43
emotional and social intelligence 78–79, 82,
  87, 88, *89*, 90–92, 95, 97, 100, 102–104,
  106, 145; emotional awareness 91–92;
  emotional intelligence 92–95; emotional
  literacy 95–97; emotional regulation
  97–100; emotional resilience 100–102;
  empathy and rapport 104–106; energy
  awareness 88, 90; energy management

90–91; optimistic outlook 103–104; self-motivation 102–103; significance of 88; social awareness 106; social intelligence 106
emotional awareness 91–92
emotional development 51, 53, 82, 88, 103, 127
emotional empathy 105
emotional engagement 187–188
emotional intelligence 62, 82–83, 87, 92–95, 94; 'fight or flight' physiological response 92–93; and NE system 93–94; self-awareness 94; unruly pupil behaviour 93; virtuous cycles 94
emotional literacy 82, 95–97, 100, 104, 122
emotional regulation 69, 87, 97–98, 97–100, 122, 210
emotional resilience 100–102
emotional state 94, 97–98, 217
emotions 69–71, 82, 86–87, 86–88, 91–106, 113, 115, 120, 122, 132, 134–135, 138, 179, 211, 230; basic 95; 'basic features' of 99; educating young boys about 92; importance of 92; misunderstanding about nature of 92; and motivation 102–103; movement features of 99; negative 82, 94, 100–102, 120; and physiological energy 87–88; sustaining helpful 98; universe of 95–96, 100, 103, 106
empathy 104–105, 122, 145, 166; across species 104; cognitive 104–105; compassionate 105; emotional 105, 172; MAP skill for developing 105–106; and rapport 104–106; types of 104–105
energy: awareness 88, 90; and emotions 120, 211; factors boosting or draining 90; levels 78, 81, 87, 90, 121, 123; management 90–91
engagement 131, 164, 173, 179, 187–189, 191, 202–203, 209–210, 212, 215, 217; agentic 188; behavioural 188; cognitive 187; definition of 187; emotional 187–188; and motivation 188–191, *189*
entropy 156–157, 176, 226
equality 16, 18, 53
equity 53, 192

equity gap 13
ESQ *See* emotional and social intelligence
Ethereum 196
evolution 2, 11, 43–44, 49, 54–55, 59, 64–65, 68, 80–81, 107, 110, 128, 139, 204, 206; of educational wave 11; framework 59; meta-steps using EDI frame 59–60; of stakeholder motivations 59
exams 13–14, 16, 25, 27–28, 40, 53, 75, 80, 91–92, 94, 130, 193
excess process 11
excitement 99, 101, 161
experiential learning 45
external assessment methods 52
extremist behaviour 27
extrinsic motivation 180, 182

Factory Act of 1802 9
Factory Act of 1833 9
FED *See* Foundation of Education Development
'fight or flight' physiological response 92–93
Finland 16, 18, 53–54
Finnish education system 16–18, 53–55; confidence in teachers and principals 54; features of 53–54; focus of 54
Finnish schools 53
Fischer, Kurt 68
formal academics, delayed introduction of 51
Foundation of Education Development 55
fragmentation of educational system 54
Friedman, Milton 25
Fuller, Buckminster R. 25

Gandhi, Mahatma 116
Gardiner, Howard 47–49, 55, 77
GCSE attainment, 'disadvantage gap' in 34
gender difference, in access to education 7
General Education Board, mission statement of 8–9
generative AI (GenAI) 205
GERM 54, 201, 202
Global Well-Being Index 234–235

Glucksberg, Sam 181
Goethe, Johann Wolfgang von 65
governance 163–165, 204, 212–213, 228
grading: and testing systems 50; types of 28
grammar schools 6, 9–10, 13–14, 19, 80
Grammar Schools Act of 1840 19
Graves, Clare 2, 2, 68, 107, 107
Greene, David 180
green value system 14, 109–110, 148, 173–174
Guay, Frédéric 203

happiness 54, 65, 73–74, 182
Harlow, Harry F. 183
Harrison, Liz 221–223, 228, 230, 232
head teachers 31, 62, 77, 97, 119, 125, 145–146, 156, 210, 221, 229–231
heart rate variability (HRV) assessment 90, 91
helicopter parenting 32
Henry, James P. 93–95
Henry's axis 93, 94
Hero's Journey 63
heuristic tasks and motivations 183
high-quality education 234
Hobbs, Elisabeth A. 47
Hobbs, John F. 47
holistic education 50, 52
homeostasis 63
home schooling 16
homework 32–33, 53, 130, 190, 205
horizontal learning *vs.* vertical development 76
human body 43–44
human development 64
human experience 36, 65
humanity 1, 67, 183

IB *See* International Baccalaureate
imagination 51
independent learning 49
individual capability 77
indu culture 8
industrial revolution 7–9, 8, 19, 24–25, 29, 183, 195–196, 206–207; leap forward central to 194–196; schooling during 8–9

inequality 33–34
inequity 128
informal schools 7
information age 195
inner development 75
inner diversity 134
inner lines of development: behaviours 86–87; emotions 86–87; feelings 86; physiology 87; *See also* development
inner maturity 75
innovation 5, 16, 124, 154, 171–172, 192, 202, 225, 234
inquiry-based learning 52
inspection, significance of 15–16
instinctive drive 183
instructional approach 19
Integrated Performance Model 85, 179
integrated special education 54
integration of subjects 46
integration phase of evolution 54
intellectual disability 13
intelligence: levels of emotional and social 88–89, 91, 100, 102, 113; as 'lines of development' 77; test 12–13; types of 48
intelligences: types of 28
interdependency 155
interdisciplinary educational systems 191–194
International Baccalaureate 51–53
internet 26, 187, 193, 195–196, 201
internet bullying 103
interoception 81–82
intrinsic and extrinsic motivation theory 180–183
intrinsic motivation 164, 180, 181, 183–185, 202, 212; critical elements for work 184–187; *vs.* extrinsic motivation 182; instinctive drive 183; rewards effect on 181
IQ testing 13
'IT'/'ITS' problem 60–61, *61*
'IT'/'ITS' solutions, designing 203

Jacques, Eliot 68
job-related stress 90

'Karoshi' 33
Kegan, Robert 68, 76, 76, 206
Kemnal Academies Trust (TKAT) 234; as catalyst for change 221; future plans 231–232; transformational journey of CEO of 227–228
Kemnal Academies Trust (TKAT) SLT developmental programme 221; benefits delivered by 227; Complete Values Profiles (CVP) 223–225, *224, 225*; developmental intervention 226; focus of 222; leadership development for headteachers 229–231; leadership model *224*; personal coaching and team development activities 228–229; Team Development Index *222*, 222–223, *223*
knowledge 12, 14, 16, 25–26, 40, 44, 46–47, 52, 62, 72, 75–76, 80, 119, 140, 147–148, 154, 192–193, 195–196, 199–201, 204, 206–207, 209–210; economy 196; transfer 23, 25, 30, 75, 80, 130, 199, 206
"knowledge doubling curve" 25, 196
Kohlberg, L. 68, 70
Kurzweil, Ray 194

Langer, Ellen 184
language 6, 12, 19, 47, 52, 69, 71, 138, 146, 169, 173, 226
large language models 205
leadership 31, 67, 86, 112, 115, 123, 151, 153, 156, 162–163, 174, 211, 218, 223, 227–228; development 143, 229; development programme 221, 229–230; model applied to education 60–61, *61*; network 162; style 226, 228, 231; team 60, 97–98, 122, 145–146, 149, 154, 157, 162–165, 169, 173, 175–176, 209, 212–214, 222–223, 230
leadership model 157, 159, 223–224, *224*, 226; Lencioni's dysfunctions mapped to *159*; Lencioni's model 157–158; TDI results mapped to *157*
leadership team developmental journey: TDI data 173–177; values analysis 169–172
Learner Profile attributes 52

learning 1, 8, 23, 26–27, 29, 31, 40, 45–51, 53–54, 71, 74–76, 80, 91, 94, 98, 128, 136, 156, 169, 176, 183, 188, 195–196, 200, 203, 206, 210–211, 214–215; as constructivism 46–47; *vs.* development 46; difficulties 32, 97; by doing 45; environment 23, 49–50, 54, 95, 204; styles 23, 48, 50–51
learning and development, disconnect between 75–82; horizontal learning 76; vertical development 76–77
LEAs *See* Local Education Authorities
Lee Kuan Yew 17
Lencioni, Patrick 157–158, 157–159, 167
Lencioni's model: 'absence of trust' 157–158; avoidance of accountability 158–159; dysfunctions of team 159–161; fear of conflict 158; inattention to result 159; lack of commitment 158
Lepper, Mark 180
level descriptions by team and leader *160*
lifelong learning outcomes *189*
life on earth, inception of 128
Linsell, David 228, 228–229
listening 105, 130–131, 133, 135, 144, 165, 231
literacy skills 33–34
LLMs *See* large language models
Local Education Authorities 12, 14
Loevinger, Jane 68
low self-esteem 27
Lyubomirsky, Sonja 103

main lesson blocks 50–51
Malthouse, Kit 233, *233*
Mandela, Nelson 1, 20, 67
MAP skill 105–106, 122, 145
marginalisation of young men 39
Maslow, Abraham 150, 183, *183*
MASTERY skills 98–100, *99–100*
Maté, Gabor 127, *127*
maturity 60, 74, 87, 112–113, 134, 145–147, 163, 200, 234; ego 68, 80–81, 87, 106, 111–112; inner 70, 75; theory 112–113, 115
McGregor, Douglas 183, *183*

mental health 28, 53, 92, 97, 127, 211
mental health crisis 82–83
mental illness 26–27
Middle Years Programme 52
'midlife crisis' 73
misogynistic influencers 27
mixed-age classrooms 49
models 36, 60, 76, 111, 149, 159, 179, 203, 210, 218, 230; corporate management 54, 201; large language 25, 205
modern educational system 23
monetary system 197
Montessori education *vs.* traditional education 49–50
Montessori, Maria 16, 49, 49–51
Montessori schools 49–50
Moss, David 230, 230
motivation 59, 80, 87, 92, 103, 105, 109, 115, 131, 145–146, 163, 169, 172, 179–181, 183, 185, 187–189, 191, 202–203, 209, 212, 215, 226; definition of 187; emotions and 102–103; and engagement 179, 188–191, *189,* 202–203, 209; and tasks 183; theory 183, 212
MYP *See* Middle Years Programme

National Association of Head Teachers 31
National Curriculum 15, 19, 24–26, 75, 79, 82; creation of 24; focus of 24, 75; obsoleting 25–26
National Schools 10
negative childhood experiences 127
network analysis 161–162
neuroendocrine system (NE) 93–94
numeracy skills 33–34

OECD Schools+ Network 55
Office of Standards in Education (Ofsted) 15, 31
Open AI 205
operational network 161
optimistic outlook 103–104
orange value system 13, 109, 123, 144, 148, 172, 225
Ornish, Dean 129
over-tuition 17

pain of affliction 73
parental anxiety 129
parental development 74–75
parenting 32–33, 74–75
parents, educational system impact on: confusion and stress 32–33; school choice 32; Tiger Moms 32–33
passion 125, 132, 169, 172, 202, 210, 215, 217
Pastoral Wave of education 6, 8
PE *See* Physical Education
peace education 50
peers 27, 47, 49, 162, 214
PEP (Positive Energy Practice) skills 100
perfectionism 26
performance pressure 17
performance system 19, 24
Performance Wave of education 6, 12–13, 16–17, 23–25, 27, 30, 37, 43; consequences of 24; and 'Cult of the Expert' 25; flaw in 13; primary goal of 16; reductionist bent of 29; root of 12–14; testing regime of 12–13
Performance Wave thinking 13, 15
Perry, Ruth 31
personal capability development 77, *78;* cognitive sophistication 79–80; ego maturity 80–81; emotional and social intelligence (ESQ) 78–79; physicality 77–78, 81; values 80–81
personal development 106
personal emotion development 103
personality 134, 166
perspective taking 132–133
physical development assessment 77–78
Physical Education 11, 53, 214, 218
physicality 77–78, 81
physiological energy and emotions 87–88
physiology 87, 91, 93–95, 179, 230
Piaget, Jean 46–47, 46–47, 68
PISA *See* Programme for International Student Assessment
play-based early education 53
play, significance of 47
Plowden Report of 1967 14
Polarities Wave of education 16–17

'political manoeuvring' 112
poor children, education for 7
poor education and poverty 38–39
populism in politics 233
positive emotion 100
positive emotional state 98
Pounds, John 9, 9
poverty 17, 38–39
power 6–7, 9, 12, 15, 64, 86, 147, 150, 152–153, 156, 187, 190, 196, 223, 233
powerfulness of belief 138
Power Wave of education 8, 11, 23–24, 43
practical life skills 49–50
primary school head teacher, developmental journey of 119–125; accelerated progress 119; BREATHE skill 120–121; E-Bank skill 121; emotional literacy 122; HRV analysis 120; openness and courage 124; situations affecting energy levels 121–122; team building 124; values profile 123–124
primary school systems 24
Primary Years Programme 52
Principle Wave of education 10–13, 23–24, 30–31, 43; downside of 11; emergence of 10–12; red values system in 11; reliance on punishment in 11
problem-solving process 41
productive member of society 23–24
Programme for International Student Assessment 14
progressive education 45
progressive thinking 14
Progressive Wave of education 5, 14, 16–17; emergence of 14–16; primary goal of 16; roots of 16
psychological safety 93, 97, 152, 157, 173
psychology 181, 191
punishment 11, 13–14, 180–183, 187
Pygmalion in the Classroom 136
PYP *See* Primary Years Programme

quality of education 54

ragged schools 9
reception 130–131

red motivational system 182
reductionism 15, 43–44
reductionist deconstruction 43–44
red values system 11, 110, 140, 143–144, 146–147, 180, 223, 225, 228, 231
reinvention of education 194, 210, 214, 217–218, 221, 233–234
relatedness 184–185, 185–186, 187, 202–203, 209, 214–215
relationship 30, 37, 73, 75, 88, 92, 94, 105–106, 128–129, 132–133, 135, 140, 145, 148, 161, 166, 169, 187, 190–192, 201, 218, 227–228; bonds 60, 105, 146, 162, 226; building 71, 106, 132; dynamics 71; and friendships 129; importance in lives 128–129; values impact on 139–141
retention crisis of teachers and leaders 111, 119, 181
rewards 13, 73–74, 180–183, 185, 187; and performance 181–183; and punishment 13–14, 180–181, 182–183
rewards-based education system 180–181
rhythmic even breathing 91
Richard II 7, 9
Rittel, Horst W. J. 35
Roberts, Karen 222, 227, 230
Robinson, Ken 29, 48, 233
Robinson, Sir Ken 29, 48, 233
Rockefeller, John D. 8, 8
Rodin, Judith 184
Rosenthal, Robert 136
Rustichini, Aldo 181
Ryan, Richard 183–185

SATs *See* Standardised Assessment Results
scaffolding 47, 61–63, 200–201
scars of early neglect 127
schizophrenia 82
school buildings 30–31
school choice 32
school days 53
School Health Service 14
schooling, during Industrial Revolution 8–9
"school leadership supply crisis" 31–32
school league tables 39

schools: business performance principles 15; control of 15; as DAOs 203–206; as DDOs 206–207; maturity 5
SDT *See* self-determination theory
secondary education 13
secondary schools 12–13, 24–25, 32, 34, 53, 185
Second Boer War and education 11
self-appreciation 103–104
self-determination 184, 187
self-determination theory 184, 202–203, 209, 214; autonomy 184; competency 184–185; engagement and motivation 187–191; potency of *186*; relatedness 185–186
self-directed learning 49
self-motivation 102–103
self-regulation 82, 90–91
self-regulation strategies, physiological and emotional 98
'self-sovereign identity' (SSI) 205
SEND agenda 31
SEND schools, case study of 210–219
Senior Leadership Team 222–223, 225, 228, 230–231
sense of autonomy 184, 188, 202–203
'serfs,' education for 7
Shaftsbury High School, developmental work of 210–219; areas of interests/projects 213–217; continuous measurement 218; engagement and competence 214; high-level strategic objectives 212; leadership team's vision 212; positive feedback loops 217; positive outcomes 218; purpose of education 211; reinvention of curriculum 217; secondary curriculum model 210–211; working groups 213–214
SHIFT skill 100–102
Simon, Theodore 12, 13
Singapore education system 16–17
Singularity University 194, 204
skills 2, 14, 17, 23, 31, 33, 47, 76, 80, 90–91, 98, 100–103, 105–106, 122, 143, 148, 169, 173, 175, 190–191, 205, 209, 215, 218, 221; emotional intelligence 104, 152; emotional self-regulation 98; mastery 214–215; problem-solving 52; social 47, 53, 104; systemic thinking 193
SLT *See* Senior Leadership Team
social awareness 106
social cohesion 34
social cost 17
social, emotional and mental health (SEMH) needs 82
social intelligence 78, 80, 82–83, 87–89, 91, 100, 102, 104–106, 113, 122, 145, 193
social interaction and collaboration 45
social media 27, 32, 88, 103, 129, 188, 190, 195
social media pressure 75
society, educational system impact on 33–34
'spare the rod ruin the child' idea 11
special education 54
specialist schools 15
Spitz, Rene 127
Standardised Assessment Results 15, 79–80, 119, 176, 199
standardised syllabus 24
State education 13
Steiner education 50–51
Steiner, Rudolf 14, 50–51
Steiner, Rudolph 14, 50, 51
Steiner schools 50–51
strategic capability 77
strategic thinking 123, 187, 231
strategy 9, 17, 98, 115, 146–148, 155–156, 163–165, 172–175, 210, 212–213; and governance 164–165, 213
stress 19, 32–33, 53, 79, 82, 85, 90, 129
student absenteeism 32
student-centred learning 47
student outcomes 97
"subject to object" (S2O) move 99
suicidal behaviours and cyberbullying, association between 129
Sunak, Rishi 29
survival 1, 112, 127–128, 137–138, 137–139, 140

sustainable relationships 106
Suvorov, Anton 182
systemic change 62, 143, 145, 191
systems development 179
systems theory 191–197; focus of 193; framework for reinventing education 191–194; industrial revolution and 193–195; shift to interdisciplinary educational model 194

talent audit 202–203, 217
Tate, Andrew 27, 27
Taunton Report 10, 14
TDI *See* Team Development Index
teacher autonomy 53
teacher professionalism 53
teacher retention 119
teachers, educational system impact on: burnout and disillusionment 30–31; 'Creativity Crisis' 31; Ofsted assessments 31; recruitment and retention problems 31–32; SEND agenda 31
teaching 6–9, 14, 18–20, 38, 48–50, 53, 68, 88, 94, 119, 130, 200–201, 203, 213, 226, 230
team and leader, level descriptions by *160*
team development 146, 148–149, 152, 154–156, 161, 175, 221, 226, 229; battling experts 150; big picture thinking 163–166; broad fellowships 154; and coaching work 221, 229; dependent experts 150–151; diverse pluralists 153–154; independent achievers 151–152; indicators 157; integrated pluralists 154; interdependent achievers 152–153; interventions 226, 228; Lencioni's model 157–158; network analysis 161–162; personal engagement 157; relationship quality 157; stages of 149, *149,* 155; strategic power 157; talented individuals 150; unified fellowships 154–155
Team Development Index 156–157, 163, 173–177, 222; results after development effort *176*; results before development effort *174*

'Team Energy Grid' 106
team engagement conditions: authority 155; commitment to development 155–156; common purpose 155; interdependency 155; leadership 156; one boat 156; team size 155
technical capability 76
technology 5, 50–51, 127–128, 194, 196, 213; as distraction or attention thief 127; negative childhood experiences and 127–128; usage and education 50, 51
teenage conflict 72
teenage wars 73
tensions 17, 134, 139, 144, 148, 150–151, 153, 171, 226
Theory of Knowledge 52
Theory of Multiple Intelligences 48, 77
thinking 2, 6, 14, 25, 30, 43, 46, 59–60, 69–70, 72, 75, 78, 86–87, 92, 105, 120, 130–131, 135, 152, 154, 162, 164, 166, 171–172, 174, 176, 179, 229–230, 234; abstract 72, 199; systemic 191, 227
thoughts 7, 25, 72, 77, 79, 86–87, 95, 130–132, 134–135, 138, 175, 188, 202, 228–230, 233
threat 7, 92–93, 112, 136, 138, 180
Tiger Moms 32–33, 47
Times Education Commission Report 17
TOK *See* Theory of Knowledge
Torbert, Bill 112
Torbert, William 68
Traditionalist approach in education 11–12
'Trads *vs.* Progs' battle 5
transformation 5, 76–77, 81, 87, 145, 152, 154, 156, 202, 228, 234
transmission of information 130
Tripartite system 14
Trump, Donald 70, 70
trust 98, 106, 144, 147, 152, 157–158, 162–166, 172, 176, 205–206, 225, 231, 234; building 93, 152; level of 165–166, 227
Tuckman, Bruce 149

universal education 10, 11
'Universe of Emotions,' galaxies in 95–98, *96,* 103

values 80–81; assessment 113; based inputs 59; and beliefs 132, 134–136, 140, 166, 188; blue value system 109; changing waves of 107; composition of 135; and ego maturity lines 145; hierarchy 110; impact on relationships 139–141; level 5, 11–12, 109–110, 140, 144–146, 172; and motivations 87, 169; profiles 146, 163, 169, 171, 173, 202–203, 227–228; spiral 5, 107, *107,* 139–140, 224, *224*; understanding 107–116

values systems 2, 4–6, 11–12, 24, 68, 107, 109–111, 123, 139–141, 143, 145–148, 169, 171, 182, 202, 223; 1st tier and 2nd tier 109; approaches to education *108,* 109; colour-coded 2, *4, 5*; ego maturity 111–116; progress through 5; shifts in 5; 'transcend and include' journey 111; upside and downside of *110,* 110–111

value waves 5; Performance Wave 6; Progressive Wave 5–6

vertical development: assessment 77–78; change capability 77; cognitive sophistication 79–80; ego maturity 80–81; emotional and social intelligence (ESQ) 78–79; *vs.* horizontal learning 76; individual capability 77; personal capability 77, *78*; physicality 77–78, 81; strategic capability 77; technical capability 76; values 80–81

virtual world and real world 190

vision 151, 163–165, 173, 211–213, 218, 229, 231

Vygotsky, Lev 47

wage cut 30

Waldorf education *See* Steiner education

Ward, Carl 55, 235

Watkins, Alan D. 44, 60, 105, 115, 155

Web2 technologies 195–196, 205

Web3 technologies 196, 204, 205

well-being of students 53–54

well-being session 97

wicked problem of education 34–41, 43, 45, 54–55, 60, 68, 75, 97, 107, 111, 132, 234; definition of 35, *35*; gnarly characteristics of 107, 109; 'I' and 'WE' problem 60–61, *61*; 'IT'/'ITS' problem 60–61, *61*; making progress on 40–41; multi-dimensional 35–36, 61–62; multiple causes of 37–38, 41; multiple solutions of 39–41, 55; multiple stakeholders of 37, 41; multiple symptoms of 38–39, 54; paradox of 41; as product of evolution 55; topography of 60

Wilber, Ken 35, *35*, 60, *60*

Williamson, Gavin 11

Winchester College 6

working class, education of 11

world views 2, *4, 5*

yellow value system 109, 124, 146, 171, 210

young people, education impact on: conditioned as factory workers 28–29; continuous assessment 28; exams 28; low expectations of educational system 29–30; marginalised individuals 27–28; mental illness 26–27; narrow academic success 29; perfectionism 26, 28; perpetual measurement and ranking 27; re-entry post exclusion 28–29; social media 27; young women 27–28

Zone of Proximal Development (ZPD) 47

For Product Safety Concerns and Information please contact our EU
representative GPSR@taylorandfrancis.com
Taylor & Francis Verlag GmbH, Kaufingerstraße 24, 80331 München, Germany

www.ingramcontent.com/pod-product-compliance
Lightning Source LLC
Chambersburg PA
CBHW081945230426
43669CB00019B/2930